Before Tom Brown

Contents

Acknowledgements		vii
Introduction		1
1	Early School Dialogues and Texts: From 2500 BC to AD 1000	5
2	Chaucer's Schoolboy	31
3	Fifteenth- to Seventeenth-Century *Vulgaria* and Colloquies	38
4	Schools and Schoolboys on the Stage	76
5	The First School Novel: *Dobsons Drie Bobbes*	122
6	Defoe's Quarrelling Schoolboys	132
7	School Life in the Early English Novel	143
8	Education outside School: *Émile*, *The Fool of Quality* and *Sandford and Merton*	172
9	The Genre Established: School Stories, 1749–85	190
Further Reading		223
Index		227

Acknowledgements

The author and publisher are very grateful to the following for permission to reproduce material:

The Chicago University Press, for permission to quote from Samuel Noah Kramer's *The Sumerians: Their History, Culture, and Character*, 1963.

Bill Harnam, Director of Publications, the Pontifical Institute of Medieval Studies, Toronto, for permission to quote from Michael Herren's translation of *The Hisperica Famina*, 1974.

Tanja Cowell at Brill for permission to quote from Yehudi Lindeman's translation of *The Rebels* by Macropedius, 1983.

Dana Sutton, University of California, Irvine, for permission to quote from her hypertext edition of Edward Forsett's *Pedantius* (1581), The Philological Museum, 1998.

Nicholas Orme for permission to quote from *Education and Society in Medieval and Renaissance England*, Hambledon Press, London, 1989.

Nicholas Orme and the Pontifical Institute of Medieval Studies, Toronto, for permission to quote from *English School Exercises, 1420–1530*, 2013.

Ben Kennedy, at Oxford University Press, for permission to quote from *A Fifteenth Century Schoolbook*, 1956.

Rachel Reeder at The Boydell Press (Boydell & Brewer Ltd) for permission to quote from Scott Gwara and David W. Porter's *Anglo-Saxon Conversations: The Colloquies of Aelfric Bata*, 1997.

Every effort has been made to trace copyright holders and to obtain their permission for the use of copyright material where necessary. The author and publisher apologise for any errors or omissions in this respect and would be grateful if notified of any corrections that should be incorporated in future printings of this book.

Introduction

The school story is one of the most enduring of all literary genres. Still popular today (witness the success of *Harry Potter*), it has existed as a distinct category of children's fiction since 1749, when Sarah Fielding's *The Governess; or, Little Female Academy*, generally acknowledged to have been the very first school story (although, as will be seen, this is slightly erroneous), was first published. Most studies of boys' school stories start with the premise that the first was *Tom Brown's Schooldays*, which was originally published in 1857. This was actually far from being the case, as numerous boys' school stories – full-length novels and short stories – had been appearing from the 1760s onwards.

However, the origins of the school story go back far beyond 1749. Some analysts of children's literature have identified the *Colloquy* of Aelfric as being the first fictional representation of English school life. Aelfric was a monk and teacher at Cerne Abbas in Dorset, and his *Colloquy*, written around AD 1000, was a dialogue between a master and his pupils, written as a teaching aid designed to give pupils a grounding in conversational Latin. This was followed by a series of *Colloquies* written by Aelfric Bata, one of Aelfric's pupils, who again set his work inside a monastic school. These *Colloquies* provide a vivid and undeniably authentic picture of school life at that time, with the added bonus of elements of entertainment and comedy, the author recognising that this would make learning more enjoyable. In addition, they also suggest the beginnings of performance, with pupils acting the roles of the dialogues' characters in the classroom.

These dialogues were, in fact, a continuation of a technique adopted by teachers as far back as at least 2000 BC, in schools in Sumeria (now part of Iraq), where the school was the setting for simple phrases, sentences and dialogues designed to teach spelling, grammar and vocabulary. Many more examples are found in texts from schools in ancient Egypt,

Greece and Rome. The format was later used in schools in the fifteenth, sixteenth and seventeenth centuries, in particular, by educationalists such as Erasmus, Claudius Hollyband and John Brinsley the Elder. Again, they provide striking pictures of school life – the curriculum, school food, punishments, schoolboy friendships and leisure activities. Some of these dialogues were very short, but others were much longer, and again it has been assumed that that they were acted in the classroom, and can be seen as another early example of staged drama.

In the meantime, Geoffrey Chaucer had featured a schoolboy in a shocking story in *The Canterbury Tales* in the 1470s, and schools and education, in particular, in terms of arguments for and against schooling, featured in several sixteenth, seventeenth and eighteenth century dramas, some of which were also notable for their satirical and mocking portraits of schoolmasters and tutors.

The very first school novel, *Dobsons Drie Bobbes*, a comic tale set in and around Durham Cathedral School, appeared as early as 1607, exactly 250 years before *Tom Brown*, and has hitherto been completely overlooked in studies of school stories or the history of children's literature. Just over 100 years later, Daniel Defoe, in *The Quarrel of the Schoolboys at Athens*, used a school as a setting to satirise the Parliament of King George I, showing that life at school reflected life outside school (or, of course, in some cases vice versa).

Schools, schoolmasters and tutors played a superficial but important part in several eighteenth-century novels, in particular, the picaresque adventures of Henry Fielding and Tobias Smollett, who showed how their heroes' characters were forged by their youthful experiences. In addition, three notable eighteenth-century novels, Rousseau's *Émile*, Henry Brooke's *The Fool of Quality* and Thomas Day's *Sandford and Merton*, portrayed education outside school, while at the same time establishing some of the themes that were taken up by later writers of school stories.

Finally, the school story as a distinct literary genre, principally but by no means exclusively aimed at children, began to emerge in the middle of the eighteenth century. *The Governess*, while set in a girls' boarding school, was less of a novel and more of a series of tales, some with a strong moral lesson, and this spawned a variety of imitators – books of loosely-connected stories, dialogues and letters – aimed at imparting lessons in behaviour, morals, religion and, occasionally, academic subjects such as natural history and geography. School stories for boys soon followed, and by 1785, the cut-off point for this study, the school story as it was to become recognised had fully emerged.

This book explores all these early texts, showing how snapshots of school life and education developed from simple sentences to complex dialogues, many with multiple participants, which can easily been seen as precursors to longer dramatic works and then to longer works of fiction. It examines the pictures of school life painted in early stage plays, which were often negative and showed schools as places of cruelty and drudgery, or showed schoolmasters as figures of fun and contempt – pompous, ignorant and scheming.

It goes on to show how school life and education began to feature more and more in longer works of fiction, with schools again often shown as being barbaric places and schoolmasters and tutors as malevolent tyrants, with some authors offering the role of a private tutor as a benevolent and more civilising way of teaching young boys. Finally, it charts the origins of the school story as we know it today, which emerged as a series of moral and educational tales into short and then longer narratives of school life, exploring some of the themes that were to become integral to the genre, creating a template that led to Tom Brown and his numerous successors.

1

Early School Dialogues and Texts: From 2500 BC to AD 1000

The first fictional portrayals of English school life appeared in the late tenth and early eleventh centuries, firstly in a dialogue by Aelfric, widely recognised as the greatest prose writer of the period, and then in a series of dialogues by one of Aelfric's former pupils, Aelfric Bata. These were written as teaching aids, designed for novices and young monks who were obliged to learn Latin in order to work and serve in their abbey. Even though there is no narrative, these dialogues still paint a vivid picture of life in a monastery school, and the dialogues of Aelfric Bata, in particular, reveal how pupils lived, worked and played, and the relationship between pupils and their master.

These were not, however, the first dialogues of their type. Written dialogues and other texts set in schools and designed as teaching aids can be traced as far back as at least 2000 BC, used by the Sumerians (in what is now part of Iraq), followed by the ancient Egyptians, and, later, the Greeks and the Romans.[1]

---

1. For a summary of texts specifically written for children in the ancient civilisations of Sumeria, Egypt, Greece and Rome, and medieval texts, see Gillian Adams, 'Ancient and Medieval Children's Texts', in Peter Hunt (ed.), *International Companion Encyclopedia of Children's Literature* (London: Routledge, 2004).

The Sumerians

The Sumerians developed the world's first technological civilisation, with many inventions that are still in use today. At the same time, they originated a system of writing on clay, and most of what is known about their land, Sumer (which was later known as Babylonia), and their society is based on the thousands of complete and incomplete clay tablets that have survived.[2] Sumerian writing emerged as a way of formalising and organising Sumerian society, which was developing a system of government, establishing institutions and technologies, and needed a skilled bureaucracy to administer the state and its activities. However, writing also became important in other areas, especially education, where texts were used to teach language and writing, and then to teach concepts such as morals, behaviour and ethics. In developing writing as a means of communication, the Sumerians created their own literature, which grew to cover religious texts, myths, tales, proverbs, fables and essays.

Amongst this Sumerian literature is a range of texts that were sometimes partly and sometimes exclusively aimed at children, and the claim has been made that these constitute the very beginnings of children's literature.[3] Many of these texts were written for use in schools, and a few, like the educational compositions of later writers such as Aelfric (see later in this chapter) and Erasmus and John Brinsley (see chapter three) reveal a great deal of what daily school life at the time was like. In addition, as examples of fictional writing, in which the writers exercised a degree of imagination, these can legitimately be described as being the very first pieces of school fiction.

Sumerian School Texts

The Sumerian school system began to mature and flourish around 2500 BC. Clay tablets from this time which have been linked to schools consist largely of lists – of gods, animals, objects and an assortment of words and phrases. Tablets from later millenia contain an assortment

---

2. For a comprehensive description of Sumerian society and a discussion of the research into their writings, see Samuel Noah Kramer, *History Begins at Sumer: Thirty-Nine Firsts in Recorded History* (London: Thames & Hudson, 1958), and *The Sumerians: Their History, Culture, and Character* (Chicago: University of Chicago Press, 1963).
3. See Gillian Adams, 'The First Children's Literature? The Case for Sumer', *Children's Literature* 14 (1986), pp. 1–30.

of exercises used by pupils as part of their daily school work, including compositions, essays and dialogues. As well as tablets containing the original texts, written by teachers, hundreds of practice tablets have been found, produced by pupils of varying ages and abilities.

The Sumerian school was known as an *edubba*, meaning 'tablet house'. The head of the school was the *ummia*, or 'expert', also known as the 'school father', while the pupil was called the 'school son'. The head's assistant, whose duties included writing new tablets for pupils to copy, examining the copies, and hearing pupils reciting studies from memory, was the 'big brother'. There were also other teachers, for example, those who taught drawing and language, and there were also monitors in charge of attendance and a 'man in charge of the whip', responsible for discipline.

The curriculum developed to consist of two main elements – scientific and scholarly, and literary and creative. The latter consisted primarily of studying, copying, memorising and imitating the growing quantity of literary compositions that had originated when writing first appeared. These ranged from simple proverbs to fables, essays, myths and epic poems, *The Epic of Gilgamesh* being one of the best-known today. Alongside these works grew a number of original school texts, written by teachers and which provide a picture of daily Sumerian school life. These show that the pupil attended school from sunrise to sunset; on arrival at school he studied the tablet he had prepared the previous day, while the 'big brother' prepared a new tablet which the pupil then copied; and finally the copy would be examined and the pupil tested on its content. Discipline was harsh, with teachers relying heavily on the cane as a means of correcting faults as well as a means of punishment for wrongdoing.

Among several long but incomplete texts[4] is one called by Samuel Kramer in his work, *The Sumerians*, 'Schooldays', which reveals the day-to-day activities of a schoolboy as recounted by a former pupil (an 'old grad'). Originally written around 2000 BC, its depiction of the schoolboy's behaviour and misbehaviour, his dislike of lessons, fear of punishment, and of his father's hopes and aspirations for his future,

---

4. As is typically the case, fragments are missing, and the condition of those that have survived is such that an accurate transcription is not always possible. The extracts quoted here are taken from Kramer, *The Sumerians*, but without the gaps and question marks inserted by Kramer to indicate undecipherable or missing text and words or phrases where the translation is uncertain.

echo down the centuries, with school dialogues written in the fifteenth and sixteenth centuries having an identical flavour.

The text opens with the former pupil being asked what he did at school, and replying:

> I recited my tablet, ate my lunch, prepared my new tablet, wrote it, finished it; then my model tablets were brought to me; and in the afternoon my exercise tablets were brought to me. When school was dismissed, I went home, entered the house, and found my father sitting there. I explained my exercise tablets to my father, recited my tablet to him, and he was delighted, so much so that I attended him with joy.[5]

However, the following day does not go as planned:

> When I arose in the morning, I faced my mother and said to her: 'Give me my lunch, I want to go to school!' My mother gave me two rolls, and I set out. ... In school the fellow in charge of punctuality said: 'Why are you late?' Afraid and with pounding heart, I entered before my teacher and made a respectful curtsy.[6]

He is then caned by various members of the school staff – for not finishing his homework, for loitering in the street and looking untidy, for talking without permission, for misbehaving in assembly, for leaving the school without permission, for taking something (the tablet is unclear on what was taken) without permission and, finally, he is caned by the headmaster for poor handwriting. Consequently, the pupil begins to hate the work he is being given and his teacher loses interest in teaching him. Aware, however, that he must learn in order to become a 'big brother' and then a scribe, he asks his father whether he would butter up the headmaster. His father agrees to invite the headmaster to dinner (in a passage where the author has changed the narrative direction and describes the events as an eyewitness):

> The teacher was brought from the school, and after entering in the house, he was seated on the 'big chair'. The schoolboy attended and served him, and whatever he learned of the

---

5. Kramer, *The Sumerians*, pp. 237–38.
6. Ibid., p. 238.

scribal art, he unfolded to his father. Then did the father in the joy of his heart say joyfully to the headmaster of the school: 'My little fellow has opened wide his hand, and you made wisdom enter there; you showed him all the finer points of the scribal art; you made him see the solutions of the mathematical and arithmetical problems, you taught him how to make deep the cuneiform script.'[7]

The father then orders his servants to anoint the headmaster with oil and announces that he wants to dress him in new clothes, give him extra salary and put a ring on his finger. The headmaster finally addresses his pupil, expressing his hope that he will go on to become a successful scholar and a leader of his fellow pupils.

As Kramer remarks, this episode records the first case of 'apple-polishing' in the history of literature.[8] Gillian Adams also points out in 'The First Children's Literature? The Case for Sumer'[9] that the message that it pays to be good to your teacher may account for the popularity of this particular text – 21 copies are known to exist – which was originally written by a teacher for pupils to copy. It is also an assertion that success at school will bring tangible rewards, not least a career as a scribe but also respect and obeisance from fellow pupils and others. Alternatively, it may have been intended as a satire, on materialism and the greed and gullibility of headmasters.

A second school composition, called by Kramer 'School Rowdies', depicts an argument between two students, Enkimansi and his older brother, Girnishag, who appears to have attained the position in the school of 'big brother'. The quarrel begins when Enkimansi refuses to do as instructed by his brother, before launching into the first of a series of insults, which both brothers are happy to trade: 'You dolt, numbskull, school pest, you illiterate, you Sumerian ignoramus, your hand is terrible, it cannot even hold the stylus properly; it is unfit for writing and cannot take dictation. And yet you say you are a scribe like me.'[10]

Girnishag responds by accusing Enkimansi of being a useless scribe and an incompetent tablet writer. In turn, Enkimansi accuses Girnishag of being lazy, careless and a hopeless mathematician. The argument carries on, although the text is poorly preserved and it is difficult to

---

7. Ibid., p. 239.
8. Kramer, *History Begins at Sumer*, p. 43.
9. Adams, 'The First Children's Literature?', p. 20.
10. Ibid, p. 241.

ascertain who is speaking. Finally, someone, probably a monitor, appears and severely admonishes Enkimansi, threatening to beat him and have him locked up:

> Why do you behave like this? Who do you push, curse, and hurl insults at each other? Why do you raise a commotion in the school? … Why were you insolent? Inattentive? Why do you curse, and hurl insults against him who is your 'big brother' and has taught you the scribal art to your own advantage? Even the *ummia* who knows everything shook his head violently saying 'Do to him what you please.' If I really did to you what I pleased – to a fellow who behaved like you and was inattentive to his 'big brother' – I would first beat you with a mace … and having put copper chains on your feet, would lock you up in the house and for two months would not let you out of the school building.[11]

Adams has pointed out that this, and the other school texts, were written to demonstrate what would-be scribes should be striving for, both in and out of school.[12] Young boys enjoy exchanging insults, and Adams suggests that the writers of these dialogues were deliberately trading on this in order to promote good behaviour and hard work. A further possibility, of course, is that the creators of these dialogues and texts used the exchange of insults and derogatory remarks, and the frequent references to physical punishment, seen safely from a distance, as a means of combining instruction with entertainment, in an effort to make learning enjoyable.

Similar dialogues include 'The Disputation between Enkita and Enkihegal' and 'The Disputation between Two School Graduates', both of which are a series of insults, boasts and vituperative remarks, the latter ending with one of the pair verbally abusing the other for no fewer than 28 lines.

The Ancient Egyptians

Education in ancient Egypt usually began at the age of four, when childhood was deemed to have ended, and boys went to schools which had a specific purpose, be it providing training for a post in a government

---

11. Ibid., pp. 242–43.
12. Ibid., p. 17.

Early School Dialogues and Texts: From 2500 BC to AD 1000

department, or temple, or the military, or as a farmer, engineer, doctor etc., with reading and writing being taught in scribal schools. One of the basic types of text from which pupils learnt to write was the model letter, along with 'instructions', in which a father instructed his son by means of a series of maxims, urging precepts such as self-control, moderation, generosity, kindness and truthfulness.

One model letter, from a father to his son, told him how to behave at school:

> I place you at school along with the children of notables, to educate you and to have you trained for this aggrandizing calling. ... When you receive your daily task be not idle ... and read diligently from the book. When you work in silence, let not a word be heard. ... Write with your hand and read with your mouth. Ask counsel of them that are clever. Be not slack, and spend not a day in idleness, or woe betide your limbs! Enter into the methods of your teacher and hear his instructions.[13]

Warnings and admonitions to pupils are widespread in surviving texts – typical was the following:

> They tell me that you have forsaken writing, and you have departed and fled; that you have forsaken writing and used your legs like horses of the riding-school. Your heart is fluttered, you are like a hy-bird. Your ear is deaf; you are like an ass in taking beatings.[14]

Discipline was strict – many surviving fragments of school texts carry sentences, written by schoolboys, such as: 'I was with you since I was a child; you beat my back and your instructions went into my ear. ... The youth has a back; he attends when it is beaten. ... Spend no day in idleness or you will be flogged.'[15]

---

13. From the *Anastasi Papyrus*, cited in Adolf Erman (ed.), *The Ancient Egyptians: A Sourcebook of Their Writings* (New York, NY: Harper & Row, 1966; originally published in Germany, 1923), p. 189.
14. Alan H. Gardiner, *Egyptian Hieratic Papyri: Series I: Literary Texts of the New Kingdom: Part I* (Leipzig: J.C. Hinrichs'sche Buchhandlung, 1911), p. 192.
15. From the *Anastasi Papyrus*, cited in Adolf Erman, *Life in Ancient Egypt*, trans. H.M. Tirard (London: Macmillan, 1894), pp. 329–31.

Whilst beating was the usual form of physical punishment, especially recalcitrant pupils were tied to a block. One boy wrote: 'You have made me buckle to since the time I was one of your pupils. I spent my time in the lock-up; he bound my limbs. He sentenced me to three months, and I was bound in the temple.'[16]

Ancient Greek and Roman School Texts

Thanks to the wealth of written records that have survived from Greece and Rome – texts written on clay and wax tablets and on papyrus – it has been possible to build up a very detailed picture of education in these societies. As was the case with the Sumerians and the Egyptians, and with later medieval schools, pupils learnt the rudiments of language and the art of conversation by using specially-written texts and dialogues, many of which portrayed school life. In addition, further fictional pictures of school life have been provided by playwrights and poets.[17]

Schools in Ancient Greece

Schools emerged in Greece between 600 and 500 BC. The earliest schools were simply rooms, often at the back of shops, hired by a teacher. Some early schools were set up on the street or under colonnades, a practice which was later followed in Rome. Pupils, who were almost always boys, girls being educated at home by their mothers, were generally accompanied to school by a *paidagogus*, a slave who carried his master's equipment and remained with him throughout the school day, watching over him, punishing him if necessary and being responsible for his moral education and inculcating good manners. The role of the *paidagogus* was illustrated in Plato's *Lysis*, a fictional dialogue written around 380 BC, about friendship, with the main characters being Socrates and two boys, Lysis and Menexenus. Socrates, the narrator, meets Lysis at a wrestling school, and begins questioning him about his activities and his family. Lysis reveals that his parents will not allow him to do as he pleases, and that they employ slaves, such as a charioteer and a muleteer.

---

16. Ibid., p. 330.
17. For a comprehensive study of education in ancient Greece (and Rome), see Henri Marrou, *A History of Education in Antiquity*, trans. George Lamb (London: Sheed & Ward, 1956).

Socrates then suggests that Lysis' parents esteem a slave as having more value than their son:

> **Socrates:** Are you your own master, or do they not even allow that?
> **Lysis:** Nay; of course they do not allow it.
> **Socrates:** Then you have a master?
> **Lysis:** Yes, my tutor; there he is.
> **Socrates:** And is he a slave?
> **Lysis:** To be sure; he is our slave.
> **Socrates:** Surely, this is a strange thing, that a free man should be governed by a slave?[18]

Not surprisingly, punishment was a perennial concern of both teachers and schoolboys. *Mimes III*, one of a series of short comic dramas written by the poet and dramatist Herodas between 275 and 270 BC, centres on the unruly and disobedient schoolboy, Kottalos, his desperate mother, Metrotime, who cannot control him, and his schoolmaster, Lampriskos. She lays a number of charges against her son in front of Lampriskos – not doing his homework, gambling, playing truant, staying away from home, getting dirty – and the schoolmaster eventually gets the message:

> **Lampriskos:** Metrotime, you may spare your imprecations. He will get just as much as deserves without them. Here, Euthies, Kokkalos, Phillos; lift him quickly on your shoulders and show him to Akeses' full moon – it has come at last. I like your goings-on, Kottalos. So you're not content to play with your knucklebones honestly like these boys, but must haunt the gambling den and play pitch-and-toss with the touts there. ... Give me my stinging whip, the ox-tail, with which I flog the 'gaol-birds' and the disgraced. Put it into my hands before I choke on my bile.
> **Kottalos:** No, no, I beseech you, Lampriskos, by the Muses, and by your beard and by your poor little Kottalos' life, don't flog me with the stinger, but with the other one.

---

18. From *The Dialogues of Plato, translated into English with Analysis and Introduction by B. Jowett, M.A.*. Vol. 1, (Oxford: Clarendon Oress, 1875), p. 51.

Lampriskos: But you're a bad boy, Kottalos. ...
Kottalos: How many strokes, Lampriskos, are you going to lay on me, please?
Lampriskos: Don't ask me. Ask your mother here.
Kottalos: Mother, how many are you two going to give me?
Metrotime: As your mother wishes you to live, you will have as many as your wretched hide can stand.[19]

Kottalos is subsequently flogged, having been hoisted into the air by three of his schoolfellows. This form of punishment went on to appear in numerous later dialogues and works of fiction.

Early Greek education was provided by three types of teacher: a physical training instructor (*paidotribe*), a music teacher (*kithariste*) and a reading/writing teacher (*grammatiste*). Pupils, who began their school education at around seven years of age, were taught how to read and write in a strict syllabus, of letters, followed by syllables, followed by words, and finally sentences, many of which were aphorisms such as, 'Work hard if you don't want a whipping.' The most important part of a boy's initial education was the reading, learning and reciting of Homer's *Iliad* and *Odyssey*.

Primary education finished at around the age of fourteen, after which boys from wealthier families had the option of going to secondary school, where they studied the theory of grammar and morphology, and the works of classical poets and writers, accompanied by exercises in composition. Other subjects included mathematics, geometry, music and astronomy.

Schools in Ancient Rome

Early Roman education was based on the home and the family, initially via the mother and then, from the age of seven, the father. Home education was nothing more than teaching the skills necessary for life, largely domestic, agricultural and military skills. Schools began to appear in the middle of the fourth century BC, being known as *ludi*, the name derived from the Latin word for play, as these schools were where children learned to socialise as well as gain a rudimentary education. The first schools were run on voluntary lines, with fee-paying schools, run by professional teachers, becoming established in the third century

---

19. Herodas, *The Mimes and Fragments*, with notes by Walter Headlam, ed. A.D. Knox (Cambridge: Cambridge University Press, 1922), p. 115.

BC. The form followed the Greek model, with most schools simply rooms at the back of shops, hired by the teacher, or rooms in private houses, or even on street corners. As was the case in Greece, teaching was poorly paid and regarded as a lowly occupaton. A teacher at a primary level was known as a *litterator* (or sometimes a *magister ludus* or *primus magister*) and he would have been helped by a *calculator*, who taught simple arithmetic.

The Latin author Juvenal wrote several poems, known as *Satires*, between the end of the first and early second centuries AD, and in *Satire VII* he condemned the lowly status and low pay of teachers, and the demands placed on them by parents:

> [Y]ou have sat from early dawn in a hole which no blacksmith would put up with ... it is seldom that the fee can be recovered without a judgment of the Court. And yet be sure, ye parents, to impose the strictest laws upon the teacher: he must never be at fault in his grammar; he must know all history, and have all the authorities at his finger-tips. If asked a chance question on his way to the baths, or to the establishment of Phoebus, he must at once tell you who was the nurse of Anchises, what was the name and birth-place of Anchemolus' step-mother, to what age Acestes lived, how many flagons of Sicilian wine he presented to the Trojans.[20]

The syllabus in these schools was similar to that in Greece, with pupils progressing from learning the alphabet to syllables, words, phrases and sentences. Most importantly, the Romans were the first to use a foreign language, Greek, to increase their mastery of their own language, Roman pupils translating Greek into Latin and vice versa. This gave rise to the bilingual school manual, which went on to become widely used throughout Europe and which gained a particular stronghold in Britain from the fifteenth century onwards (see chapter three).

At the age of nine or ten, boys from wealthier families would move on to a secondary school (often referred to simply as a *schola*) under a *grammaticus*, who taught Greek and Latin literature, and polished the pupils' writing and speaking. As a teacher, the *grammaticus* was better paid but was still poor by the standards of skilled workers. Hours in Roman schools were long, from around sunrise to sunset, a feature of

---

20. From *Juvenal and Persius*, trans. G.G. Ramsay (London: Heinemann, 1918), p. 157.

Roman life which did not meet with universal approval. Undoubtedly, children would not have liked the early start and certainly adults complained, as evidenced by Marcus Valerius Martialis (better known as Martial), a poet whose fame rests on his twelve books of epigrams, published in Rome between AD 86 and 103:

> What right have you to disturb me, abominable schoolmaster, object abhorred alike by boys and girls? Before the crested cocks have broken silence, you begin to roar out your savage scoldings and blows. ... We, your neighbours, do not ask you to allow us to sleep for the whole night, for it is but a small matter to be occasionally awakened; but to be kept awake all night is a heavy affliction. Dismiss your scholars, brawler, and take as much for keeping quiet as you receive for making a noise.[21]

At a fairly early stage in the development of Roman education, the Romans adopted the Greek custom of a slave-companion, called similarly a *paedagogus*, one of whose particular roles was to assist in the teaching of Greek. In Plautus' play *Bacchides* (or *The Two Bacchises*), a comedy about two sisters who work in a brothel, and the two men who fall in love with them, written around 190 BC, a picture of the role of the *paedagogus* and of Roman school life is provided by Lydus, an obviously disgruntled teacher:

> But you, who are pleading his cause for a son so profligate, was this the same as your own training, when you were a young man? ... when you were reading your book, if you made a mistake in a single syllable, your skin would be made as spotted as your nurse's gown. ... But now-a-days, before he is seven years old, if you touch a boy with your hand, at once the child breaks his tutor's head with his tablet. When you go to complain to the father, thus says the father to the child: 'Be you my own dear boy, since you can defend yourself from an injury.' The paedagogus then is called for: 'Hallo! you old good-for-nothing, don't you be touching the child for this reason, that he has behaved so boldly'; and thus the despised paedagogus becomes just like a lantern with his oiled linen

---

21. From *The Epigrams of Martial, translated into English prose* (London: George Bell & Sons, 1890), p. 429.

rags. Judgement pronounced, they go away thence. Can this preceptor then, on these terms, keep up his authority, if he himself is to be beaten the first?[22]

The most detailed picture of school life in ancient Rome is provided by the *Hermeneumata Pseudodositheana*, a series of bilingual (Greek and Latin) school textbooks, the first of which was written around AD 300. They contain vocabularies, word-lists, short passages, fables and dialogues, and they formed the model for those that were developed in the Middle Ages. One passage demonstrates how these manuals taught not only conversation but also set out to increase a pupil's vocabulary, with its lists of words and phrases:

> I go out to the school of the accountant, of the stenographer, of the Greek grammarian, of the Latin grammarian, of the orator. I entered the school and said: 'Hello teacher, hello instructor.' He greeted me in return. He gives me a lectern and tells me to read five pages to him, and I read accurately and clearly. Then I give the book to another student. Later I go off to the assistant-teacher. I greet him and my fellow-students, and they greet me in return. Then I sit in my place, on the bench or seat or step or stool or chair. As I sit there my slave who is carrying my writing-case hands me my tablets and my writing-case, my straight-edge, my tablet, and my lupines.[23]

Another passage provides a description of the beginning of a schoolboy's day, opening with a detailed description of him getting up, washing, dressing (assisted by his slave), greeting his parents, and then going to school:

> My schoolfellows come and meet me; I say hello to them and they say hello back. I come to the staircase. I go up the stairs quietly, as I should. In the hall I take off my cloak, run through my hair with my comb, and go in, saying: 'Good morning,

---

22. From *The Comedies of Plautus*, trans. Henry Thomas Riley (London: Henry G. Bohn, 1852), pp. 173–74.
23. *Lupinum*, nt., or *lupinus*, m., is Latin for a lupin (bean), sham money or, in this instance, counters. Quoted in Mark Joyal, Iain McDougall and J.C. Yardley, *Greek and Roman Education: A Source Book* (London: Routledge, 2009), pp. 169–170.

master.' The master embraces me and returns my greeting. The slave hands me my writing-boards, my inkstand and my ruler. 'Good morning, everybody. Let me have my seat. Squeeze up a bit.' 'Come here.' 'This is my place!' 'I got it first!' I sit down and set to work.

Another extract shows that the idea of older pupils teaching younger ones may have originated around this time:

I go to school. I enter and say: 'Good morning, teacher.' He gives me a kiss and says hello to me. My slave gives me the tablets, the case; I take out the stylus and sit down at my place; I erase and copy according to the model. Afterwards, I show my writing to the teacher, who makes every kind of correction. He asks me to read and then I give the text to another pupil; I learn the colloquia and I recite them. 'Give me a dictation', I ask. Another student dictates to me. … When the teacher bids them, the little ones engage in letters and syllables, and one of the older students pronounces them aloud for them. Others recite in order the words to the assistant teacher and write verses. Being in the first group, I take a dictation. Then, after sitting down, I study commentaries, glosses, and the handbook of grammar.[24]

Early English and Irish School Texts

The teaching of Latin in medieval Britain relied heavily on colloquies, dialogues which taught simple conversational skills alongside grammar, vocabulary and punctuation. Some of these dialogues were between a schoolmaster and his pupils, and were dictated, written down and memorised by the pupils, and then read aloud in class. Their purpose was not just to help in the learning of Latin as a written language but also as a spoken one, not only formally but also colloquially.

The use of colloquies as a teaching aid appears to have arisen in England and Ireland in the early Middle Ages. The most famous colloquies are those of Aelfric, the abbot of Cerne Abbas and one of the most prolific writers of his era, and his pupil, Aelfric Bata, both being particularly notable for their vivid portraits of eleventh-century

---

24. Quoted in Raffaella Cribiore, *Gymnastics of the Mind: Greek Education in Hellenistic and Roman Egypt* (Princeton, NJ: Princeton University Press, 2001).

monastic life. However, these works were simply following a long tradition of English and Irish pedagogical dialogues going back to at least the seventh century.

The Hisperica Famina *and* De Raris Fabulis

One of the earliest surviving texts of this sort is the *Hisperica famina*, a manuscript that probably originated in Ireland around AD 650.[25] Its exact purpose is unclear, as is its author, or authors – it is not known whether it was produced by a schoolmaster or a schoolboy, or both. It is written in an obscure and artificial Latin, utilising Hebrew, Greek and Celtic, and appears to be a school exercise, beginning with a dialogue between two or more scholars which is followed by a series of short compositions. The origin of the text may be monastic, as there are brief references to God and prayer, and there is a description of a chapel, but otherwise the tone is strictly secular.

The opening dialogue portrays a group of visiting foreign scholars. It was not unknown for English people to travel to Ireland to study in the seventh century – for example, Bede, in his *Ecclesiastical History of the English People*, noted that many people, from both the nobility and 'the lower ranks of the English nation', were in Ireland in the seventh century, some of them for the purpose of religious study, where they were warmly-received and given free food and books, and taught free of charge.[26]

The manuscript describes the activities of the visiting scholars, with one of them describing daybreak, how the noises of the farm animals and labourers drive them out of bed, and, after studying all morning, they go off in search of food: 'Let us visit the domain around us that they might offer sweet food to the famished.'[27] They therefore make their way to nearby farms where the inhabitants 'feed the choirs of wandering scholars', although they have to be wary of 'brigands'. They then arrive at an inn where they wash and place their satchels on the walls to impress the locals:

---

25. There are, in fact, four surviving copies, with various textual differences, although only one is complete. There is a comprehensive analysis of this along with an English translation in Michael Herren, *The Hisperica Famina: 1. The A-Text* (Toronto: Pontifical Institute of Medieval Studies, 1974).
26. Bede, *The Ecclesiastical History of the English People* (London: George Bell & Sons, 1907), Book III, ch. 27.
27. Herren, op cit., p. 81.

> Fill the steady hand basin with water and wash your dirty feet with flowing draughts; wipe clean your muddy soles with the clear liquid. Hang your white booksacks on the wall, set your lovely satchels in a straight line, so that they will be deemed a grand sight by the rustics.[28]

After lighting a fire, they go round to the townsmen, whom they must address in Irish, and beg for food. The same exercise is repeated in the evening, with excess food being carried back to school before they do their homework and then prepare for bed, with some of the scholars reading on into the night and others keeping watch.

School dialogues appear to have developed in Wales and Cornwall in the ninth century, one of the earliest being *De raris fabulis* ('On Uncommon Tales'), which is contained in a manuscript, the *Codex Oxoniensis Posterior*, at Oxford's Bodleian Library.[29] This is a series of 24 short dialogues centring on the daily activities of monks, oblates, boys and abbots. Like its Roman predecessor, it begins with rising and dressing:

> Get up, my friend, from your bed: it is time, if you are going to get up today.
> I will indeed get up. Give me my garment, and then I will rise.
> Show me where is your garment.
> It is on the stool which is at my feet, or which I placed near you, or which is nearby.
> Give me my shoes so that they may be on my feet when I walk. Give me my staff, which supports me on my journeys, so that it may be in my hand.[30]

This is yet another example of how these dialogues were sometimes written so that they provided a framework for performance, while also allowing for words or phrases to be interchanged – as in 'at my feet, or which I placed near you, or which is nearby'. Another example centres on a schoolmaster going to bed:

> O boy, make up my bed in the dormitory and put on it a blanket, pillow, bolster, bedroll, rug, or covering. Shake, fluff, or plump

---

28. Herren, op cit., p. 83.
29. MS. Bodl. 572.
30. Cited in Nicholas Orme, *Medieval Schools: From Roman Britain to Renaissance England* (New Haven, CT: Yale University Press, 2006), p. 44.

the straw. Help make up my or our bed carefully, so that I may sleep in it tonight, or whatever night in fact, should God wish and permit me. Men, be quiet and sleep and rest, because it's time to sleep, and don't wake or rouse us from sleep.[31]

A third reads:

> Listen, boys or students! Go to the river, spring or well and bring back clear water so that I may wash my hands, eyes, and my whole face with it, because I have not yet washed a single one of my limbs today.[32]

The manuscript containing *De raris fabulis* seems to have made its way to Winchester and then on to Canterbury. Some sources have suggested that Aelfric (see below) would possibly have encountered it during his time studying at Winchester, and used it as a model for his *Colloquy*, a hypothesis that also takes into account circumstantial evidence that Aelfric was taught Latin by a Welsh layman, Iorwerth, who had himself been trained in this dialogue fashion.[33] More importantly, it is now accepted that Aelfric Bata, one of Aelfric's pupils who became a monk and a teacher, used *De raris fabulis* as a source for his own dialogues.

Aelfric's *Colloquy*

Little is known about the life of Aelfric, even though he was one of the most prolific writers of his age. He was born around AD 950, and educated at the Benedictine monastery school at Winchester, where he was taught by Aethelwold (later St Aethelwold), Bishop of Winchester.

Aelfric left Winchester in 987 and became a novice at the newly founded abbey at Cerne Abbas in Dorset. Shortly afterwards he wrote

---

31. Cited in Scott Gwara, *Education in Wales and Cornwall in the Ninth and Tenth Centuries: Understanding "Der Raris Fabulis,"* (Cambridge: Hughes Hall and Department of Anglo-Saxon, Norse, and Celtic, University of Cambridge, 20024), p. 58.
32. Ibid., p. 40.
33. See Michael Lapidge, 'Aelfric's Schooldays', in S. Rosser and E. Treharne (eds), *Early Medieval English Texts and Interpretations: Studies Presented to Donald G. Scragg*, Medieval and Renaissance Texts and Studies Series, Volume 252 (Tempe: Arizona Centre for Medieval and Renaissance Studies, 2003).

the first of what was to become around 130 homilies – these were largely sermons, based on earlier writings, and instructive texts, dealing with subjects such as the life of Christ, the history of the apostles, and the foundation of monastic life. These were written – according to a prefix added by Aelfric at a later date – as a way of teaching the uneducated. Indeed, most of Aelfric's writings were pedagogic in nature, hence he is often referred to as 'Aelfric the Grammarian' or the 'Grammaticus'.

Typical of his later writings were a Latin grammar and a Latin-English glossary, or vocabulary, both written for his pupils. Also written as a teaching aid was his *Colloquy*, written in order to teach boys conversational Latin, and which consists of a dialogue between the master and various workers – a ploughman, shepherd, hunter, fisherman, merchant etc. – followed by a dialogue between the master and his pupils.[34]

Contrary to some early interpretations of the *Colloquy*, which assumed that the master was conversing with real labourers and artisans, the pupils would have taken the parts of the various workers themselves, and firstly learned the individual speeches by heart, and then, possibly, translated them into Old English. On this basis, it can be said that the *Colloquy*, and those of Aelfric Bata which followed this, are the earliest forms of English drama.

It opens with pupils asking their master 'to teach us to speak Latin correctly, for we are ignorant and we speak badly'. The pupils then, in one of the most widely-quoted passages, admit their willingness to be beaten as an encouragement to their learning: 'We would rather be flogged that we may learn, than remain ignorant, but we know that you are kindly, and that you will not lay strokes upon us, unless we oblige you to do so.'[35]

The dialogue continues with the master asking questions of various workers, which reveal the hardships of daily life in middle- and lower-class Anglo-Saxon England. A ploughman, oxherd, hunter and birdcatcher describe their day's routine, followed by other tradesmen: a merchant, tanner, salter, baker and cook, and the conversation then moves away from description, with the master asking a lawyer what he considers to

---

34. For a study and textual analysis, see G.N. Garmonsway (ed.) *Aelfric's Colloquy*, Exeter Medieval Texts and Studies Series, rev. edn (Liverpool: Liverpool University Press, 1991) (originally published by Methuen in 1939). This only provides the original Latin and later Old English translation. There are at least two modern English translations of the *Colloquy*: in S. Harvey Gem, *An Anglo-Saxon Abbot: Aelfric of Eynsham* (Edinburgh: T. & T. Clark, 1912); and in Michael Swanton (ed. and trans.), *Anglo-Saxon Prose* (London: J.M. Dent & Sons, 1975).
35. Harvey Gem, op cit., p. 183.

be the most important skill. The lawyer replies that the service of God is the most important. The master then asks him what the most important secular skills are – the lawyer suggests agriculture, because it provides food. The blacksmith then argues that without his skill there would be no ploughs; the carpenter points out that everyone uses his skills; and the lawyer finally urges everyone to practise their art more conscientiously.

The dialogue then turns to describing the day-to-day life of the school, the master asking one boy what he has done that day:

> I have done many things. This night, when I heard the call, I rose from my bed, and went out to the church, and sang nocturns with the brethren; then we sang of all the saints, and the matin song of praise; after that prime, and the seven psalms, with litanies, and the first mass, then terce, and we performed the mass of the day; after that we sang sext; then we ate and drank, and had our sleep, and rose up again, and sang nones, and now we are here before you, prepared to hear what you may say to us.[36]

Later on, the master asks a boy what he has to eat and drink:

> I am allowed meat, because I am still a boy, living under the rod.
> What do you eat besides?
> Vegetables and eggs, fish and cheese, butter and beans, and all clean things I eat, with giving of thanks.
> You are very voracious, to eat everything that is put before you.
> I am not such a glutton as to be able to eat all these kinds of food at the same meal.
> Then how do you manage?
> I eat sometimes this food, and sometimes that, with moderation, as befits a monk; I do not eat voraciously, for I am not a glutton.
> And what do you drink?
> Beer, if I have any, or water, if I have no beer.
> Don't you drink wine?
> I am not rich enough to buy myself wine, and wine is not a drink for boys, or foolish persons, but for elders, and wise men.[37]

---

36. Ibid., p. 194.
37. Ibid., p. 194.

Finally, the master addresses all the pupils:

> O good boys, and pleasant scholars, your instructor exhorts you to be obedient to the rules of divine discipline, and to behave yourselves decorously, wherever you may be. Walk with steadiness when you hear the bells of the church, enter into the house of prayer, and bend reverently before the holy altars. Stand in good order, and sing together, ask forgiveness for your faults, and go out again, without playing the fool, into the cloister or the schoolroom.[38]

Hence the *Colloquy* was aimed not just at teaching Latin, but was also a forum for discussing labour and trade, a philosophical essay on the value of education, and a way of instructing or reminding pupils how they should behave. It also reveals that the teaching of Latin was not confined to vocabulary and grammar – boys were taught how to converse in Latin (even, as the later works of Aelfric Bata showed, colloquially) and such lessons involved role-play and, presumably, opportunities to depart from the script and improvise when the boys had become proficient.

Only four copies of Aelfric's *Colloquy* exist, two held by the British Library, one being incomplete, with another incomplete copy in the Plantin-Moretus Museum, Antwerp. The fourth is held by St John's College, Oxford.

All four manuscripts have a range of additions and alterations, one in particular containing a continuous interlinear translation of the original Latin text into Old English.[39] All the embellishments have been attributed to one of Aelfric's pupils, Aelfric Bata, who added them some time after the originals had been written, and who went on to write his own *Colloquies* which provide an even more vivid and detailed picture of Anglo-Saxon monastic school life.

The *Colloquies* of Aelfric Bata

Aelfric Bata is the only one of Aelfric's pupils whose name is known. It is thought that he was a pupil under Aelfric at Eynsham, and then went on to teach at Canterbury, and possibly elsewhere.[40]

---

38. Ibid., p. 195.
39. Held at the British Library: BL Cotton MS Tiberius A III.
40. The most complete discussion and translation of Aelfric Bata's *Colloquies*, and conjectures as to his life, are in Scott Gwara (ed.) and David W. Porter

He began writing his own *Colloquies* around AD 1000, using the earlier *De Raris Fabulis* as source material. Like Aelfric's *Colloquy*, Bata's dialogues were designed to teach conversational Latin, but unlike Aelfric, Bata went to extremes to make his dialogues entertaining as well as educational. They are full of wit, satire and abuse, and paint a picture not only of monastic life as it should have been led, but also of how it actually was led, and revealing, in far more detail than Aelfric's *Colloquy*, the way in which monastery boys learned to read and write, how they played, how and why they were punished, what they ate and drank, how they interacted with each other and with their master, and how their lives were regulated by the monastic regime, and what they thought of their restrictions and the limited freedoms they enjoyed.

Bata wrote 29 colloquies, and a further thirteen *Colloquia Difficiloria* (i.e. more difficult dialogues). Some are extremely short – one or two sentences only (in the original Latin) – whereas others are very long, and would have proved troublesome to have been learnt by heart.

Scott Gwara and David Porter in their volume on Bata, *Anglo-Saxon Conversations*, point to the differences between Aelfric and his pupil – Aelfric is described as 'sober, serious and taciturn, an abstemious monk adhering to a monastic ideal', whereas Aelfric Bata (who describes himself at the beginning of his *Colloquies* as 'a very short monk') is 'a devoted drinker, a garrulous talker with a huge vocabulary, a comic dramatist with a deft sense of the satirical and a most lukewarm regard for Benedict's taboos'.[41]

The differences are reflected in the dialogues themselves, in which drunkenness, gluttony and verbal abuse are common, as are violations of monastic custom, such as the ownership of private property, the carrying on of trade and bartering, and, indeed, an occasional disregard for the strict monastic routine that governed, or should have governed, the pupils' lives, and frequent bad behaviour, excess, disrespect and hardship. This is, however, balanced by a willingness to learn, an acceptance of discipline and the rigours of school life, and an adherence, albeit occasionally loosely, to doctrine and religious practice.

The fact that both sides of the coin, so to speak, are so obviously revealed suggests that the picture could hardly be more authentic.

(trans.), *Anglo-Saxon Conversations: The Colloquies of Aelfric Bata* (Woodbridge: Boydell Press, 1997). See also Gulliver Grisbrooke-Campbell, 'Aelfric Bata's *Colloquia*: Reassessing an Eleventh-Century Latin Textbook' (unpublished MA thesis, University of Wales, Trinity Saint David, 2021).

41. Gwara (ed.) and Porter (trans.), *Anglo-Saxon Conversations*, p. 12.

Aelfric Bata wrote his *Colloquies* both as a former pupil and as a young monk who had experienced, at first hand, the problems of teaching. The parallels between eleventh-/twelfth-century school life – in particular, the resentments, drudgery, fear of punishment, stoicism and occasional enthusiasm for academic work – and that of the nineteenth, twentieth and twenty-first centuries are obvious. Aelfric Bata wrote about the reality of the daily life of his pupils – and his *Colloquies* have an aura of verisimilitude that cannot be denied.

Of course, the intention behind the *Colloquies* was not to leave a portrait of school life for future generations, but rather to teach conversational Latin. In addition, Gwara and Porter suggest that Aelfric Bata was training a new generation of Latin teachers – many of the dialogues give gentle hints as to how masters, rather than pupils, should behave and, furthermore, they allow for role play, when boys could briefly become adults, not just schoolmasters but also farmers, fishermen, merchants etc.

Occasionally, a dialogue fails to make clear who is speaking – some dialogues have a clear authorial voice but they could be spoken by a pupil, presumably an older pupil, who may well have taken a minor teaching role himself.

The life of the boys in Bata's 'fictional' monastery is delineated in great detail. In *Colloquy 5*, a master arrives in the classroom and asks the boys what they have been doing, and receives a lengthy reply setting out when they sang, said prayers, attended mass, went to the toilet, had their meals and so on.

The timelessness of pupils begging to be spared punishment, on a promise of better behaviour or harder work, and the innate suspicion of the schoolmaster, is portrayed in *Colloquy 6*, where a pupil, threatened with a whipping for not preparing his lesson, is let off on the promise that he will work harder.

Colloquy 7 reveals the boys at play:

> It seems to me it's almost the hour of vespers now.
>   We think so, too, but it's still not vespers yet.
>   Master, let us play a little while – since we very well know our assignments, lections, responses and antiphons already.
>   Very well, you may, because it's a feast day. I now give you permission this time to play until the vespers signal.
>   Now it's good for us to be alive! Let's all go together to play outdoors with our sticks and our ball or hoop.

> You, boy, lend me a stick, and I'll give you back two sticks right away, please.
>
> I have plenty. And if you want to play with a hoop together, I'll give you a flail so we can both play taking turns. If you want to play with a ball, I'll lend you both my ball and my stick to play with.
>
> Do that. Bless you always. Now I've realised that you're my friend and because of that I want to love you sincerely and well in true and honest friendship.[42]

Here, we have both a picture of Anglo-Saxon games, and, perhaps, a suggestion of romantic friendship.

Colloquy 14 reveals the pupils' methods of working, with its list of items echoing earlier texts:

> I don't have a wax tablet or a stylus or a penknife or a knife or an awl or a razor – or a whetstone for sharpening my razor so I can sharpen my pen. No craftsman can work well without tools!
>
> What you say is true, brother. We have to get you wax tablets and styluses, penknives and knives, awls and rules, vellum scraps and parchment, ink and razors, and whetstones and pens enough for writing and painting so that you have no excuse in this thing.[43]

The second part of this dialogue shows the master providing all that has been requested, with all the items listed, albeit in a slightly different order.

Elsewhere, the *Colloquies* reveal much about the relationships between master and boys. *Colloquy 5* portrays boys behaving in much the same way as they do now, with one boy being instructed to keep an eye out for the master, and another boy warning the class to make sure they are working when the master arrives. Other colloquies cover subjects such as food and drink, the contents of the monastery, telling the time and the days of the week, and exhortations to study and not to misbehave.

One of the longest dialogues, *Colloquy 25*, consists of a tirade by the master aimed at a pupil, who is always late and troublemaker, and the pupil's equally as verbally vicious response:

---

42. Ibid., p. 95.
43. Ibid., p. 113.

> You idiot! You goat shit! Sheep shit! Horse shit! You cow dung! You pig turd! You human turd! You dog shit! Fox shit! Cat turd! Chicken shit! You ass turd! You fox cub of all fox cubs! You fox tail! You fox beard! You skin of a fox cub! You idiot and halfwit! You buffoon! What would you have me for? Nothing good, I think.
>
> I would like you to be totally beshat and depissed for all these words of yours. Have shit in your beard! May you always have shit in your beard, and shit and turds in your mouth, three and two times and eight and one, and I none at all ever! Now your words reveal the truth, that you are a buffoon and a fool and a silly blabbermouth. You don't know how to do anything better than to use your stinking stupid words to beshit and befoul those who come to you. I'm not learned yet, or as smart as you. I can in no way use wisdom; I don't know how at all, because my young age is entirely unable to do so.[44]

It goes on and on, the master revealing in the next passage that the pupil he is haranguing is fifteen or sixteen years old. The invective, from both parties, is astonishing – surely exaggerated, and not, by modern standards, what would be considered appropriate for classroom use, let alone in a religious classroom. However, this irreverence is not uncommon in Bata's dialogues, and fully in keeping with his character and teaching philosophy – situations are pushed to an extreme in order to drive home both a moral and pedagogic message. This is typified by several references to drinking and drunkenness, perhaps reflecting Bata's own proclivities – the word 'bata' meant 'fifty pints' or 'the barrel'.

The problems of personal hygiene are highlighted in *Colloquy 23*, with a boy complaining that no one has any shears (for cutting hair), soap, razors or hot water and that their clothes are dirty, with *Colloquy 26* seeing a boy complaining that he only has one cover on his bed, no strong shoes or overcoat, and only one pair of trousers, which are stained with blood following a beating. He asks for a 'a fur robe, a shirt, a good cowl, hose, stockings, tunic, cloth, gloves, belt; and knife and penknife, and various dishes – cup, jug, bowl and dish; and writing tablet, stylus and a cover for my seat'. The master's response is that God will provide their necessities, and the boy agrees.[45]

---

44. Ibid., p. 139.
45. Ibid., p. 161.

One of the commonest themes in the eighteenth- and nineteenth-century school story was the robbing of orchards or the stealing of fruit – presumably an allegorical device, a metaphor for forbidden fruit and the serpent's tempting of Adam and Eve in the Garden of Eden[46] – and, perhaps not surprisingly, given the religious background to Bata's teaching, this is the theme of *Colloquy 28*, which also deals with the issue of other types of theft, and, rather dramatically, punishment. When a master accuses two boys of stealing apples, which they deny, another boy accuses them, only for the two boys to turn the tables on him and point out that he is a known liar and thief, providing a long list of items he has stolen in the past, including clothes, money, books and food. The boy acknowledges his guilt, but claims he wants to stop stealing and do penance. The boys ask the master to punish him, although the master places the onus onto the two pupils:

> Take two rods. One boy stand on the right side of his ass and one on the left. Take turns like this beating his ass and back. First you two beat him well and I will afterwards.
>
> Be lenient this time, father, and spare me. That's enough.
>
> Hit harder, you fool! He's making fun of your blows. He doesn't feel them at all.
>
> Father, from this moment I'll stop the lying I'm suffering for. I've been beaten and punished enough this time. Show me some kindness and leniency. I'm about to die.
>
> You're not dead yet.
>
> This is hurting me. I'd rather be dead now than to bear such lashes. Woe is me, why was I ever born? It would be better for me to die now than to live so miserably ...
>
> Will you ever steal anything again?
>
> No, sir, no. I'm very sorry that I ever stole. I'll swear to you by God that from now on I'll stop all thieving and lying for as long as I have life.
>
> Do so, poor boy, do so. Stop now, brothers, stop. Don't beat him any longer. Get up, silly boy, and dress yourself. Don't cry. Sin no more so nothing worse overtakes you.
>
> I'll be careful for as long as life remains in my body and God lets me live on earth.[47]

---

46. Alternatively, of course, it may simply be a reflection of a childish liking of fruit and other sweet things, reinforced by a diet lacking in sugar.
47. Ibid., pp. 167 and 171.

This dialogue also introduces the concept of the reformed sinner, another integral part of the eighteenth- and early nineteenth-century school story. Of course, without a narrative, we are not to know whether the sinner did reform – but the harshness of the punishment points towards it being a distinct possibility. The punishment itself is also of interest, in that the thief is beaten by two of his schoolfellows – a precursor of the later, officially sanctioned punishments carried out by prefects, monitors, praepostors etc.

Bata's *Colloquia Difficiloria*, which follows his *Colloquies*, was designed to teach more difficult Latin speech, and is also rather more reverent. Of the thirteen additional dialogues (in fact, most are monologues, spoken by the master), around half are devoted to learning and the need to serve God. This is a much more sober Aelfric Bata, one who has, it seems, forsaken the irreverent debauchery of some of his earlier *Colloquies* and who has, perhaps belatedly, remembered his position and role.

2

Chaucer's Schoolboy

Geoffrey Chaucer's contribution to the history of the boys' school story has, until now, been wholly overlooked. Yet, within his epic poem *The Canterbury Tales* there is an embryonic school story – an overtly shocking tale, but one in which the hero's school life is an integral element, and, as such, it is, arguably, the first 'genuine' school tale ever written.

Chaucer was born around 1340 (the exact date is not known). His parents lived in the parish of St Martins-in-the-Vintry in London, his father having associations with the wine trade. His early schooling was possibly at St Paul's Almonry, although there is no evidence for this. After his education was finished he became a page in the household of the Countess of Ulster. In 1359 he was sent to France to fight in what became known as the Hundred Years' War; in 1374 he became a comptroller of customs at the Port of London; in 1385 he became a justice of the peace for Kent. He died in 1400.

It is, of course, as a poet that he is now remembered and, in particular, for his epic poem *The Canterbury Tales*.[1] This is a description

---

1. The publication history of *The Canterbury Tales* is very complex. The first printed version was published by William Caxton in 1476 or 1477. Later editions were published by Pynson, Wynkyn de Worde and William Thynne. Over 60 manuscript copies, pre-dating the printed editions, have survived. In addition, numerous edited and revised editions have been published since the late 16th century. The text quoted here is taken from William Wordsworth's translation, published in *The Poetical Works of William Wordsworth*, New Edition (London: Longman, Rees, Orme, Brown, and Green, 1827), Volume IV.

of a pilgrimage from London to Canterbury, in which each of some 30 pilgrims tell stories to each other. The pilgrims represent a cross-section of late fourteenth-century society – including a knight, yeoman, monk, miller, cook, prioress, physician, clerk, merchant and squire. The tales they tell are, in most cases, based on earlier tales – from England, Europe and, occasionally, the Far East – both contemporary and historical, and all have an important moral or philosophical purpose.

A handful of these tales are concerned with education, although this is in a general sense, and more a plea for the education of mankind as a whole rather than a discussion of the education of the young. Two of the stories – *The Wife of Bath's Tale* and *The Squire's Tale* – place a special emphasis on the training and education of the young, although these are philosophical in nature rather than descriptive. Chaucer was, if anything, more interested in university education than school education, although there is no evidence that he attended university himself.[2] He owes his place in the history of the school story to *The Prioress's Tale* – a story which had its basis in legend but which even today is rather disquieting.

The tale that the Prioress tells her fellow pilgrims centres on a young schoolboy who is murdered by some Jews for his Catholic faith. The setting is Asia:

> *There was in Asia, in a mighty town.*
> *'Mong Christian folk, a street where Jews might be,*
> *Assigned to them and given them for their own*
> *By a great Lord, for gain and usury,*
> *Hateful to Christ and to his company;*
> *And through this street who list might ride and wend;*
> *Free was it, and unbarred at either end. (Stanza VI)*

> *A little school of Christian people stood*
> *Down at the farther end, in which there were*
> *A nest of children come of Christian blood,*
> *That learned in that school from year to year*
> *Such sort of doctrine as men used there,*
> *That is to say, to sing and read also,*
> *As little children in their childhood do. (Stanza VII)*

---

2. It is known that Chaucer's son, Lewis – to whom he dedicated *A Treatise on the Astrolabe* in 1391 – was a student at Oxford.

Nicholas Orme, in his article on 'Chaucer and Education',[3] suggests that the school attended by the schoolboy closely resembles an English elementary school or the elementary department of a grammar school.

The schoolboy is 'a Widow's son, a little scholar, scarcely seven years old ... ', who is extremely pious:

> *day by day unto this school hath gone,*
> *And eke, when he the image did behold*
> *Of Jesu's Mother, as he had been told,*
> *This Child was wont to kneel adown and say*
> *'Ave Marie', as he goeth by the way. (Stanza VIII)*

He has presumably only just started his school education – he is described as studying his primer, which was a simple schoolbook containing the alphabet and basic Latin prayers. Whilst at school he hears other pupils singing the hymn to the Virgin, *Alma Redemptoris Mater* ('Loving Mother of the Redeemer'). He listens carefully until he knows the opening verse by heart, although he has no idea what it means:

> *This Latin knew he nothing what it said,*
> *For he too tender was of age to know;*
> *But to his comrade he repaired, and prayed*
> *That he the meaning of this song would show,*
> *And unto him declare why men sing so;*
> *This oftentimes, that he might be at ease,*
> *This child did him beseech on his bare knees. (Stanza XI)*

His schoolfellow explains the purpose of the hymn, although he, too, is ignorant of its translation:

> *His Schoolfellow, who elder was than he,*
> *Answered him thus: – 'This song, I have heard say,*
> *Was fashioned for our blissful Lady free;*
> *Her to salute, and also her to pray*
> *To be our help upon our dying day.*
> *If there is more in this, I know it not;*
> *Song do I learn, – small grammar I have got.' (Stanza XII)*

---

3. Nicholas Orme, 'Chaucer and Education', *Chaucer Review* 16 (1981), pp. 38–59.

The younger boy determines to learn the entire song by heart, even if this means forgoing learning his primer and being beaten:[4]

> *'I will use my diligence*
> *To con it all ere Christmas-tide be spent;*
> *Although I for my Primer shall be shent,*
> *And shall be beaten three times in an hour,*
> *Our Lady I shall praise with all my power.' (Stanza XIII)*

The older boy therefore teaches his younger schoolfellow the words and music every day as they are going home after school:

> *His Schoolfellow, whom he had so besought,*
> *As they went homeward taught him privily;*
> *And then he sang it well and fearlessly,*
> *From word to word according to the note*
> *Twice in a day it passed through his throat;*
> *Homeward and schoolward whenso'er he went,*
> *On Jesu's Mother fixed was his intent. (Stanza XIV)*

---

4. Chaucer was not an advocate of corporal punishment and its mention here is simply a reflection of the reality of school life at the time – schoolchildren were beaten if they failed to learn their lessons. In *The Parson's Tale*, Chaucer makes clear his distaste of corporal punishment of children, and makes a plea for patience:

> Upon a time a philosopher would have beaten a disciple for his great misdoing, at which the philosopher had been much annoyed; and he brought a rod wherewith to scourge the youth; and when the youth saw the rod he said to his master: 'What do you intend to do?' 'I will beat you', said the master, 'for your correction.' 'Forsooth,' said the youth, 'you ought first to correct yourself who have lost all your patience at the offence of a child.' 'Forsooth,' said the master, weeping, 'you say truth; take the rod yourself, my dear son, and correct me for my impatience.' From patience comes obedience, whereby a man becomes obedient to Christ and to all to whom he owes obedience in Christ. And understand well that obedience is perfect when a man does gladly and speedily, with entire good heart, all that he should do. Obedience, generally, is to put into practice the doctrine of God and of man's masters, to whom he ought to be humble in all righteousness.

The Prioress then goes on to say that the hearts of the Jews in the town are possessed by Satan, who objects to the boy singing a Christian hymn, and as a result they arrange for the young schoolboy to be murdered:

> *From that day forward have the Jews conspired*
> *Out of the world this Innocent to chase;*
> *And to this end a Homicide they hired,*
> *That in an Alley had a privy place,*
> *And, as the Child 'gan to the School to pace,*
> *This cruel Jew him seized, and held him fast*
> *And cut his throat, and in a pit him cast. (Stanza XVII)*

The boy's mother waits up for him all night, and in the morning she goes to the school to look for him:

> *Now this poor widow waiteth all that night*
> *After her little Child, and he came not;*
> *For which, by earliest glimpse of morning light,*
> *With face all pale with dread and busy thought,*
> *She at the School and elsewhere him hath sought,*
> *Until thus far she learned, that he had been*
> *In the Jews' street, and there he last was seen. (Stanza XX)*

She approaches the Jewish residents of the street but they deny all knowledge of the boy and, eventually, she finds his body in the pit where he had been dumped. However, even though his throat has been cut, he begins singing – other Christians who are passing by stop in wonder, and the boy is then taken to the nearest abbey. The provost is sent for and he curses the Jews who had conspired in the child's murder, and orders them to be drawn apart by horses and then hanged.

As the boy is being prepared for burial, the abbot asks him how he is able to carry on singing. The boy replies that, when he died, the Virgin Mary placed a grain on his tongue that allows him to speak and sing, and that he can only ascend to heaven when the grain is removed. The abbot thereupon touches the boy's tongue and removes the grain, and the boy dies peacefully. The tale ends with a lament for the young boy and a curse on the Jews who murdered him.

The precise aim of the story, even today, is unclear. It has obvious anti-semitic overtones, yet these are, in the narrative, expressed by the Prioress – a character for whom Chaucer clearly had little sympathy. Yet, there is still great scope for debate as to how far the tale was a reflection of Chaucer's own views,[5] particularly in the context of the time in which he wrote the tale.

Jews had been expelled from England in 1290, by King Edward I, a hundred years after 150 Jews had been massacred in York in an uprising which followed the coronation of Richard I. Following this, popular culture in the fourteenth century was imbued with anti-Jewish sentiment, with stories of the 'Blood Libel' – the belief that Jews would kidnap, torture and murder Christian children during Passover – widely disseminated.

Indeed, Chaucer's tale is a clear version of one of these stories and was almost certainly based on the legend of 'Hugh of Lincoln', as evidenced by the Prioress's lament:

> *Young Hew of Lincoln! In like sort laid low*
> *By cursed Jews – thing well and widely known,*
> *For not long since was dealt the cruel blow. (Stanza XXXIV)*

Hugh, an eight-year-old boy, was the alleged victim of ritual murder by Jews in Lincoln in 1255. He disappeared and his body was eventually found in the well (or cesspit) of a house belonging to a Jew, who was induced to confess that the boy had been murdered by a number of Jews who were visiting Lincoln. Although he had been pardoned by a priest, in return for his confession, the pardon was revoked by King Henry III, who ordered that he be dragged around Lincoln tied to the tail of a horse, and then hanged. Ninety-two Jews were subsequently arrested and taken to London, where eighteen were executed.

The story was notorious, as there was no evidence behind it, and it was far more likely that Hugh fell into the well while chasing a ball and was drowned purely by accident.[6]

Nevertheless, the legend persisted, with a shrine to Hugh being erected over his tomb in Lincoln Cathedral and with Hugh being seen

---

5. See, for example: Helen Cooper, *Oxford Guides to Chaucer: The Canterbury Tales* (Oxford: Oxford University Press, 1989); Albert Friedman, 'The *Prioress's Tale* and Chaucer's Anti-Semitism', *Chaucer Review* 9 (1974), pp. 118–29; Emmy Stark Zitter, 'Anti-Semitism in Chaucer's *Prioress's Tale*', *Chaucer Review* 25, no. 4 (1991), pp. 277–84; and John Matthews Manly, *Some New Light on Chaucer: Lectures Delivered at the Lowell Institute* (Gloucester, MA: Henry Holt & Co., 1926).

6. See, for example, Bernard Grebanier, *The Truth about Shylock* (New York, NY: Random House, 1962), pp. 24–25.

as a Christian martyr. The shrine was replaced in 1955 with a plaque explaining that the legend was fiction and that it and similar medieval tales had led to many innocent Jews losing their lives.

* * *

The death of the schoolboy in *The Prioress's Tale* has faint echoes in later children's literature, where children who are deeply pious die uncomfortable (or more usually comfortable) deaths. One notable exemplar of this tradition was James Janeway's *A Token for Children: Being an Exact Account of the Conversion, Holy and Exemplary Lives, and Joyful Deaths of Several Young Children*, first published in England in 1672 and which later enjoyed great success in America (see chapter nine).

Pious children continued to die in eighteenth and nineteenth century children's literature,[7] including in school stories, where such deaths were almost always in the context of heavily evangelical fiction, in which religion and a strict adherence to biblical precepts and God's law was the central theme. Death, even that of very young children, was God's will, and something to be celebrated rather than mourned. The basis of such stories was therefore far removed from the apparent bigotry of *The Prioress's Tale*, with its cruelty and its rather unpious narrator.

Yet, despite the story's unsavoury taste, and the debate that has raged over Chaucer's motives in writing the story – or rather reviving an old legend – the tale itself remains the first to portray a schoolboy, something of his daily school life, and the effect of his actions on both himself and others. This, after all, is the bedrock of most later school fiction, and so *The Prioress's Tale* can be seen as the moment when the English school story germinated, growing from the brief snatches of school life portrayed in the dialogues of Aelfric and Aelfric Bata, and beginning its development into a longer, self-contained narrative.

---

7. See, for example, Rowland Hill, *Instructions for Children; or, a Token of Love for the Rising Generation* (London: G. Thompson, 1794), which includes *A Short Account of the Lives and Deaths of Good Children that Died Rejoicing in the Lord*.

3

Fifteenth- to Seventeenth-Century *Vulgaria* and Colloquies

The use of colloquies as an aid to teaching Latin re-emerged in the fifteenth century (indeed, had probably never gone away) and were often found alongside *vulgaria* – conversational phrases, sentences and passages. Again, some of these had school settings, which, having been invented by their creators, can be seen as a further forerunner of the school story.

One of the best introductions to the way that Latin was taught in schools in England in the fifteenth and sixteenth centuries is in Nicholas Orme's *Education and Society in Medieval and Renaissance England*.[1] In particular, Orme highlights the importance of texts – phrases and sentences – which were written by schoolmasters and used as teaching aids:

> Translation sentences are one of the most accessible and appealing genres of school literature in the fifteenth and sixteenth centuries. They indicate the content and level of the curriculum – the grammar, syntax and vocabulary which the master was teaching, and also something of his policy and methods. Medieval and Renaissance schoolmasters used translation sentences to impart wisdom and morality

---

1. Nicholas Orme, *Education and Society in Medieval and Renaissance England* (London: Hambledon Press, 1989).

as well as Latin. They set proverbs and wise quotations for translations, and they tried to capture the pupil's interest by choosing topics of humour, school affairs, news and life outside the school. ... As a result, the sentences preserve a great many cultural references. They reveal the master himself, his duties and status, the pupils, their families and prospective careers, classroom procedures and customs.[2]

In particular, Orme makes a point which few historians of children's literature have picked up on, when he points out that the writers of these phrases:

can be said to have discovered a major topic of interest in modern English literature: the evocation of childhood. Here too what began as an educational device ended as a literary influence. The schoolmasters of the later middle ages had the same general objective as their modern successors. Their task was to prepare their pupils for adult life, and this they did by introducing into their teaching as many precepts as possible about the ethics and standards required of adults at that time: religious observance, self discipline, obedience, courtesy and so on. But like their successors today, they found that their teaching was more effective if it made concessions to their pupils and dwelt to some extent on childish things: the everyday life of children, their humour, pleasures, problems, and emotions. Matters of this kind not only held the attention of the class but actively assisted its progress to adulthood.[3]

Collections of sentences which boys were expected to translate became known, in the late 1400s, as *vulgaria* – because they were written in a colloquial, or common, manner. The word first appears (in Latin) as the title of a collection of phrases and sentences taken or adapted from the plays of the Roman playwight Terence and compiled by John Ankwyll, Master of Magdalen School in Oxford in 1483.[4] One famous early phrase, written by John Drury, a Suffolk schoolmaster, in 1434,

---

2. Ibid., p. 75.
3. Ibid., p. 69.
4. *Vulgaria quedam abs Terencio in Anglicam linguam traducta* (Oxford, 1483).

deals with the schoolboy's universal fear: 'Myn ars comyng to scole xal be betyn.'[5]

The earliest of these teaching aids exist only in manuscript form, particularly in school notebooks compiled by schoolmasters (and, occasionally, by pupils). It wasn't until the end of the fifteenth century, after the introduction of printing in England by William Caxton in 1476, that texts written by schoolmasters for use in schools were made widely available beyond their individual classrooms, although texts in manuscript form did circulate amongst schools prior to this.

Nicholas Orme brought several of these manuscript texts together in *English School Exercises, 1420–1530*, published in 2013.[6] One of the earliest texts, from around 1427, is preserved in a collection of manuscripts compiled by Thomas Schort, a west country priest, and now held in the Bodleian Library, Oxford.[7] Amongst the texts are *vulgaria* comprising 115 sentences and passages in English, each followed by a Latin equivalent. While these were transcribed by Schort, their likely author was Robert Londe, the master of Newgate School in Bristol. The text tells us that school began at six o'clock in the morning, with pupils going hungry until breakfast or dinner: 'Me comyth to scole yn the mortyde sory, but me goyth to dyner mery and glad.' The school contains a mixture of pupils from wealthy and poor backgrounds: 'Chyldryn stond yn a row, sum wel a-rayd, sum evel a-rayd.'

Learning Latin can be difficult: 'A hard latyn to make, my face wexyth blakke'; 'The mayster hath yrebukyd me for my defawtys.' The threat of corporal punishment is never far away: 'My felow y-bete with a byrch zerd, y ham to be bete with a whyppe.' There are other universal complaints and observations: 'Y have no spendyng money' and 'My gowne ys y-steynyd.' Elsewhere the manuscript provides indications of daily classroom life – boys being examined by the schoolmaster and also reading; there are occasional fights amongst the pupils; school food includes cabbage stalks, herrings and rashers of meat; and games are played.

---

5. John Drury – *Parue latinitates de termino Natalis Domini sed non pro forma reddicionis* – transcribed by Sanford Brown Meech in 'John Drury and His English Writings', *Speculum* 9, no. 1 (1934), pp. 70–83.
6. Nicholas Orme, *English School Exercises, 1420–1530* (Toronto: Pontifical Institute of Medieval Studies, 2013).
7. MS Lat. 129 (E). See Orme, *English School Exercises*, pp. 48–69, for a full discusssion and transcription.

A manuscript from Exeter Grammar School, held by Gonville and Caius College, Cambridge,[8] shows a slight disdain for schoolmasters:

> We were deceived today when we came to the school after the established hour, thinking that the master had not arrived there, because previously he was accustomed to stay in his bedroom for longer; we believe, however, that fleas troubled him with their bitings or else he lacked a good drink overnight, a medicine that causes and compels a man to sleep.

It also reveals the hardships experienced by families who strive to give their children a good education: 'My parents, who live in the country in great penury, are put under a great strain by sending me to school to learn grammar in Exeter, and with a large family at home, acquiring food and clothes takes immense efforts.'

Boys being late for school, and punishments, were key themes in some manuscripts, especially in one created in London at some time between 1450 and 1470, held by the British Library[9] and again transcribed by Nicholas Orme:

> Two scholars today being beaten for late arrival are shamed by the lies with which they excused themselves, saying that their friends detained them at home, it having been openly known that they had lain overlong in bed.
>
> It was displeasing to the master at six o'clock to find so very few boys sitting in school, who came from distant places while truants who dwell nearby were lying in bed.

Magdalen School Manuscripts

Some of the best-known school *vulgaria* emanated from Magdalen Grammar School in Oxford, in particular, those written by John Stanbridge and Robert Whittinton and published in the early sixteenth century. Two other notable *vulgaria* exist only in manuscript.

Magdalen College, Oxford, had been founded in 1448 by William of Waynflete, who later (in 1480) established a grammar school alongside it (in much the same way that Winchester had been established, in 1382,

---

8. MS 417/447. See Orme, *English School Exercises*, pp. 148–76.
9. Additional MS 37075. See Orme, *English School Exercises*, pp. 177–236.

as a sister foundation to New College, Oxford). Waynflete had been a grammar master at Winchester, before becoming Provost of Eton in 1442, and then Bishop of Winchester in 1447.

Magdalen Grammar School's first Master (or Informator) was John Ankwyll, who published the first Latin grammar aimed at schoolboys in 1483.[10] Appended to this was his *vulgaria* using phrases from Terence (see above).

Arundel Manuscript

A second *vulgaria*, which, unlike Ankwyll's, is wholly original in composition and which has many references to school life, is preserved in a collection of manuscripts in the British Library,[11] and discussed and transcribed by William Nelson in *A Fifteenth Century School Book*.[12] Nelson dates this manuscript, which comprises 387 passages, to between 1493 and 1498, although its author remains unidentified. There can be little doubt, however, that it originated from Magdalen Grammar School – there are numerous references to Oxford and its environs, including Headington and Carfax.

In his analysis of the manuscript, Nelson comes up with a composite portrait which represents a late fifteenth-century schoolboy and his life, at school and at home:

> He began his education – and underwent his first professional beating – at the local 'absey' or primary school. At the age of eleven he was sent off to Oxford where he now lives with other boys under the care of a 'creanser' or house tutor. ... It may be five years before he sees his parents again for the roads are poor and the thieves are many.[13] But he writes letters to them if a friend or the carrier happens to be going in the right direction. Sometimes they send him a present of fruit. If he

---

10. John Ankwyll, *Compendium totius grammaticae* (Oxford: T. Rood & T. Hunt, 1483).
11. MS Arundel 249.
12. William Nelson (ed.), *A Fifteenth Century School Book: From a Manuscript in the British Museum (Ms. Arundel 249)* (Oxford: Clarendon Press, 1956). The manuscript is now in the British Library.
13. This was echoed in the first half of the nineteenth century, in the policy of many boarding schools, particularly those in Yorkshire, having 'no vacations' and highlighted by Charles Dickens in *The Life and Adventures of Nicholas Nickleby*, published in 1839.

is lucky, someone from home turns up on fair day and buys him such requisites as a penknife to cut his quills and keep them sharp, a pen case, writing tablets, and most important of all, books. He loses these things from time to time, or they are stolen.

The thought of food is never far from his mind. His basic diet is monotonous and meagre; he is often so hungry that he is tempted to take more than his portion or to steal from his neighbour. But he would rather eat poorly with his fellows than fare better sitting quiet and well-behaved with his elders. ...

Above all, he hates waking before dawn on winter mornings and sitting down to hours of study before breakfast, but if he doesn't get up the creanser will beat him, and if doesn't have his 'vulgars' written his grammar master will. Then there are errands to run for the creanser, so that the boy may get to school late, his work unfinished, with the inevitable consequence. The schoolmaster and his assistant are kindly enough, but they would not hurt the scholar by sparing him the rod. ...

Inevitably, our scholar sides with his fellows against his teachers, and he giggles gleefully when he learns that his master suffers from toothache. At the same time, he has caught something of his master's enthusiasm for the glories of Latin, and he has begun to think that hard study may stand him in good stead in later life. His master may be able to further his career; either for that reason or because of a growing respect for him the boy strives for his good opinion.[14]

All this, and much more – about life outside school, holidays, sport, entertainment and so on – can be gleaned from the 387 passages.

The very first passage is described by Nelson as a 'beautifully imagined soliloquy of an eleven-year-old suffering from the shock of immersion in grammar school life, in particular the need to get up early: "nowe at fyve of the clocke by the monelyght I most go to my booke and lete slepe and slouthe alon."' Later on, a boy complains of the cold:

> The moste part of this wynter my handes wer so swellynge with colde that I coulde nother holde my penn for to wrytt nother my knyff for to cutt my mete at the table, and my fete

---

14. Nelson, *A Fifteenth Century School Book*, pp. xxii-xxiv.

also thei wer arayde with kybblayns that it grevyde me to go enywhere.[15]

As other extracts show, the life of a schoolboy was sometimes harsh, and many of the passages have a palpable sense of poignancy. In one, a boy (presumably an orphan) laments that he has to stay at school while his fellow pupils are allowed to go home: 'Well is my scole felows which have leve to go se ther fathers and mothers to sport them. as for me, I cannot so moch as a moment departe from my maisters side.'[16]

Corporal punishment, or at least the fear of being beaten, especially for unprepared or poorly prepared work, was also a common theme: 'Felow, I besech the hertely to kepe oure counsell lest the maister know how unthriftely we myspent oure tyme yesterday, for yff he may know he wyl be verey angrye and not without a cause.'[17]

A master reveals how his pupils present excuses to escape the classroom:

> As sone as I am cum into the scole this felow goith to make water and he goyth oute to the comyn drafte [i.e. privy]. Sone after another askith licence that he may go drynke. another callith upon me that he may have licence to go home. thies and such other leyth my scholars for excuse oftyntyms that they may be oute off the waye.[18]

Boys reflect on friendship and death:

> John, methynkith that there is no man more ungentle nother mor uncurtese to me then thou art, for allway thou complanest upon me withoute a cause to my Creanser. After my mynde I have not deservede thy evyll wyll but rather thy frendeshipe, for I have benn allway very delygent to do the a pleasure.[19]

> I was very sory when I herde say that thy brother was dede in this pestilence for I have lost a gentle frende and a trusty. from oure first acquentance, the which was sens we

---

15. Ibid., p. 6.
16. Ibid., p. 14.
17. Ibid., p. 29.
18. Ibid., p. 39.
19. Ibid., p. 41.

were childern, we were companyde togedre in on house and undre onn maister and lightly we hade onn mynde in every mater. I cannot tell in goode faithe what losse may be comparede with this. the philosopher thought ther was nothynge more to be praisede than a goode frende.[20]

Nelson also highlights the short step that the manuscript occasionally takes from individual sentences/speeches to dialogues – as in the earlier colloquies by Aelfric and Aelfric Bata – and he hints that these may have involved some degree of action and acting: 'We have no way of knowing whether or not they were acted out as rudimentary playlets in the classroom. If the author of the vulgaria was as clever a teacher as he seems, he would not have missed the opportunity.'[21]

Royal Manuscript

A second Magdalen manuscript, fully discussed and transcribed by Orme, and which features the life and work of a grammar school, is preserved in the British Library.[22] This consists of 87 passages of Latin prose each followed by an English translation, a reversal of the usual format of *vulgaria*, in which English passages are to be translated into Latin. Orme suggests it was written between 1526 and 1527.

As with the Arundel manuscript, it is possible to compile a detailed composite picture of a Magdalen schoolboy and his daily life, and also that of the master, who appears in many of the passages. Orme describes the latter as:

> both wise and stern, sometimes giving encouragement but more frequently admonitions, which can escalate into reprimands, threats, and the promise of punishment. Beating, however, which features prominently in other schoolbooks, is strangely underemphasised. The master is a single man, since there is no reference to his wife or family, and this accords with what we know of his real-life Magdalen counterparts, most of whom were either priests or unmarried clerks. He sometimes finds teaching in Oxford tiresome, because of the criticism he gets from others who think they know his

---

20. Ibid., p. 45.
21. Ibid., p. xxvi.
22. Royal MS 12.B.xx. See Orme, *English School Exercises*, pp. 378–414.

business better than he does himself, but he is represented as a diligent teacher and a sober citizen out of school hours, taking his recreation by gentle walking and by dining out with a friend.[23]

Orme also points out that the text provides evidence of a move towards the recognition of schoolmasters as important members of the community, thanks largely to the establishment of growing numbers of endowed schools, whereby schoolmasters no longer had to rely on fees for their income, but instead had a guaranteed wage and a large degree of job security (although this recognition and acceptance was a slow process, evidenced by the frequent negative portrayal of schoolmasters in the drama of the period – see the next chapter).

The boys at the school were either day boys or, probably in the majority of cases, boarders, who lived within the school or in lodgings in Oxford, many with tutors (creansers) appointed by their parents to look after them and supervise their studies. The unwelcome return to school after the Christmas holiday is portrayed in one of the opening passages of the manuscript, spoken by the master:

> Me semeth it is tyme to leve owre plays, sportes and mery conseittes that we have fullyd your myndes with this cristinmes holidays, and to fall in hand a-nother while with mater of sadnes, for and if we give your selfe styll a-pease to maters of sport, it wilbe long or we cum to connyng [i.e. learning], wich must be gotten with grett labour and diligence.[24]

The master's threats as to what will happen if boys do not resume their studies diligently after another holiday are reiterated in a later passage:

> Ye had your liberte now a grette whill to play at dise, at cardes, at tables, at chestes, to syng, to daunce, to drynke, to revell and to do suche thynges as ye thowght pertynyd to the pleasur of mynde. Now this day begynges in another maner of lernyng that requirith other manores. It is your parte therfor to go a-bowght other thynges, that is to say go se a-nother whyll your bokes and renew your studis that have ben discontinuyd

---

23. Orme, *Education and Society*, p. 128.
24. Orme, *English School Exercises*, p. 383.

and set your myndes to them, for and you begynne all to pla styll a-pece ye shall never cum to the lernyng that ye desire.'[25]

Pupils complain that learning doesn't always come easy, and some pupils regret not applying themselves to their lessons. Conditions at the school were harsh, especially in winter, although there is sympathy for others in a similar plight: 'For all my clothis iet I am often tymes a-cold. I mervell in what case the be that be kept in wardes and prison this cold season, which have nother fier nother covering to their bodis. In a veri evill case me semeth the be.'[26]

Ill health was not uncommon:

> Ther be tow scolers in owre howse that be veri sike in ther stomakes, of the wiche oon wytes all his disease to the etyng of a heryng, the other knowis not the cause of his disease. God grant the both scape ther siknes and recover, for and if fortune them to die ther deth will make not only us but many other to fle from the universite.[27]

Even death is portrayed:

> This day senett oon of my bretheren that I lovid best of any man in the world died upon a consumption, whose deth thawght it can be bot hevines to me, yet be-cause I ever knew hym vertuose in all his lyffe, I am more glad of his vertuosnes than I am hevy for his dethe.[28]

Orme points out that the author's references to ill health reflected a real situation, with Oxford being hit by epidemics of one sort or another regularly in the early sixteenth century. Magdalen School was itself evacuated en masse to the country in 1500, 1502 and 1507, for example, with the pupils lodging in farms and cottages.[29]

Another hazard of school life, theft, is revealed when a boy's fruit, a gift from home, is stolen:

---

25. Ibid., p. 405.
26. Ibid., p. 384.
27. Ibid., p. 389.
28. Ibid., pp. 387–88.
29. Orme, *Education and Society*, pp. 132–33.

> My father sende me fygges and resyns in the begynnyng of lent, the wich I layd up in my cofer thinkyng not to take them with-owt tyll werey nede compellyd me, but sum-body hath cumyn – I can not tel who – that hath broken up the loke and emptyd my cofer clene and lefte nother fyge nor resyng for me. If he had taken parte, who so ever he was, I wold have ben content, but to have all takyn a-wa I can do no nother wise but be discontent.[30]

Finally, the use of foul language, and a hint that boys had a role in moderating each other's behaviour, is given in a passage which has many echoes in the evangelical school story of the nineteenth century:

> If thu woldyst refrayn thi-self from the fowle communicacion that thu usist dayly, ther shold be no man in the world that I wold desire to company wit more. If thu dydist understande how evyll hit be commyng the and thu grettly thu dost a-myse with thi spekyng in that faschon, y dowte not but thu woldyst refrane from all suche comunicacion.[31]

Stanbridge, Whittinton and Horman

Ankwyll was succeeded as Master of Magdalen School by his usher (assistant teacher), John Stanbridge, in 1488. Stanbridge (born in 1463) had been educated at Winchester College and then at New College, Oxford, where he was admitted as a Fellow in 1481. He published his *Vulgaria* in 1519, although he had been using it as a teaching aid for some years prior to this. Such was its popularity that it subsequently ran to 107 editions before 1540.

Beatrice White, who edited Stanbridge's *Vulgaria* alongside a later *Vulgaria* by Robert Whittinton,[32] reiterates the general point made by Orme when she says that Stanbridge 'realised a fact that was grasped by all his successors ... that a text-book should have some topical interest to appeal to schoolboys', and, as such, his *Vulgaria* is not only just a

---

30. Ibid., p. 407.
31. Ibid., pp. 397–98.
32. Beatrice White (ed.), *The Vulgaria of John Stanbridge and the Vulgaria of Robert Whittinton* (London: Kegan Paul, Trench, Trubner & Co., 1932). The introduction comprises a lengthy and informative essay on 'Early Tudor Grammarians', which discusses the life and works of several schoolmasters who wrote Latin schoolbooks.

Fifteenth- to Seventeenth-Century *Vulgaria* and Colloquies

collection of sentences to be translated into Latin, but is also a valuable social document, with many vivid allusions to school life:

> I was sent to scole when I was seven yere olde.
> I was beten this morning.
> All my fellowes hate thy company.
> He hath taken my boke fro me.
> My heed is full of lyce.
> Wolde god we might go to playe.
> My gowne is the worste in all the scole.[33]

Some of these sentences have a rather sad and pathetic air, an indication of the writer's sympathy with his pupils, and a reflection of the realities of school life for many boys at that time.

Stanbridge's successor at Magdalen Grammar School was Robert Whittinton. Born around 1480, he had been educated at the school of St John's Hospital in Lichfield before studying under Stanbridge at Oxford. He went on to become a prolific writer of school textbooks (his first book was published in 1512), including his own *Vulgaria* (1520), which, like that of his predecessor, contained many sentences reflecting school life:

> Peace – the mayster is comen into the schole. He is as welcome to many of us as water unto the shyppe.
>
> May mayster hath bete me so naked in his chaumbre I was not able to do of nor upon myn owne clothes.
>
> He hath torn my buttokkes so that theyr is left noo hole skynne upon them.[34]

Although this last phrase is followed by 'If ever I be a man I wyll revenge his malice', a suggestion either of boyish dreams, or, perhaps more likely, that boys, if they applied themselves to their learning, could become schoolmasters themselves.

Another well-known grammarian from this period was William Horman, who published his *Vulgaria* in 1519.[35] Born in Salisbury,

---

33. Ibid., pp 14, 15, 16, 16, 19, 28 and 30.
34. Ibid., pp. 88, 90 and 102.
35. William Horman, *Vulgaria* (London: Richard Pynson, 1519), reprinted with an introduction by Montague Rhodes James (Oxford: Roxburghe Club Publications, 1926).

Horman was educated at Winchester and became a Fellow of New College, Oxford, in 1475. In 1485 he was appointed Headmaster of Eton. Nine years later he accepted the headmastership of Winchester, and then returned to Eton as Fellow in 1503, subsequently becoming Vice-Provost. He died in 1535.

He wrote around 30 books during his lifetime, on a wide range of subjects, although only two appear to have survived. One of these was his *Vulgaria*, written whilst he was teaching at Eton and intended for the use of the boys there, rather than for public circulation. It comprises some 3,000 English sentences with Latin translations, arranged in chapters in such a way that they form a compendium of Tudor knowledge on almost every subject, ranging from gastronomy, medicine, law and sport to religion and education. Most of his sentences relating to education are in a chapter called 'De Scolasticis':

> I have lefte my boke in the tennys playe.
>
> I have wrytten Virgil.
>
> Tell me in laten: what he sayeth in greke.
>
> This copy is truly correcte and without faute.
>
> I have fogot my lernyng.[36]

Particularly notable is his suggestion that a form of football was being played at Eton in, or before, 1519: 'We wyll playe with a ball full of wynde.'

Horman also indicates that he utilised drama, alongside the more conventional methods, as a way of teaching Latin (and Greek): 'We have played a comedi of greke / latten.'

He also used his *Vulgaria* to discuss his views on teaching: 'A dogged mynde is the worse for betynge' and 'The moste parte of techers of grammer make most of the worst authors',[37] the second being a thinly-veiled attack on earlier writers of Latin textbooks and *vulgaria* (although this was a little premature – Whittinton's *Vulgaria*, one of those Horman objected to, ran to no fewer than 181 editions, compared with only four for Horman's).

---

36. Ibid., pp. 131, 126, 145 and 133.
37. Ibid., pp. 141 and 129.

Desiderius Erasmus

The use of dialogues as a method of teaching conversational Latin found a particular voice in the sixteenth century through the writings of Desiderius Erasmus, a Dutch educationalist who helped to establish the curriculum at St Paul's School, London, alongside its founder, John Colet.

St Paul's had been established in 1509, in the churchyard of St Paul's Cathedral. Colet and Erasmus wrote many textbooks specifically for use in the school, Erasmus, in particular, adapting a set of dialogues he had earlier used whilst teaching in Paris.

Erasmus was born in 1466 in Holland. After the death of his parents, he was sent to a religious school before entering an Augustinian monastery in 1485 and being ordained as a priest in 1492. He began writing his dialogues while teaching in Paris. He first met John Colet on a trip to England in 1499. In 1509 he began lecturing at Cambridge University, before returning to Europe in 1514 and becoming a prolific and influential, if controversial, philological scholar. He died in Switzerland in 1536.[38]

His *Colloquies* were originally written between 1497 and 1500. His manuscript was published, without his approval, in Switzerland in 1518, followed by an authorised version in 1519. Erasmus revised and expanded this several times before his death, with the final version, containing just over 60 colloquies, constituting a textbook on almost every aspect of early sixteenth-century life – education, sport, social issues, war, religion, philosophy, politics, food, morals, courtship and marriage.[39]

In his biography, *Erasmus of the Low Countries*, James D. Tracy points out that some of these colloquies were like plays, and that Erasmus:

> had a dramatist's eye for situations and scenes, [although] what he writes are not dramas in any formal sense, for the action is recalled or implied or described; we 'see' it or imagine it through the author's art in setting it forth within dialogue.

---

38. For a comprehensive biography and discussion of the writings of Erasmus, see James D. Tracy, *Erasmus of the Low Countries* (Berkeley: University of California Press, 1966).
39. There have been several 'modern' editions of Erasmus' *Colloquies*, including Erasmus, *The Colloquies of Erasmus*, trans. N. Bailey (London: Reeves & Turner, 1878), and Desiderius Erasmus, *Colloquies*, trans. and annotated by Craig R. Thompson, Collected Works of Erasmus, Vols 39–40 (Toronto: University of Toronto Press, 1997). The extracts here are from the 1878 edition.

> None the less, like much good fiction it has the potentiality of being staged, of becoming theatre.[40]

Indeed, many of the dialogues do read as short plays, with the characters even being given names, an important step forward from the anonymity in previous dialogues.

The dialogues associated with school life begin with one called 'The Schoolmaster's Admonitions', (or *Monitoria paedagogica*), in which a master instructs a boy as to how to behave:

> You seem not to have been bred at court, but in a cow-stall; you behave yourself so clownishly. A gentleman ought to behave himself like a gentleman. As often or whenever anyone that is your superior speaks to you, stand straight, pull off your hat, and look neither doggedly, surlily, saucily, malapertly, nor unsettledly, but with a staid, modest, pleasant air in your countenance, and a bashful look fixed on the person who speaks to you; your feet set close one by the other; your hands without action. Don't stand titter, totter, first standing upon one foot, and then upon another, nor playing with your fingers, biting your lip, scratching your head, or picking your ears.[41]

A further set of instructions follows – how to speak, how to greet various people, how to behave at mealtimes, and so on – the whole dialogue having a clear pedagogical purpose beyond that of simply being a Latin translation exercise. However, the next dialogue is far less didactic, showing how a group of boys persuades their master to grant them a holiday, so that they can play. This dialogue has a definite air of learnt and rehearsed drama, with four named participants – Nicholas, Jerome, Cocles and the Master. Furthermore, the dialogue delineates the different characters of the boys: Nicholas the realist, Jerome the cynic, Cocles the cheeky and brave, and the Master who is both stern and kindly:

> **Nicholas:** I have a great mind a good while, and this fine weather is a great invitation to go to play.
> **Jerome:** These indeed invite you, but the Master don't.

---

40. Tracy, *Erasmus of the Low Countries*, p. xxvii.
41. *Erasmus*, trans. Bailey, p. 72.

Nicholas: We must get some spokesman that may extort a holiday from him. ...

Jerome: We must pick out a messenger that is not very bashful. ... There is nobody fitter for this business than Cocles.

Nicholas: Nobody in the world, he has a good bold face of his own, and tongue enough; and besides, he knows his humour too.

Jerome: Go, Cocles, you will highly oblige us all.

Cocles: Well, I'll try, but if I do not succeed, do not lay the fault on your spokesman. ...

Master: What does this idle pack want? ...

Cocles: Your whole school beg a play-day.

Master: You do nothing else but play, even without leave.

Cocles: Your wisdom knows that moderate play quickens the wit, as you have taught us out of Quintillian.

Master: Very well, how well you can remember what's to your purpose? They that labour hard, had some need of relaxation. But you that study idly, and play laboriously, had more need of a curb, than a snaffle.

Cocles: If anything has been wanting in times past, we'll labour to make it up by future diligence.

Master: O rare makers up! Who will be sureties for the performing of this promise?

Cocles: I'll venture my head upon it.

Master: Nay, rather venture your tail. I know there is but little dependance upon your word; but however, I'll try this time what credit may be given to you. If you deceive me now, you shall never obtain anything from me again. Let them play, but let them keep together in the field, don't let them go a tippling or worse exercises, and see they come home betimes, before sunset.

Cocles: We will, Sir. I have gotten leave, but with much ado.

Jerome: O brave lad! We all love you dearly.

Cocles: But we must be sure not to transgress our orders, for if we do, it will be all laid upon my back. I have engaged for you all, and if you do, I'll never be your spokesman again.

Jerome: We'll take care. But what play do you like best?

Cocles: We'll talk of that when we come into the fields.[42]

The boys are then shown at a variety of games and sports: 'playing at ball', 'bowls', what appears to be a primitive form of croquet and 'leaping'. These games are not simply played for the sake of playing – a competitive element is introduced by, for example, gambling in the first game, between Nicholas and Jerome, with the latter declaring: 'Which hand soever shall get the first three games, shall pay the sixth part of a groat to the other; but upon condition that what's won shall be spent among all the company alike.' Two other boys, however, also playing bowls, are opposed to gambling, with one saying: 'It is a mean thing to play for money; you are a Frenchman, and I a German, we'll both play for the honour of his country.'[43]

The poor quality – or lack of – school food is hinted at during the opening exchanges of another dialogue in this sequence:

> **Vincent:** Have you a mind to jump with me?
> **Laurence:** That play is not good presently after dinner.
> **Vincent:** Why so?
> **Laurence:** Because that a fullness of belly makes the body heavy.
> **Vincent:** Not very much to those that live upon scholars commons, for these oftentimes are ready for a supper before they have done dinner.[44]

Again, one can see the writer's innate sympathy for his schoolboy subjects, no doubt based on his memories of his own schooldays. Furthermore, it is not too fanciful to imagine these dialogues, having been learnt by heart and used in the schoolroom, later being performed publicly, to an older, adult, audience who would appreciate the subtle comedy and dry wit and, perhaps, recognise something of themselves in some of the characters. This is reinforced by the absence of any obvious pedagogical purpose behind these particular dialogues (although that is not true of most of the others in Erasmus' work) – these dialogues are not aimed at teaching conduct or behaviour, and they do not have any theological purpose, but rather have a feel of being written, partly at least, with an element of entertainment in mind.

---

42. Ibid., pp. 75–76.
43. Ibid., pp. 77 and 80.
44. Ibid., p. 83.

Nevertheless, while Erasmus obviously sympathised with his pupils, and was aware of the privations they suffered and the drudgery of learning, he still believed that they should take learning, and literature, to their hearts.

A further, and at times equally as irreverent, picture of school life is given in a brief dialogue under the heading 'Scholastic Studies'. In this, Sylvius meets John hurrying to school:

> **Sylvius:** What makes you run so, John? ...
> **John:** Because unless I am there in time, before the bill is called over, I am sure to be whipped.
> **Sylvius:** You need not be afraid of that, it is but a little past five: look upon the clock, the hand is not come to the half hour point yet. ...
> **John:** But there is something else that I am more afraid of than that – I must say by heart a good long lesson for yesterday, and I am afraid I can't say it. ... And you know the master's severity. Every fault is a capital one with him: he has no more mercy of our breeches, than if they were made of a bull's hide.
> **Sylvius:** But he won't be in school.
> **John:** Who has he appointed in his place?
> **Sylvius:** Cornelius.
> **John:** That squint-eyed fellow! Wo to our backsides, he's a greater whip-master than Busby himself.[45]
> **Sylvius:** You say very true, and for that reason I have often wished he had a palsy in his arm.
> **John:** It is not pious to wish ill to one's master: it is our business rather to take care not to fall under the tyrant's hands.

---

45. 'Busby' refers to Richard Busby (1606–95), headmaster of Westminster School for over 55 years and notorious for his liberal use of corporal punishment. In Erasmus' original (Latin) text, Cornelius was compared to Lucius Orbilius Pupillus (*c*. 114 BC– *c*. 14 BC), a Roman grammarian and teacher who was also noted for his violence towards his pupils. The poet Horace, who was taught by Orbilius when the latter was in his sixties, called him 'plagosus', meaning 'causing wounds' or 'abusive'. Erasmus' rendering of his name was 'Orbilio plagosior'. This would probably have meant little to pupils in the seventeenth and eighteenth centuries, whereas Busby's notoriety would have been well-known, hence the translator's subtle change.

> **Sylvius:** Let us say one to another, one repeating and the other looking in the book.
> **John:** That's well thought on.
> **Sylvius:** Come, be of good heart; for fear spoils the memory.
> **John:** I could easily lay aside fear, if I were out of danger; but who can be at ease in his mind, that is in so much danger?
> **Sylvius:** I confess so; but we are not in danger of our heads, but of our tails.[46]

These sentiments are as true today as they were in the mid-sixteenth century.

A further dialogue reaches back to those of Aelfric Bata, with its list of alternative words or phrases (indicating its underlying purpose as a teaching aid), and forward to what has been a common complaint amongst boys at boarding school for generations:

> What signifies letters without money? What signifies empty letters? What do empty letters avail? What good do they do, what do they profit, advantage? To whom are letters grateful or acceptable without money? What advantage do empty letters bring? What are idle letters good for? What do they do? What use are they of? What are they good for? What do they bring with them of moment? What use are empty letters of? They are useful, fit, proper, to wipe your breech with. They are good to wipe your backside with. If you don't know the use of them, they are good to wipe your arse with. To wipe your breech with. To wipe your backside with. They are good to cleanse that part of the body that often fouls itself.[47]

Nonetheless, Erasmus the pious and religious teacher is never far away and in a later dialogue he shows us his ideal of the perfect schoolboy – one who is diligent in his learning and, more importantly, a devout and God-fearing Christian. This model child, Gaspar, who reveals himself to be not quite seventeen years old, is met by his friend Erasmus, who asks him where he has been. Gaspar reveals that he has been to church, although he (or the author) retains a degree of cynicism:

---

46. Ibid., pp. 102–103.
47. Ibid., pp. 106–107.

> **Erasmus:** You have more religion than is common to one of your age.
> **Gaspar:** Religion is becoming to every age.
> **Erasmus:** If I had a mind to be religious, I'd become a monk.
> **Gaspar:** And so would I too, if a monk's hood carried in it as much piety as it does warmth.[48]

There is a curious passage in which Erasmus asks Gaspar how he prepares for sleep at night:

> **Gaspar:** I don't lie upon my face or my back, but first leaning upon my right-side, I fold my arms across, so that they may defend my breast, as it were with the figure of a cross, with my right hand upon my left shoulder, and my left upon my right, and so I sleep sweetly, either till I awake of myself, or am called up.[49]

It is not wholly clear what Erasmus (the author) means by this passage – although it appears that he may be recommending such a posture, with the hands on each shoulder in a form of embrace, as a safeguard against the temptation to masturbate.

Erasmus later asks Gaspar to expand on his religious devotions, which he does with enthusiasm and rather in the manner of a sermon, and he then asks about confession:

> **Erasmus:** [H]ow do you stand affected as to confession?
> **Gaspar:** Very well, for I confess daily.
> **Erasmus:** Every day?
> **Gaspar:** Yes.
> **Erasmus:** Then you ought to keep a priest to yourself.[50]

Erasmus (the author) clearly had an ear for comedy.

---

48. Ibid., p. 87.
49. Ibid., p. 91.
50. Ibid., p. 95.

Juan Luis Vives

The dialogues of Erasmus were widely used in schools throughout Europe, as were those of Juan Luis Vives, whose *Linguae latinae exercitatio*, better known as *School Dialogues*, first published in 1539, went into over 100 editions. Again, this consisted of a series of dialogues in Latin, written specifically with the aim of helping boys who were learning to speak, rather than write, Latin. It was required reading at Eton, Westminster and Shrewsbury; editions with translations were published in Spain, France, Germany and Italy, although the only English translation did not appear until 1908.[51]

Juan Luis Vives was born in Spain in 1493, educated at the town school in Valencia, and then studied at university in Paris between 1509 and 1512. He met Erasmus in France in 1518 when he was working as a tutor. In 1523 he took up the readership in Humanity at Oxford University, before returning to Bruges, where he died in 1540.

As with many other writers of school dialogues, Vives used the entire day to paint a picture of school, and home, life. The first dialogue, for example, features two boys getting up in the morning, ordering their mother to provide various items of clothing and in turn being ordered to wash and comb their hair (similar to many earlier dialogues). The third dialogue sees a father taking his son to school for the first time, having discussed the merits of two schoolmasters with a neighbour, and deciding to send his son to Philoponus, who has the smaller number of pupils. This provides an interesting insight into how schoolmasters were paid:

> **Father:** What is the charge for your instruction?
> **Philoponus:** If the boy makes good progress, it will be little; if not, a good deal.
> **Father:** That is acutely and wisely said, as is all you say. We share the responsibility then; you, to instruct zealously, I to recompense your labour richly.[52]

The fourth dialogue shows a group of pupils loitering on the way to school, and this is followed by a series of dialogues painting a picture of learning and school life. A teacher (the praeceptor) instructs his pupils

---

51. Foster Watson, *Tudor School-Boy Life: The Dialogues of Juan Luis Vives* (London: J.M. Dent & Co., 1908), from which the extracts here are taken. This also contains a brief biography of Vives in the Introduction.
52. Watson, *Tudor School-Boy Life*, p. 10.

in the rudiments of reading, after which two pupils discuss the nature of school:

> **Lusius:** We are not playing today.
> **Aeschines:** No, for it is a work-day. What, do you think you have come here to play? This is not the place for playing, but for study.
> **Lusius:** Why, then, is a school called ludus?
> **Aeschines:** It is indeed called *ludus*, but it is *ludus literarius*, because here we must play with letters as elsewhere with the ball, hoop, and dice. And I have heard that in Greek it is called schola, as it were a place of leisure, because it is true ease and quiet of mind, when we spend our life in studies. But we will learn thoroughly what the teacher has bidden us, quite in soft murmur, so that we don't become a hindrance to one another.[53]

The seventh dialogue deals with school meals, with Vives continuing the old tradition of introducing lists of words as a way of extending his reader's vocabulary:

> **Piso:** Our early breakfast is a piece of coarse bread and some butter or some fruit as the time of year supplies. For lunch, there are cooked vegetables or pottage in pottage-vessels, and meat with relishes. Sometimes turnips, sometimes cabbages, starch-food, wheat-meal, or rice. Then on fish-days, buttermilk from butter which has has been turned out in deep dishes, with some cakes of bread, and a fresh fish, if it can be bought fairly cheap in the fish-market, or if not, a salt-fish, well soaked. Then pease, or pulse, or lentils, or beans, or lupines.[54]

Later in the same dialogue Vives provides a short introduction to the rules of gender and tenses, before finishing with instructions on manners, using as his focus the ending of a meal:

> **Praeceptor:** Here, you, Gangolfus, don't wipe your lips with your hand or on your cuff, but wipe both lips and hands

---

53. Ibid., pp. 19–20.
54. Ibid., pp. 27–28.

> with your napkin, which has been provided you for the purpose. ... You, Dromo, don't you observe that you are putting your coat-sleeves into the fat of the meat? If they are open, tuck them up to the shoulders. If they are not, turn them or fold them to the elbow. If they slip back again, fix them firm with a needle, or what would be still more suitable for you, with a thorn. You, delicate little lordling, you are reclining on the table. Where did you learn to do that? In some hog-stye? ... Prefect of the table, see that the remains of the dinner don't get wasted. Put them away in the store-room. Take away first of all the salt-cellar, then the bread, then the dishes, plates, napkins, and lastly the table-cloth. Let each one clean his own knife and put it away in its sheath. You there, Cinciolus, don't scrape your teeth with your knife, for it is injurious. Make for yourself a tooth-pick of a feather or of a thin sharp piece of wood, and scrape gently, so as not to scar the gum or draw blood. Stand up all of you and wash your hands before thanks are returned. Move the table away, call the maid that she may sweep the floor with the broom. Let us thank Christ. Let him who said grace return thanks.[55]

Here, therefore, in an echo of Aelfric Bata, is not just a translation exercise but also a manual of etiquette.

The art of writing is covered in the tenth dialogue, particularly in practical terms, with sections on the making of a quill pen, ink and paper. The pupils are then shown struggling to get to grips with this new part of their curriculum, before one complains that his ink is too thick, with the other diluting it with water. They then return to their teacher, who gently criticises their work ('In the future let there be a greater space between the lines so that I may be able to alter your mistakes and correct them').

Claudius Hollyband

Fictional dialogues became a popular and effective way of teaching not just Latin but other languages, and not just in schools – they were particularly used, for example, by merchants in the fifteenth and sixteenth centuries, for foreign trade was becoming more and more important. Conversely, books were also appearing on the continent for

---

55. Ibid., pp. 37–38.

the benefit of Europeans who wished to learn to write and speak English. Jacques Bellot's *The English Schoolmaster* was published in 1580 – this was aimed at the recent influx of French immigrants, many of whom, like Bellot, were Protestants who had come to England to escape religious persecution. Indeed, it is another French refugee, Claudius Hollyband, who has left us with another glimpse of sixteenth-century school life through a series of dialogues set in and around a boys' school.

Hollyband (whose original name was Claude de Sainliens) was born in Moulins, France, a staunchly Protestant town from which Huguenots were ordered to leave in 1562. Hollyband, however, stayed on until at least 1566, before fleeing to England. In 1568, he was recorded as living in the City of Westminster, along with John Henrycke (i.e. Jean Henri), a teacher who presumably fled France at the same time.

By 1573, Hollyband had opened a school in Lewisham; in 1576, or thereabouts, he moved the school to St Paul's Churchyard in London. After spending a few years in Germany, he again took up teaching in St Paul's Churchyard, and in 1597 he was known to be living in Bartholomew Lane, near the Royal Exchange. After this, no more is known about him – he may well have returned to France after the Edict of Nantes (by which French Protestants were guaranteed freedom of worship) in 1598.

He is best-known for his three books of educational dialogues: *The French Schoolmaster*, *The French Littleton* and *Campo di Fior*.[56] The original editions of the first two of these books (1573 and 1576, respectively[57]) were both dedicated to Robert Sackville, who had earlier provided the inspiration for Roger Ascham's 1570 treatise on education, *The Scholemaster*. He based much of his texts on the work of Juan Luis Vives, either simply translating Vives' original Latin into French and English, or taking ideas from Vives and making up his own dialogues.

---

56. *The French Schoolemaster, wherein is most plainlie shewed, the true and most perfect way of pronouncing of the Frenche tongue, without any helpe of Maister or teacher* (London: Abraham Veale, 1573) (this was not written for use in schools, despite its title, but, as the title goes on to explain, it was: *set foorthe for the furtherance of all those whiche doo studie privatly in their owne study or houses*); *The Frenche Littelton. A Most Easie, Perfect, and Absolute way to learn the frenche tongue* (London: Thomas Vautroullier, 1566 [i.e. 1576]); and *Camp di Fior, or else The Flovrie Field of Foure Languages* (London: Thomas Vautroullier, 1583).

57. The earliest extant edition of *The French Littleton* is dated 1566 – however, this was almost certainly a typographical error. See Alfred W. Pollard, *Transactions of the Bibliographical Society*, vol. 13 (1913–15), pp. 253–72.

The school dialogues from these three books were reworked into *The Elizabethan Home: Discovered in Two Dialogues* (edited by Muriel St Clare Byrne and published by Frederick Etchells and Hugh Macdonald in 1925, with a new and revised edition published by Methuen in 1949). Peter Erondell was also a Huguenot refugee from France, who wrote *The French Garden*, a phrase book specifically written for women, in 1605. This was included in *The Elizabethan Home*, alongside some of Hollyband's dialogues.

Hollyband's first school dialogue – between Francis, a schoolboy, and Margaret, a maid – appeared in *The French Schoolmaster*, and is an echo of the dialogues of Aelfric Bata, with its list of words inserted into one of Francis' speeches, although it is also a vivid picture of a spoilt brat and the nature of the relationship between children and their servants at the time:

> **Margaret:** Ho Fraunces rise, and get you to schoole: you shalbe beaten, for it is past seven: make yourself readie quickly, say your prayers, then you shall have your breakfast …
> **Francis:** [W]here have you layde my girdle and my inckhorne? Where is my gyrkin of Spanish leather of Bouffe? Where be my sockes of linnen, of wollen, of clothe? Where is my cap, my hat, my coate, my cloake, my kaipe, my gowne, my gloves, my mittayns, my pumpes, my moyles, my slippers, my handkarchif, my poyntes, my sachell, my penknife and my bookes? Where is all my geare? I have nothyng ready: I will tell my father: I will cause you to be beaten … geve me a towell: mayden, now geve mee my breakfast, for I am readie: make haste.[58]

Hollyband himself, in his real-life role of a schoolmaster, appears in a dialogue in *The French Littleton*, when a father, taking his son, John, to school, is stopped by a friend (called Gossip):

> **Gossip:** [W]hether go you so early? Whether lead you your sonne?
> **Father:** I bring him to schoole, to learne to speake Latin and French: for he hath lost his time till now: and you know

---

58. St Clare Byrne, *The Elizabethan Home*, pp. 1–2.

well that it were better to be unborne than untaught: which is most true. ...
Gossip: [W]hether goeth he to schoole?
Father: In Paules Churcheyard, hard by the signe of the Lucrece: there is a Frenchman which teacheth bothe the tongues: in the morning till eleven, the Latine tongue, and after dinner the French: and which doth his dutie ...
Gossip: [W]hat is his name?
Father: I cannot tell truely: I have forgotten it.
Gossip: John, how is thy maister called?
John: He is called M. Claudius Hollyband.
Gossip: Is he maried? what countreyman is he?
John: He is a Frenchman: he hath wife and children.[59]

Hollyband goes on to reveal much about the life of a schoolmaster, his fees, and the curriculum he taught:

Father: I have brought heere unto you my sonne, praying you to take some paine with him that he may learne to speake Frenche, reade and write ... what take you by moneth, by weeke, by quarter?
Master: A shilling a weeke, a crowne a moneth, a reall a quarter, fourtie shillings a yeare.
Father: It is to much: you are to deare.
Master: If it be to much, bate of it: but I will tell you one thing, that if your sonne learneth well, it is not to much: but if he learneth nothing, though I should teache him for a groate a month, it would be to deare both for you, and him.
Father: Call me that boy which is there in the corner: Gabriel, have you bene here long? how long have you bene here?
Gabriel: About half a yeare, Sir. ...
Father: What book readeth your maister unto you?
Gabriel: As his scholars are fit for: unto some, he readeth Terence, Virgill, Horace, Tullies offices: unto others Cato, pueriles, their accidentes, their grammar, according to their capacitie: as for me, I learne onely Frenche, and to read and writ, and sometimes to cipher.

---

59. Ibid., p. 3.

> **Father:** Maister Hollyband, take a littell paine with my sonne. he is somewhat hard of wit, understanding, memorie: he is shamefast, wanton, wicked, liar, stuburne unto father and mother: correct, chasten, amende all these faultes, and I will recompense you: Hold, I will pay you the quarter beforehand.
> **Master:** I thanke you: hath he a sachell, bookes, inck, quilles and paper?
> **Father:** No, but I go and buy unto him an inckhorne, a penknife and all that he hath neede of.[60]

A picture of life in the classroom, as it was then and still is now, is provided in another dialogue from *The French Littleton*:

> **Nicholas:** Maister, John Nothing-worth hath sworne by God, plaid by the way, solde his poyntes, chaunged his booke, stollen a knife, lied twise, lost his cappe.
> **Master:** Is it true? come hether companion, untrusse you: untie you: put your hosen down, dispatche.
> **John:** Nicholas doth mocke me, plucketh me by the heare, by the eares: hath stroken me with his fist upon the head: hath stroken me: hath made me bleede.
> **Master:** You shall be beaten both for companie, for ye have deserved it well.[61]

Proceedings are then interrupted when a boy arrives late, and, after the master has listened to his excuses and forgiven him, Nicholas is telling tales again:

> **Nicholas:** William hath spitted on my paper: torne my booke: put out my theme: broken my girdle: trod my hat under his feete: marred my copie: spoken Englishe.
> **Master:** Ah littell fellow, you pratell, brabell, cakell, play the vice. Geve me my roddes: stretch your hand: you speake with the nose: you are a snoty one: blow your nose.[62]

Here, elegantly and comically portrayed, is the eternal naughty schoolboy – boisterous, lazy, devious and a tell-tale.

---

60. Ibid., pp. 4–5.
61. Ibid., p. 5.
62. Ibid., p. 6.

Hollyband reveals himself to be slightly ambivalent as to how to treat his pupils – he threatens corporal punishment but, on occasion, is clearly distracted before delivering it. Indeed, there is more than a faint hint of the stereotypical French master of nineteenth- and twentieth-century school fiction – the ineffectual, bumbling and weak butt of his pupils, easily upstaged by the cleverest boys and the victim of countless practical jokes.

Several more school dialogues appear in Hollyband's *Campo di Fior*, a manual written in four languages – Latin, English, French and Italian.[63] One, between two boys called Nepotulus and Pison and their master and usher, describes school food and, later, a meal itself. As with some earlier dialogues, the description of school food is little more than a lesson in vocabulary, with its list of foodstuffs, although it also gives a fascinating insight into late sixteenth-century cookery:

> **Pison:** The first dishe of the supper is a salat cut small with salt upon it, and moistened with oile of olives put foorth of a vessell with a long necke, and with vinaiger (a thing of evill taste and unhealthsome). And mutton sodde in a large platter, with dry prunes, or small rootes, or chopped herbes. Sometimes a very good gallimafrie [a French meat stew], now and then a minced meat of merveillous savor. In certaine dayes of the weeke a little roste-meate, specially veale, and sometimes kidde. Upon fasting days, we have egges, rosted, fried or poched – every one hath his owne as he will – or made after the fashion of a pannecake in a frying panne with vinaiger or vergis [a sour fruit juice]. Therto is added sometimes a little fishe, and after the cheese, come nuttes.[64]

Nepotulus, obviously not a pupil at the same school as Pison, is impressed:

> **Nepotulus:** May I come and suppe with you?
> **Pison:** Easely, if thou aske licence of our maister, the which I know he will willingly graunt. Otherwise it should be an unmanerly part, to bring thee to dinner with us without telling our maister of it.[65]

---

63. This is based partly on the dialogues written by Juan Luis Vives in *Linguae latinae exercitatio*.
64. St Clare Byrne, op cit., p. 9.
65. Ibid, p. 9.

The master readily agrees, and then instructs the boys to lay the table, fetch ale and water, and to wash their hands.

Hollyband was the first writer to provide Elizabethan England with suitable and practical French school books. Like his predecessors, who taught Latin, he used dialogues to teach the 'true phrase of the language' – i.e. as it was spoken, and not just written. He also, as has been shown, used dialogues to impart practical lessons on behaviour both in and out of school. He is now mainly remembered for his dialogues which focus on domestic life – the homes and parents of his pupils – which paint a fictional yet wholly authentic picture of the day-to-day life of ordinary Elizabethan people. Yet his school dialogues should not be overlooked – they followed what had become a well-established tradition, and, in many respects, were an even stronger forerunner of the later boys' school story.

John Brinsley

Another influential teacher associated with pedagogic dialogues was John Brinsley, whose *Ludus literarius, or the Grammar Schoole* (1612) provides a picture of life in a seventeenth-century provincial grammar school, as does his *Pueriles confabulatiunculae*, a series of dialogues most of which are set in a boys' school.

Brinsley was educated at Christ's College, Cambridge, graduating in 1588. He later became master of the grammar school at Ashby-de-la-Zouch in Leicestershire, where he made his reputation as a brilliant teacher of Latin and Greek. His religious views – he was a strict Puritan – eventually led to him being removed from the school, and he moved to London where he lectured and concentrated on writing. Brinsley believed that Latin was best taught by translating texts into English, with pupils then expected to render the English translation back into Latin. He argued the case for this in his first book, *Ludus literarius*,[66] which takes the form of a dialogue between two schoolmasters, one a successful and confident teacher, the other less experienced and anxious to improve his skills. It was written for teachers in the 'poore countrey schooles', and a note at the beginning reveals that the best way of teaching Latin is:

> by causing the Scholar first to understand the matter which hee learneth: secondly, to construe truly: thirdly, to parse

---

66. *Ludus Literarius, or the Grammar Schoole* (London: Thomas Man, 1612). The text here is taken from an edition published in 1917 by Liverpool University Press and Constable & Co. in London.

Fifteenth- to Seventeenth-Century *Vulgaria* and Colloquies

exactly: fourthly, to translate into English plainly: fifthly, to translate out of the English into the Latine of the Author againe: and so after to compare with the Author how neere he came unto it.[67]

Chapter one is headed: 'A Discourse between two Schoolemasters, concerning their function. In the end, determining a conference about the best way of teaching, and the manner of their proceeding in the same.' It begins in much the same way as a stage play, with the two teachers meeting, and one of them, Spoudeus, complaining about his choice of career:

> I myselfe have so long laboured in this moiling and drudging life, without any fruit to speake of, and with so many discouragements and vexations in stead of any true comfort, that I waxe utterly wearie of my place, and my life is a continuall burden unto me. Insomuch as that it causeth me to feare, that God never called me to this function, because I see his blessing so little upon my labors; neyther can I find any delight therein.[68]

His friend therefore proceeds, over the next 222 pages, to provide a detailed illustration of the techniques of teaching Latin grammar appropriate to a seventeeth-century provincial grammar school. Chapters on Greek, Hebrew and religion follow, and these are followed by chapters on the qualifications and qualities of schoolmasters and ushers, the organisation of a school, school government and authority. Corporal punishment is discussed in some depth, with, for example, ten pages devoted to the execution of justice in schools by punishment, which is justified by religious authority.

The unenviable(?) role of schoolfellows in helping with punishment (already seen in one of Aelfric Bata's colloquies) is also described:

> To this end appoint 3 or 4 of your Schollars, whom you know to be honest, and strong inough, or moe if neede be, to lay hands upon him together, to hold him fast, over some fourme, so that he cannot stirre hand nor foot; or else if no other remedy will serve, to hold him to some post (which is farre the safest and free from inconvenience) so as he cannot any way hurt himselfe or others, be he never so peevish. Neither

---

67. Ibid., p. xxv.
68. Ibid., pp. 2–3.

that he can have hope by any device or turning, or by his apparell, or any other meanes to escape.[69]

In 1615, Brinsley published *The Parsing of the Parts*, in which pupils are taught the rudiments of Latin by means of questions and answers, much like a catechism. Two years later, he published *Pueriles confabulatiunculae*.[70] This was a translation of a work by Evaldus Gallus (the rector of a Latin school in Weert, Holland), first published in 1555 and which comprised a series of dialogues in Greek and Latin.[71] There are several clues in Brinsley's translation to its original source, including a reference to a schoolmaster called Evaldus Gallus in the last dialogue.

A second translation of Gallus' work, by Joseph Webbe, appeared in 1627,[72] and a third, by Charles Hoole, a London schoolmaster, appeared in 1659.[73] Both of these new translations restored several dialogues from the original that Brinsley had omitted, on the grounds that they were unsuitable for teaching purposes, as they were 'unsavourie, Popish, or both'.[74] However, it is John Brinsley's translation of *Pueriles confabulatiunculae* that is best-known today.

Like his predecessors, especially Aelfric Bata and Claudius Hollyband, Brinsley was not averse to the use of colloquialism in terms of everyday conversation, although his enthusiasm for this tends to disrupt the natural flow of his translations. An indication of this is given in the subtitle he chose for *Pueriles confabulatiunculae*: *Children's dialogues, little*

---

69. Ibid., p. 289.
70. *Pueriles confabulatiunculae: or Childrens dialogues, little conferences, or talkings together, or little speeches togather, or Dialogues fit for children* (London: Thomas Man, 1617). A facsimile edition was published by The Scholar Press (Menston, England) in 1971.
71. *Pueriles confabulatiunculae: a mendis repurgatae* (Cologne: Arnold Birckman, 1555).
72. *Pueriles confabulatiunculae, or Childrens talke: claused and drawne into lessons, for such as desire to breed an habit in themselves … of that kinde of dialogicall, or common-speaking Latine, after the method of Dr. Webbe* (London: F.K., 1627).
73. *Childrens talk, English & Latin: divided into several clauses: wherein the propriety of both languages is kept. That children by the help of their mother-tongue may more easily learn to discourse in good Latin amongst themselves* (London: Company of Stationers, 1673).
74. 'To the loving Reader', note at the end of Brinsley's *Pueriles Confabulatiunculae*.

conferences, or talkings together, or dialogues fit for children – a series of synonyms that establishes a pattern for the dialogues themselves. Almost every sentence has alternative words or phrases in a marginal column printed alongside the text, ranging from the simple: 'It shall be done, or, I will do it', to the more complex: 'I thank you, or, I have (or give) thanks to you (or I give you thanks).'

The book opens with a series of phrases which might be found in any foreign phrase book – saying hallo, goodbye, an invitation to supper etc. There is even guidance on how to ask to leave the classroom to go to the toilet:

> Reverend master I pray you give me leave,
> That I may purge my belly.
> That I may go to the privy.
> That I may go to make water.
> That I may lighten my bladder.[75]

This reversion to the style of earlier *Vulgaria* is echoed in a sequence of sentences revealing boys telling tales:

> Peter hath beaten mee with his fists.
> He hath made water upon my shooes.
> He hath blotted my paper.[76]

The bulk of *Pueriles confabulatiunculae*, however, is taken up with a series of dialogues, of varying lengths, delineating a typical day-in-the-life of schoolboys. Early on, for example, one boy is shown waking up in the morning and explaining to his mother his fear of being late for school and not having the time to have a wash. In a later dialogue, Gerarde and Henry argue over seating arrangements:

> **Gerarde:** Give place a little.
> **Henry:** Hast thou not place enough there?
> **Gerarde:** No.
> **Henry:** Neither can I give place any thing at all.
> **Gerarde:** But where shall I sit? …
> **Henry:** Sit where dogs sit.

---

75. *Pueriles conffabulatiunculae*, 1617, p. 3.
76. Ibid., p. 4.

> **Gerarde:** And where do dogs sit?
> **Henry:** Upon their buttocks.⁷⁷

Several dialogues centre on boys being late for school, or absent altogether, and some are vivid pictures of schoolboys misbehaving. The perennial problem of school hygiene (and poverty) is brought up in a dialogue between Erasmus, the schoolmaster, and Fredericus, a pupil:

> **Erasmus:** Ought you not to komb your head, before you came to the schoole?
> **Fredericus:** We have not a combe.
> **Erasmus:** Why doe you not buy?
> **Fredericus:** My parents say that they want money.
> **Erasmus:** Sell yee corne, that you may have money.
> **Fredericus:** We have no corne.
> **Erasmus:** But ye may borrow a comb otherwhere.
> **Fredericus:** No man will lend us.
> **Erasmus:** Wherefore?
> **Fredericus:** We have most of us scabbed heads: I think men doe shun that.
> **Erasmus:** Dow your parents spend so many pots of ale, and can they not spare so much from their throat, that they may buy a combe?
> **Fredericus:** In truth I know not.
> **Erasmus:** Either come to mee more handsome to the schoole, or come not at all.
> **Fredericus:** I will tell my parents.⁷⁸

The somewhat lowly status of schoolmasters, and their desire to ingratiate themselves with the families of their pupils, is vividly illustrated when a master (Matthew) sets out to punish boys that have been absent. One boy makes the excuse that his father sent him into the fields (and poses the pertinent question: 'Will you not, that we obey our parents?'), another that he was making bread, and another that his family had entertained guests the previous evening, to which the schoolmaster responded by asking why he hadn't been invited.

One dialogue centres on boys who speak English in class when they should be conversing in Latin, and another deals with the learning of

---

77. Ibid., pp. 6–7.
78. Ibid., pp. 13–14.

grammer. However, school work is not everything, as shown in a dialogue in which a boy promises always to obey the master and study hard if the boys are allowed to play. The boys' leisure activities are later delineated in a dialogue between Conrade and Didimus, which concludes with a humorous touch that was typical of many dialogues:

> **Didimus:** [D]oth fishing please you?
> **Conrade:** Whether? fishing with hook, or fishing with net?
> **Didimus:** Either of them.
> **Conrade:** Truely I am drawen with neither.
> **Didimus:** For what cause?
> **Conrade:** The one makes us slothful, the other makes us wet.[79]

Conrade goes on to discuss his dislike of wrestling, riding, hunting and shooting (i.e. archery) and, after explaining that his bow was broken and being asked why he couldn't mend it, he goes on to say that if he had money he would rather spend it on books. Finally, an exasperated Didimus, unable to persuade Conrade to do anything other than read his books, questions whether anyone could endure to play with him.

Finally, in a dialogue worthy of Richmal Crompton's mischievous William Brown, Gisbert and Hubert discuss changing a letter from Gisbert's father to his schoolmaster:

> **Hubert:** What will you? tell me in a word.
> **Gisbert:** That you expound unto me this letter. ...
> **Hubert:** Doe you bid me to open other mens letters?
> **Gisbert:** They are not other mens. My father writ them. ...
> And hee commanded mee to beare them to my master. ...
> Now I am much affraide, lest these letters complain of me.
> **Hubert:** What have you done?
> **Gisbert:** Nothing that I know.
> **Hubert:** Why then doe you say, lest they complaine of you?
> **Gisbert:** Because my father said, that they were letters of
> comendations, where I suspect to be some fraud.
> **Hubert:** You say that which is like to be true.
> **Gisbert:** Looke upon the letters quickly. They will dispatch
> all the matter unto us.
> **Hubert:** Hearken. Hermane Ceratine sendeth hearty
> commendations to Evaldus Gallus. Hee that delivereth

---

79. Ibid., p. 28.

> these letters is most deare unto me, because he is my
> sonne; I pray you seeke to amend him, lest I begin to hate
> him, for his naughtiness, I can doe no good by words, or
> by rebuking or chiding. I have tryed. Wherefore I earnestly
> pray you, that you would effect the matter with rods. Take
> heed you do not hurt his boanes, I can easily endure that
> you should beat his skin and his flesh. Farewell.
>
> **Gisbert:** Truely I did conjecture so. …
> **Hubert:** What will you do?
> **Gisbert:** I will change them.
> **Hubert:** Will not this bee knowne to our master?
> **Gisbert:** Not at all. He knoweth not my fathers hand.
> **Hubert:** But how will you change it?
> **Gisbert:** Will you heare?
> **Hubert:** If you shall say briefly.
> **Gisbert:** Hermane Ceratine sendeth commendations to
> Evaldus Gallus. Hee that delivereth you these letters, is
> most dear unto me, because he is my sonne. I pray you,
> that you begin not to hate him for the fraude of others. If
> he shall in any thing offend, labour to amend him with
> words: you may doe much good with blaming and chiding.
> I have made experience. Wherfore I earnestly intreat you,
> that you would not doe it with rods. It is so farre off that
> I would have his bones to be hurt, that indeed I cannot
> easily suffer his skin or flesh to be beaten. Farewel.
> **Hubert:** In very deed an artificiall change. But take heed lest
> either of them know the imposture.
> **Gisbert:** I will have a care of these things.[80]

The editions of *Pueriles confabulatiunculae* by Joseph Webbe and Charles Hoole are almost identical, in their translations, to that of Brinsley, although neither give the extensive marginal alternatives that Brinsley provides. There are occasional differences – for example, in the opening of a dialogue between Conrade and Didimus, Brinsley's version simply reads:

> **Conrade:** I wonder that our master can suffer us to sit idle
> here in so faire weather.[81]

---

80. Ibid., pp. 31–34.
81. Ibid., p. 27.

Whereas Webbe's has a rather more sacrilegious opening:

> **Conrade:** I would all the Gods and Godesses would cast some misfortune upon our Master!
> **Didymus:** What evill hath our Master done you? that you so storme against him?
> **Conrade:** Because he suffers us to sit idle here in so faire weather.[82]

Mathurin Corderius

Mathurin Corderius (1479–1564) was a French-born theologian and teacher who worked in France and Switzerland. He wrote several books aimed at teaching children, the most famous being *Colloquiorum Scholasticorum*, first published in 1564. This was later translated into English by John Brinsley in 1636,[83] with further translations by: Charles Hoole in 1652; John Clarke, a grammar school master in Hull, in 1718; John Stirling in 1739; Samuel Loggon, a Basingstoke schoolmaster, in 1745; and John Farrer in 1807.

The English translations of Corderius' *Colloquiorum scholasticorum* – particularly that by John Clarke – were popular textbooks both in Europe and America, and were widely used in English schools from 1652 (when it was translated by Charles Hoole) up until the mid-nineteenth century (one of the last editions was published in 1830).

As with *Pueriles confabulatiunculae*, Corderius' *Colloquiorum* comprises a series of dialogues between schoolboys and between schoolboys and their master. Many concern day-to-day school life – boys discussing what time they got up, what they have been doing, asking for help with their school work, or asking permission to play or leave the school. The first six dialogues, in John Clarke's *Corderii colloquiorum centuria selecta*,[84] centre on lessons and pupils helping each other (or not helping

---

82. *Pueriles confabulatiunculae, or Childrens talke*, Webbe (1627), p. 87.
83. *Corderius dialogues translated grammatically; For the more speedie attaining to the knowledge of the Latine Tongue, for writing and speaking Latine* (London: Andrew Hebbe, 1636).
84. John Clarke, *Corderii colloquiorum centuria selecta; or, A select century of Cordery's colloquies: With An English translation as literal as possible, design'd for the use of beginners in the Latin tongue* (York: Thomas Hammond Jr, 1718). This was reprinted numerous times. The quotes which follow are from an edition published by J. Binns (Glasgow) in 1790.

each other) and several later dialogues concern the borrowing of items such as pens and books, and two dialogues show boys borrowing money.

The age-old problem of poverty amongst schoolboys (and the reaction of parents to the demands made by schools, still relevant today) is brought up in a later dialogue:

> Alas, wretched me! lo, we have changed our form, and I have no money whence I may buy books.
> Does not your father give you?
> He gives indeed, but too sparingly.
> He is covetous then.
> It does not follow.
> What hinders then, that he does not allow you money?
> Poverty; besides, when I ask, he wonders that we have need of so many books.
> No wonder, especially when he is poor; but in the meantime be of good courage, and not afflict yourself I pray. I will do my endeavour that my father may help you, for he bestows to the poor willingly, especially to those whom he knows to be studious of good letters.[85]

In much the same way as earlier dialogues, the desire of boys to escape the classroom is not forgotten:

> Master, may I speak a few words?
> Speak boldly.
> I and my school-fellows have been fixed to our books almost these whole three days; may we relax our minds a little by play?[86]

A later dialogue reveals the boys' chosen form of sport:

> In what game shall we exercise ourselves?
> None is pleasanter to me than hand-ball.
> Nor to me indeed.
> Let us see then whether or no the rest have chosen their parts, for if we should play alone there would be less of pleasure.[87]

---

85. Clarke (1790 edition), p. 74.
86. Ibid., p. 131.
87. Ibid., p. 144.

There is a similarity across all these dialogues – in particular those by Erasmus, Evaldus Gallus and Mathurin Corderius (and their translators) – in that, as well as revealing how conversational Latin was taught, they portray schoolboys in everyday situations, and focus on aspects of school life that are of most concern to boys: school work (and school work that should have been prepared but hasn't been); lost pens, books etc.; boredom and the desire to escape the classroom; games; school food; and the constant threat of corporal punishment (although this is largely absent from the dialogues of Corderius).

What lifts them above the ordinary, in the same way as some of those by Aelfric Bata, is their humour, at times gentle and at times sharp and crude. The authors recognised that teaching Latin, especially to pupils who may have been reluctant to learn, had to have an element of entertainment in order to maintain interest.

Moreover, portraying as they do schoolboy life, they have an unmistakeable air of authenticity, even though they are, in a real sense, pure fiction. They must, of course, be seen in their context of being simply part of the school curriculum at the time. While there is plenty of evidence as to their widespread use, they formed only a part of the overall teaching of Latin and other languages, and their portrayals of school life were, in some cases, a small part of their overall range.

Nevertheless, these school-based episodes remain, alongside the dialogues of Aelfric and Aelfric Bata, genuine fictional depictions of life in boys' schools and, as such, provide us with a clear origin for the school novel which developed in later centuries.

4

Schoolboys and Schoolmasters on the Stage

As chapters one and three have shown, dialogues, used in schools as a way of teaching Latin (and other languages), could be seen as a primitive form of drama, requiring pupils to learn lines and act them out – not necessarily by means of a 'performance' but in order to utilise the conversational and colloquial style of the text with some degree of realism.

It is not a big step from dialogues to full-length drama and, indeed, drama was a major feature of Tudor school life. Its importance was emphasised by Richard Mulcaster, headmaster of Merchant Taylors' School, in his 1581 treatise on education, in which he urged that schoolboys should be trained to 'pronounce without booke, with that kind of action which the verie propertie of the subject requireth, orations and other declamatory arguments'.[1]

William Malim, headmaster of Eton between 1561 and 1563, had held similar views – according to T.H. Vail Motter, in his book, *The School Drama in England*, 'The art of acting, he wrote, is a trifling one, but when it comes to teaching the action of oratory and the gestures and movements of the body, nothing else accomplishes these aims to so high

---

1. Richard Mulcaster, *Positions Wherein those Primitive Circumstances be Examined, which are Necessary for the Training up of Children, either for skill in their booke, or health in their bodie* (London: T. Vautrollier, 1581).

a degree.'² Westminster School, at its refounding in 1560, incorporated drama into its statutes, with the declaration that within twelve days of Christmas the scholars should perform one play in Latin and another in English.³

However, the growth of drama, both in schools and commercially, was not universally welcomed, and opposition came particularly from the Puritans, who objected to drama's basis in mimicry, which allowed people to be presented as or become that which they were not.⁴ Nonetheless, drama in schools was tolerated, just, with the clergyman John Northbrooke cautioning that comedies could be performed as long as they did not include 'ribaudrie and filthie termes and wordes', and that acting should be educational, and in Latin only.⁵

Later, and rather ironically, Ben Jonson (1572–1637) used Westminster, where he had been educated in the 1580s, as a target of savage criticism voiced by three gossips – Mirth, Tattle and Censure – in his 1625 play, *The Staple of News*.⁶ The gossips have been watching a play and, in their animated discussion after the first act, Mirth, referring to the play's author, reminds Tattle that a friend had once pointed out that: 'he was a profane Poet, and all his plays had Devils in them: that he kept School upon the Stage, could conjure there, above the School of Westminster'. Their criticisms are stronger after the third act, with Censure complaining that schoolmasters: 'make all their scholars play-boys! Is't not a fine sight, to see all our children made enterluders? Do we pay our money for this? We send them to learn their grammar, and their Terence, and they learn their play-books?'

The objection here, of course, is not on religious grounds, but rather on the grounds that boys were sent to school to be educated, rather than

---

2. T.H. Vail Motter, *The School Drama in England* (London: Longmans, Green & Co., 1929), p. 51.
3. See F.H. Forshall, *Westminster School, Past and Present* (Wyman & Sons, 1884), p. 468.
4. See, for example, J. Barish, *The Antitheatrical Prejudice* (Berkeley: University of California Press, 1981), p. 96.
5. John Northbrooke, *A Treatise Wherein Dicing, Dauncing, Vaine Playes or Enterludes with other idle pastimes etc. commonly used on the Sabboth day, are repreved by the Authoritie of the word of God and auntient writers* (London: George Byshop, 1577[?]).
6. It was first published in 1631. The extracts here are taken from W. Gifford, *The Works of Ben Jonson, with Notes Critical and Explanatory, and a Biographical Memoir* (London: W. Bulmer & Co., 1816).

to learn to act. While Jonson was obviously being satirical, the text reflected a degree of public opinion that existed at the time.

Some of the dialogues of Aelfric and Aelfric Bata allowed pupils to play the role of adults outside school, in various trades and professions, as a way of preparing them for adulthood. In his dissertation, '*Ludi Magister*: The Play of Tudor School and Stage', Paul Sullivan suggests that the Tudor grammar school did a similar thing, providing 'an arena in which boys of widely different social origins experimented publicly with self-dramatisation as a preparation for – and a miming of – social advancement'.[7] He goes on to point out that: 'Tudor schoolmasters used play, both competitive and dramatic, to teach children to perform coveted roles of authority in church, city, and state.'[8]

School drama played an important role in demonstrating a school's ability to transform schoolboys, from a variety of backgrounds, into gentlemen, able to attend university or achieve upward social mobility. The school play was as telling an advertisement as to a school's status as sports teams were to become in the nineteenth and twentieth centuries. However, while schools were staging plays in the fifteenth, sixteenth and early seventeenth centuries – both internally and for public performance – hardly any of these were actually about school, or school life.[9] Schools, schoolboys and schoolmasters did, however, make occasional appearances in Tudor drama, in particular, in plays which were concerned with education and the family. Unlike the dialogues which had preceded them, which were written for use inside schools and therefore had a limited audience, plays were aimed at a much wider – public – audience, and plays concerning schools and education therefore have to be seen alongside the public perception of these issues, which in turn was governed by the changes in and the growth of education in the Tudor period.

---

7. Paul Vincent Sullivan, '*Ludi Magister*: The Play of Tudor School and Stage' (PhD dissertation, University of Texas, 2005), p. 7.
8. Ibid., p. 21.
9. The most famous companies of boy actors in the sixteenth century were the Children of the Chapel (later the Children of Blackfriars), a theatre company affiliated to the Chapel Royal, and Children of St Paul's, affiliated to the choir school at St Paul's Cathedral. They achieved a small degree of notoriety for the way they occasionally pressganged boys into joining. They performed for wealthy and influential audiences, although they were twice closed down, in the 1580s and then the early 1600s, when the dramas they were staging, which were often politically satitrical, fell foul of censorship laws.

Schooling in the fifteenth and sixteenth centuries was subject to major upheavals, particularly the movement of the control of schools away from the Church to secular authorities, and the adoption of a more humanist curriculum. Education became, for many families, free or at least inexpensive – schools were established by means of endowments from wealthy benefactors, and schoolmasters were no longer obliged to charge fees. The huge growth in the number of schools meant that education became available to many more children, and to children from a wider cross-section of society.[10]

The nobility, however, remained largely untouched by this. Ursula Potter, in her thesis, 'Pedagogy and Parenting in English Drama, 1560–1610', suggests: Book learning was regarded by the elite as a sedentary occupation, which was potentially unhealthy and therefore not consonant with images of masculinity.'[11] (Indeed, this attitude was reflected in some eighteenth-century school stories). The nobility and the gentry tended to limit the education of their sons to the arts of riding, hunting, shooting and so on, preparing them for their roles as inheritors of estates and protectors of their lands and, indeed, protectors of the country itself. This attitude to learning amongst the upper classes led to an ambivalence in the social status of many schoolmasters – treated with respect, because of their education and skills, amongst the lower and middle classes, but shunned by the aristocracy. As Ursula Potter puts it:

> Underlying all the critical commentary on schoolmasters is a social paradox: schoolmasters were in status little different to servants, hired by parents or civic authorities, and as such they were entitled to little social prestige. By dint of their learning, however, which was presumed to be superior to that of the parents, they were entitled to a professional respect within the community.[12]

However, teachers of very young children – aged between four and eight – were often incompetent. Many taught in parish schools, dame schools, petty schools and other types of 'elementary' school, where education usually centred on learning the alphabet and reading, and

---

10. For a detailed study of education in this period, see Nicholas Orme, *English Schools in the Middle Ages* (London: Methuen, 1973).
11. Ursula Potter, 'Pedagogy and Parenting in English Drama, 1560–1610' (PhD thesis, University of Sydney, 2001), p. 23.
12. Ibid., pp. 38–39.

religious instruction. Teachers were poorly paid and often themselves poorly educated. In addition, many schools had only one schoolroom and one schoolmaster for pupils ranging in age from six to sixteen (or even older), and the difficulties of teaching such a range of ages are obvious. Schoolmasters also frequently had jurisdiction over their pupils outside school, thereby blurring the role that they shared with parents. Children could be expelled from school because of their behaviour outside it. This both cemented the authority of the schoolmaster within the community itself, while at the same time leading to tensions with parents.

Such tensions lay at the heart of several plays, written during the Tudor and Jacobean periods, which focus on the relations between school and parents, and the attitudes of parents to the schooling their children were being given. Some plays portrayed schools – and education – in a negative light, whereas others were more positive, and were an encouragement to learning. Other plays also took the opportunity to poke fun at school – and in particular schoolmasters, who were often portrayed as pompous and semi-literate buffoons, characters who either provided light relief or who were central to a plot which condemned verbosity and delusions of grandeur.[13]

One of the earliest stage dramas to touch on education was *The World and the Child (Mundus et Infans)*, a morality play published by Wynkyn de Worde in 1522 (although it may have been performed as early as 1508).[14] This is an allegorical play in which the World follows a man from birth to adulthood – the man is initially christened Child, then Wanton, Lust-and-Liking and Manhood, when he meets characters such as Conscience, Folly and Perseverance.

As Wanton, he declaims to the audience an element of childhood behaviour – the stealing of fruit – which harks back to Aelfric Bata, and which had vivid echoes in the eighteenth- and early nineteenth century school story:

> and every day
> When I to school shall take the way,

---

13. For a detailed discussion of drama and education in this period, see Darryll Grantley, *Wit's Pilgrimage: Drama and the Social Impact of Education in Early Modern England* (Aldershot: Ashgate, 2000).
14. The play has been published several times. See, for example, W. Carew Hazlitt (ed.), *A Select Collection of Old English Plays* (London: Reeves and Turner, 1874), from which the extract here has been taken (volume 1, pp. 246–47).

> Some good man's garden I will assay,
> Pears and plums to pluck.
> I can spy a sparrow's nest.
> I will not go to school but when me lest,
> For their beginneth a sorry feast
> When the master should lift my dock [i.e. when his
>   schoolmaster prepares to beat him].[15]

A similar morality play was *The Play of Wit and Science*, written around 1540 by John Redford, a composer of early English keyboard music and vicar choral at St Paul's Cathedral. The play only survives in manuscript form and in modern reprints.[16] In this play, each of the characters are personifications of human behaviour – e.g. Reason, Instruction, Wit, Diligence, Idleness etc. It was written for the choristers of St Paul's to perform at Court and, like many morality and allegorical dramas, portrays a journey, undertaken in this case by Wit, who gains understanding and knowledge on the way. Education is, of course, a central theme in Wit's journey, although, as with other allegorical plays, this is in a general sense rather than as a reference to school or institutional learning.

There is, however, one comic scene in which Ignorance is schooled by Idleness, who, possibly uniquely in the drama of the time, takes the role of a schoolmistress. Ignorance (whose character is spelt 'Ingnorance' in the manuscript, in order to match the contrived method by which he is taught his name) is not allowed to attend school by his mother, so Idleness sets out to teach him how to spell his name, breaking it down into its constituent syllables. 'Ing' is the first half of England; 'no' is his answer to the suggestion that Idleness should beat him; 'ran' refers to a dog; and 'hiss' is what a goose does: the whole being pronounced 'Ing / no / ran / hiss'.

In a later version of this play, *The Marriage of Wit and Science*, published by W. Marsh in or around 1570,[17] Wit is warned by his mother, Nature, that, if he wants to marry Science (the daughter of Reason and Experience), he must work hard, over a period of time, before he will be in a position to do so. She then goes on to emphasise the value of

---

15. Hazlitt, p. 246.
16. See, for example, James Orchard Halliwell (ed.), *The Moral Play of Wit and Science* (London: Printed for The Shakespeare Society, 1848).
17. For a modern reprint, see John S. Farmer (ed.), *Five Anonymous* Plays (London: Early English Drama Society, 1908).

education, as impressed on her by a higher power: 'he will'd me to inspire, the love of knowledge and certain seeds divine'. Wit is sent to be educated under Instruction, Study and Diligence, although he soon tires of this and it is only after a series of mishaps that he comes to realise that learning is the key that unlocks success, in life as well as love.

In plays such as these, education and learning were seen simply as steps on a journey. Other plays, however, focussed much more closely on education, and, in some cases, school and school life were integral features.

The Rebels and *Petriscus*

The foundations for drama with a school setting were laid in *The Rebels*, written by the Dutch writer Macropedius in 1535, and in a similar play by the same author, *Petriscus*, written in 1536. Both of these early plays were translated and performed beyond the Netherlands and they also inspired other plays, in particular, English plays such as *Nice Wanton*, *The Disobedient Child* and *The Glasse of Governement* – which feature the dire consequences of pupils who reject learning or neglect their education.

Macropedius was born Joris van Lanckvelt in Holland in 1487. After attending the local parish school, and then a grammar school, he became a member of the Brothers of the Common Life, and changed his name to Brother George Macropedius. After ten or so years he was ordained as a priest and started teaching Latin. He went on to become headmaster of St Jerome's school in Utrecht, where he also wrote Latin textbooks and plays. He died in 1558.

The Rebels, the first stage play to centre on school life, is also the precursor of many later plays and stories which feature four key themes in the development of the boys' school story: the influence of indulgent mothers, the effects of neglecting education, the brutality of schoolmasters, and the reform of rebellious and disobedient boys. In this case, as in most other similar plays and stories, the central message is based on the biblical precept of 'spare the rod, spoil the child'.[18] As such, it seems remarkable that it has hitherto been wholly overlooked in the history of school drama and fiction.[19]

---

18. Proverbs 13:24.
19. For a modern translation of the play, see Macropedius, *Two Comedies: Rebelles (The Rebels), Bassarus*, ed. and trans. from the Latin, with an introduction, by Yehudi Lindeman (Leiden: Brill/Hes & de Graaf, 1983).

Although *The Rebels* breaks new ground with its subject matter, it still draws on earlier drama – medieval folk tradition and, in particular, Roman comedy. Most notable, perhaps, is the portrait of the two mothers, Philotecnium and Cacolalia, who are soft-hearted and have lost all control over their sons' education and moral progress.

The play begins with a Prologue which suggests that the play was written, initially at least, for an audience of schoolboys. We then see Philotecnium, the mother of Dyscolus, on stage, alone, bemoaning the fate of both herself – with 'the burden of a coarse man for a husband' – and the fate of her children, for whom she wishes to have a 'rich and respectable life', which they would do if it were not for:

> the wicked, mindless attitude of the teachers who have been beating his delicate young boy's skin ... we have seen nothing but hard and cruel measures: always the same story, the lad returns home from school with his buttocks black and blue, thus showing through the punishment he receives (oh woe is me) the venom and hatred of the master.[20]

Philotecnium and her friend, Cacolalia, the mother of Clopicus, decide to place their sons with Aristippus, a schoolmaster with a reputation for gentleness. When the two boys learn of this, they are naturally delighted:

> **Dyscolus:** I know what our parents have decided to do.
> **Clopicus:** Please tell me, what is it?
> **Dyscolus:** They demand that we be instructed without being beaten.
> **Clopicus:** No beating?
> **Dyscolus:** Correct.
> **Clopicus:** No beating?
> **Dyscolus:** Without beating.
> **Clopicus:** Oh immortal God, how very foolish is a mother's mind, yet how convenient for us.[21]

The mothers then take their sons to the school run by Aristippus, who agrees to take them in as pupils but not wholly acquiescing with the mothers' plea to treat them gently, saying that he will apply discipline if necessary. These are the first examples in school literature of indulgent

---

20. Lindeman, p. 35.
21. Lindeman, p. 41.

mothers, although they are motivated largely by an aversion to corporal punishment.

The second act reveals the two boys, some time later, revelling at their good fortune at being under a schoolmaster who is apparently lax and who doesn't beat them, despite their idleness:

> **Dyscolus:** Oh Hercules, oh my dear Clopicus, how cleverly we escaped this time, in spite of the master's threats. I hate to think how that lash of the teacher's whip would crack against us if he were to check the nitty-gritty details of our behaviour more fully. The fact is that, except for stories, we haven't done or learned a thing all year. And all the notes we took in class have either been lost or destroyed.
>
> **Clopicus:** By Pollux, we would have been whipped to a froth a long time ago and would now be black and blue like scurfy sheep. But this time we once again got out without any harm to our buttocks. If it could only happen more often, then nothing on earth would be more welcome or more delightful. I think that he is afraid to beat us, because of our parents.[22]

The two boys then gamble with each other, only to start arguing when one is accused of cheating, and consequently they start fighting. They are interrupted by Aristippus, who sends them inside to be punished. Immediately afterwards, the two boys make up and decide to take the opportunity of their master's cruelty as a way of abandoning their education and embarking on adulthood, by complaining to their mothers and showing them the injuries caused by the schoolmaster's punishment. Calcolia is horrified: 'how this boy has been mutilated and torn to shreds with lashes of the whip'. The two mothers confront Aristippus, who defends himself and points the finger of blame for the boys' behaviour at them: 'through your blindness and your pampering (and nobody else's) each of the boys is led to his certain destruction. Not knowing the meaning of control, they are destined, in the end, to hang on the dreaded gallows.' After receiving further insults and threats, Aristippus threatens to beat the mothers themselves, until they retire gracefully, promising to withdraw their sons from the school and set them up in business.

Having left school, and with plenty of their parents' money in their pockets, the two boys fall into bad company, gambling with two pimps

---

22. Lindeman, p. 47.

in a local tavern. Having been fleeced of all their money, and beaten up when they protested, they decide to rob a farmer by way of recouping their losses. However, they are caught, and hauled up before the magistrates, who sentence them to be hanged. They are saved by the intervention of Aristippus, who claims that he, rather than the magistrates, has authority over the boys. Nevertheless, he flogs the boys again, and this time they accept his discipline. Their mothers are equally as repentant, bemoaning the fact that they rejected the 'advice of a good and honest man'. Philotecnium acknowledges that she is displeased by the 'overly liberal education' that her son has had and Cacolalia attributes the benevolence of Aristippus to God. Both mothers set off to go to church to give thanks and then to prepare a banquet for their sons and, of course, for Aristippus.

Macropedius' other school play, *Petriscus*, also features an indulgent mother, but is much more carnivalesque in nature. Set on Shrove Tuesday, it focusses on a young boy, the titular Petriscus, who is cossetted by his mother, Mysandra, and bullied but otherwise pretty much ignored by his father, Galenus. When Galenus learns from his servant, Liturgus, that Petriscus is responsible for several thefts of food and money from within the house, he asks the schoolmaster, Didasculus, to beat him and in return invites him to dinner. When Petriscus arrives at school, he is ordered to remove his trousers and is held down by four fellow pupils and beaten, tearfully confessing to be a thief and promising to change. He also reveals that that he has been sharing the things he has stolen with two friends, Cabiscus and Stypiscus, who are that moment cavorting in a nearby brothel.

When Mysandra hears of his punishment, and claims from Patriscus that Liturgus was the guilty party and had laid false charges against him, she vows revenge on both Liturgus and her husband. In the meantime, Didasculus has gone to the brothel to apprehend his two truanting pupils. There, beaten back by a barrage of stones and chamber pots, he resorts to summoning two officers of the law, who drag the boys back to the school where they are both flogged. They immediately leave the school and the authority of their scholmaster.

More farce follows when Petriscus is free to pilfer more food and money in the absence of his parents and Liturgus. He is accosted by his father on his way to the brothel and, claiming to be heading for school, is obliged to show his books, which he had fortuitously brought with him. This is observed by Mysandra, who is slightly drunk and assumes that that her husband is bullying her son. The two parents argue, with Mysandra refusing to believe that a fourteen-year-old boy could be guilty of stealing and visiting prostitutes. She ends the row by hitting her husband with her stick.

Later, Cabiscus and Stypiscus rob a peasant of all his money, but are caught hiding in the brothel and thrown into jail. Back at Petriscus' home, his father has discovered the latest theft of money, and Mysandra lays the blame on Liturgus. The servant is arrested, but his innocence is quickly established and it is Petriscus who ends up in jail. When Mysandra discovers this, she suddenly admits her shortcomings in mollycoddling her son and begs Didasculus for help. He successfully persuades the sheriff to release Petriscus, in particular, because, as a schoolboy, he is subject to his schoolmaster's rule. The other two boys, however, are taken away to be immediately hanged.

The play ends with a family dinner, attended by Didasculus, and a plea to the audience from Galenus that mothers should not pamper their children and fathers should punish misbehaviour.[23]

Other Plays with Similar Themes

The issue of indulgent parents became a familiar theme, and was the subject of stark warnings by dramatists – for example, by Robert Wever (or Richard – his exact name is uncertain) in *Lusty Juventus*, written around 1550 and first published in 1565:

> For as much as man is naturally prone
> To evil from his youth, as Scripture doth recite,
> It is necessary that he be speedily withdrawn
> For concupiscence of sin, his natural appetite:
> An order to bring up youth Ecclesiasticus doth write,
> An untamed horse will be hard, saith he,
> And a wanton child wilful will be.
> Give him no liberty in youth, nor his folly excuse,
> Bow down his neck, and keep him good awe,
> Lest he be stubborn: no labour refuse
> To train him to wisdom and teach him God's law.[24]

---

23. There appears to be no English translation of *Petriscus*, but for a detailed summary and analysis of both this play and *The Rebels*, see Thomas W. Best, *Macropedius* (New York, NY: Twayne Publications, 1972), pp. 42–66.
24. John S. Farmer (ed.), *The Dramatic Writings of Richard Wever and Thomas Ingelend*, (London: Early English Drama Society, 1905), p. 3.

Similarly, Tom Tospot, in *Like Will to Like*, written around 1568 by Ulpian Fulwell, a schoolmaster, warns:

> Oh all ye parents, to you I do say,
> Have respect to your children and for their education,
> Lest you answer therefore at the latter day,
> And your need shall be eternal damnation.
> If my parents had brought me up in virtue and learning
> I should not have had this shameful end.[25]

William Wager gave a similar warning in his play, *The Longer Thou Livest, The More Fool Thou Art*, written around the years 1560 to 1568:

> Two things destroye youth at this day,
> Indulgentia parentium, the fondness of parents
> Which will not correct their naughty way,
> But rather enbolden them in there entente,
> Idlenesse alas idlenesse is an other.[26]

The consequences of this neglect, in particular the likelihood that children will fall into bad ways or, even worse, turn to crime, were fully explored in plays from the mid-1500s such as *The Disobedient Child* (which centres on a boy's recklessness in entering into marriage at too young an age), *Nice Wanton*, and *The Glasse of Governement*, all of which were direct descendents of Macropedius' *The Rebels*.

The Disobedient Child was written possibly in or just before 1553 by Thomas Ingelend, of whom nothing is known other than that, according to the title page of the first published edition (*c.* 1560) of his play, he was educated at Cambridge University.[27] It is based on a Latin play – *Juvenis, Pater, Uxor* – by Ravisius Textor, although its setting is London and, later, a town some 40 miles away.

There is little doubt that it was written for, and performed by, schoolboys, with Michael Shapiro, in his book, *Children of the Revels*,

---

25. Hazlitt (ed.), *A Select Collection of Old English Plays*, vol. 2, p. 45.
26. Alan Stewart (ed.), *The Broadview Anthology of Tudor Drama* (Peterborough, ON: Broadview Press, 2021), pp. 464–65.
27. Thomas Ingelend, late student of Cambridge, *A Pretie and Mery New Enterlude: The Disobedient Child* (London: Thomas Colwell, 1560[?]). The text was reprinted in Hazlitt (ed.), *A Select Collection of Old English Plays*, vol. 2.

suggesting that it was staged 'by pupils of provincial grammar schools rather than by the London schoolboy or chorister troupes who brought plays to Court each Christmas'.[28] There are numerous occasions in the text where the actors address the audience as 'masters, children, parents, young men' etc. – indicating a school audience.

There are no school scenes, but it deals briefly with Tudor school life and paints a vivid and horrifying picture of brutality and misery, outlined by a young boy as he pleads with his father, in a lengthy opening scene, to be permitted to marry as an alternative to going to school. (This suggests that the boy is at least fourteen years old, then the legal age for marriage for boys.) His father acknowledges that school can be irksome but that learning and knowledge can bring pleasure. The boy then begins to reveal the real reason for his antipathy towards school, based on what he has heard from other boys the schoolmaster is a brutal tyrant:

> Their tender bodies both night and day
> Are whipped and scourged, and beat like a stone,
> That from top to toe the skin is away.[29]

His father suggests that, whilst some children deserve punishment, this cannot be an accurate reflection of school life, but his son is adamant, claiming that he knows of a boy who died after being hung by his heels and whipped. The boy eventually reveals his desire, which is to be married while he is 'young, lively and lusty'. His father, after pointing out that a wife would be a burden and a 'yoke' all his life, reluctantly concedes, while at the same time warning his son that he will be on his own, and would not be able to turn to his father for help if it was needed.

The play goes on to portray the initially happy marriage of the young boy to a loving wife, but the relationship eventually degenerates – his wife bullying and beating him – to the extent that he returns to his father and confesses that his marriage is not what he had hoped, and that his father's warnings were correct. Nonetheless, while his father is sympathetic, he refuses to intervene, leaving the boy to face the consequences of his actions.

---

28. Michael Shapiro, *Children of the Revels: The Boy Companies of Shakespeare's Time and Their Plays* (New York, NY: Columbia University Press, 1977), p. 152.
29. Hazlitt, op cit., p. 273.

Like *Nice Wanton* (see below), the play is a plea for education, with its message that, if education is ignored, the consequences can be dramatic. The impact in this case is less severe – a life of wedded drudgery and servitude with a cruel wife rather than early death – but the message is plain. The boy's father, in particular, makes the point that education is a preparation for life, in the case of boys, a life in which wealth and property (the father is described in the play as 'a rich man') are to be inherited and a life of marriage, with its responsibilities, if this is entered into at an appropriate age.

The importance of education is emphasised throughout the play – in the prologue, in the dialogue between the father and the son, in a comic scene between two cooks, one of whom reveals she learnt Latin at school, by the Devil (who appears on stage in a brief scene towards the end) and by the father when he refuses to take his son back. A final scene, in which a Perorator recapitulates the play, drives the message home, with its references to a child being a twig that can be bent[30] and the biblical exhortation not to spare the rod. The Perorator also places responsibility for the young boy's misfortunes on his parents, with its suggestion that mollycoddling was to blame. However, the father (the mother being entirely absent from the play) is deserving of some sympathy – he is gentle, affectionate, full of good advice and, although eventually unmoved, dignified in his acceptance of his son's position and in his refusal to reverse his own position.

In the context of *The Disobedient Child* as a precursor of the school story, its importance is in its depiction of school life. The father sees school as a place of friendship, learning and a preparation for life, whereas his son sees school as a cruel, violent and demeaning place. The picture he paints is one gained at second hand, having never been to school himself and, whilst it is horrific, there is evidence to suggest that it wasn't necessarily inaccurate – the various treatises on school teaching by writers such as Erasmus indicate that schoolchildren were abused in a similar way to that described by the son. Having said that, the play's aim is to refute the arguments against schooling which were prevalent at the time. The author uses the son's allegations, and his eventual fate, as a way of pointing out the dangers of anecdotal evidence and rumour. The father rejects his son's stories, suggesting that no schoolmaster could be as cruel as he alleges. While that may not have been the case, this

---

30. 'As the twig is bent, the tree inclines' (Virgil), meaning that adulthood is affected by childhood experiences.

is irrelevant to the play's purpose, which is to point out that schooling was the best preparation for adult life, with all that adult life, including marital responsibilities, involves.

Another early example of an indulgent parent appeared in *A Pretty Interlude Called Nice Wanton*, which was first published by John Kynge in 1560,[31] although internal evidence suggests it was written between 1547 and 1553, during the reign of King Edward VI. It was almost certainly written for performance by schoolboys, possibly one of the London companies (the Chapel Royal or St Paul's), or a provisional grammar school.[32]

The play's moral is clearly signposted in a prologue, delivered by a messenger, who (again) quotes the biblical precept not to spare the rod. The opening of the play itself sees Barnabas, the good son, trying to persuade his brother and sister, Ismael and Dalilah, not to play truant, but Ismael is unimpressed:

> Go, get thee hence, thy mouth full of horse-dung!
> Now, pretty sister, what sport shall we devise?
> Thus palting to school, I think us unwise:
> In summer die for thirst, in winter for cold,
> And still to live on fear of a churl who would?[33]

After they have thrown away their school books, a neighbour, Eulalia, berates their mother, Xantippe, for their behaviour, which includes swearing and bullying Eulalia's own children, and she urges Xantippe to punish them. However, Xantippe is unsympathetic to her complaints, and instead is full of sympathy for her children:

> Alas, poor souls, they sit a-school all day
> In fear of a churl; and if a little they play,
> He beateth them like a devil; when they come home,
> Your mistress-ship would have me lay on.[34]

---

31. A second edition was published by John Allde in 1565. For a modern text, see Hazlitt (ed.), *A Select Collection of Old English Plays*, vol. 2, from which the extracts here are taken.
32. See, for example, Shapiro, *Children of the Revels*.
33. Hazlitt, op cit., p. 165.
34. Ibid., p. 167.

Ismael and Dalilah then gamble with a character called Iniquity, which takes the play, for a while, into the realms of allegory, while at the same time their behaviour is rooted in reality – Iniquity, for example, being aware that Ismael has stolen money from his father. Having lost all his money gambling, Ismael vows to rob the next person he meets. For her part, Dalilah is revealed as having no sexual morals – both Iniquity and Ismael refer to her as a whore, and when Iniquity strikes her after she tries to hide her winnings from him, she retaliates by saying that she has a number of male friends, more or less confirming her position as a prostitute.

However, she soon returns to the stage ragged and disfigured, leaning on a staff, and confessing to being in pain, with her 'flesh eaten with pox'. She goes on to blame her parents for her plight, telling the audience that they indulged her and failed to discipline her. Barnabas, on seeing this pathetic figure, takes pity on her, not realising that it is his sister, and offers to help her both bodily and spiritually. Dalilah responds by revealing who she is and again regrets her past, bemoaning her decision to play truant. Barnabas then offers Dalilah his brotherly love, while at the same time imploring her to beg forgiveness from God.

In the next scene, Ismael appears before a judge, charged with 'felony, burglary and murder'. The judge rejects attempts by Iniquity to bribe him, and the jury finds Ismael guilty. On being sentenced to be executed, Ismael blames Iniquity for his sins and, after turning on Ismael, Iniquity himself is arrested. Wordly Shame, another allegorical character, then reveals to Xantippe that her daughter has died of the pox and her son has been hanged. Xantippe acknowledges her guilt in their demise, and is about to kill herself with a knife when Barnabas intervenes and comforts her, and, as with Dalilah, urges her to seek forgiveness from God.

Barnabas finally addresses the audience, pointing out the dangers of letting children run wild. He urges parents to teach children by example and children to apply themselves to learning and to obey their elders.

Nice Wanton is a clear and explicit plea for education, in terms of both learning and discipline, and, following on from *The Rebels*, uses two motifs that became a staple of the eighteenth- and early nineteenth-century school story to drive home its message – first, that of an indulgent mother and, second, the fatal consequences if education is neglected. Interestingly, in the eighteenth- and nineteenth-century school story, the first of these themes is sometimes seen as a refutation of the educational theories of Rousseau, although that clearly cannot be the case here and with other plays from this period.

While the moral of the play is clear, what is unclear is why Barnabas was different from his siblings. There is no hint as to whether he is older, and more mature, or younger. In addition, the play indicates that Xantippe treated Ismael and Dalilah differently to him – Dalilah tells Barnabas that, while they were 'tiddled' (i.e. treated with fondness), he was beaten, which suggests straightforward favouritism.

On a wider level, Barnabas represents the authority of the school, evidenced by the absence of a schoolmaster, who would otherwise confront Xantippe with evidence of her childrens' truancy and misbehaviour. Instead, it is Xantippe who proffers a negative image of schoolmasters. She refers to her childrens' master as a 'churl' and also, with her references to the children being beaten, as cruel and harsh. She is also critical of the lack of exercise in schools, and she values looks more than learning, saying that Eulalia disdains her children because they are well-dressed. Finally, the father is absent, although his existence is signposted several times. Xantippe is thus made the scapegoat, although there is the underlying message that her husband is equally to blame.

A further play which was inspired by *The Rebels* was *The Glasse of Governement*, written by George Gascoigne and first published in 1575.[35]

Gascoigne was born between 1530 and 1535 and educated at Trinity College, Cambridge. In 1575 he helped devise the masques which entertained Queen Elizabeth on her visit to Kenilworth Castle. He died in October 1577, noted as both a playwright and a poet.

The premise of *The Glasse of Governement*, which is set in Antwerp, is very similar to that of *The Rebels* – two parents decide to send their sons (two pairs of brothers) to a 'godly' teacher, before sending them to university. One notable difference is that the parents in this drama are the fathers, who are shown as taking an active interest in their sons' education. A second difference is that the schoolmaster lives up to his reputation as 'godly' – corporal punishment does not feature at all, although this is possibly because the boys are rather old (described as 20 and nineteen).

---

35. *The Glasse of Governement – A tragicall Comedie entituled bycause therein are handled the rewards for Vertues, as also the punishment for Vices*, (London: C. Barker, 1575). For an edition of his works, including *The Glasse of Governement*, see *The Complete Works of George Gascoigne*, ed. John W. Cunliffe, 2 vols (Cambridge: Cambridge University Press, 1910), from which the extracts here have been taken.

The play opens with the fathers, Phylopaes and Phylocalus, meeting the schoolmaster, Gnomaticus, and asking him to take their sons into his school, both being aware of his reputation as a 'vertuous enstructer'. Phylopaes emphasises the value he places on education, and that 'there is no money so well spent as that which is given to a good Schoolemaister'.[36] Phylocalus goes on to explain that, while the boys have already been well educated, they need a little more instruction before they go off to university.

Gnomaticus readily agrees to take in the four boys – Phylautus, Phylomosus, Phylosarchus and Phylotimus – as pupils (and as boarders) and, when they have been summoned and have introduced themselves, he is impressed with their demeanour. When he asks the boys to outline the extent of their education, Phylautus, the elder son of Phylopaes and brother of Phylomosus, explains: 'Sir, my Brother here, and I have bene taught first the rules of grammer, after that wee had read unto us the familiar comunications called the *Colloquia* of *Erasmus*, and next to that the offices of *Cicero*, that was our last exercise.'[37] Phylosarchus, the elder son of Phylocalus and brother of Phylotimus, adds: 'Sir: my Brother and I have also bene taught our grammer and to make a verse, we have redde certaine Comedies of *Terence*, certaine Epistles of *Tully*, and some parte of *Virgill*, we were also entred into our greeke grammer.'[38]

Gnomaticus then proceeds to teach, at insufferable length, a variety of philosophical, religious and moral lessons, all of which are greeted with enthusiasm by the younger brothers but prove to be rather cumbersome to the older boys, with Phylosarchus declaiming that he would rather be at a university and that being at school is wasting his time. They subsequently do very little work, finding a more enjoyable outlet for their energies in the company of a courtesan and her friends.

News of the older boys' extra-curricular activities reaches the ears of their fathers via a servant and they decide to consult Gnomaticus, who is surprised at the boys' apparent misbehaviour. Consequently, he agrees that it is time for all four boys to leave his school after he had given them a task which the two younger boys performed well, while the two older boys had wasted their time writing 'loving sonets' and 'verses in praise of Marshiall feates and pollycies'. The boys' fathers hope that, by sending their sons to university together, the younger siblings will exercise some

---

36. Cunliffe, p. 12.
37. Ibid., p. 16.
38. Ibid., pp. 16–17.

degree of moral control over their brothers, but this is not to be, and both older brothers again waste their time and neglect their studies.

While the younger brothers go on to achieve academic and professional success – as a secretary to a palsgrave (a feudal lord) and as a preacher in Geneva, respectively – Philautus is found guilty of robbery and is executed and Phylosarchus, charged in Geneva with fornication, is whipped 'openly three severall dayes in the market' and then 'banished the Towne with great infamie'.

Another unpleasant picture of school life appeared in *July and Julian*, an anonymous comic play written around 1560, which exists only in manuscript form[39] and in a modern reprint.[40] It was clearly written for performance by boys – the prologue declaiming 'we are come hither to trouble you as boys', although there is no evidence as to who wrote it and where it was performed. The text, with its references to the audience as 'most worshipful' and 'right worshipful' suggests an adult, gentlemanly audience rather than one of schoolboys. Giles Dawson, the editor of the modern reprint, suggests that the author was a schoolmaster, evidenced by the appearance within the play of a grammar school master, a song school master and schoolboys,[41] although their roles are superfluous to the play itself.

The plot centres on the efforts of a mother and father to thwart the plans of their eldest son, July, to marry the mother's maid, Julian. A subplot involves the release from bondage of two servants, who are instrumental in bringing the marriage plot to a successful conclusion. As such, the play borrows a great deal from Roman comic drama.

However, within the play are intriguing vignettes of sixteenth-century school life, and the attitude of boys and parents to education. The focus of this is the schoolboy, Dick, the younger brother of July, and who is far from enamoured of school life. Not long after the play has begun, he complains that boys are badly treated at home and at school, and goes on lament the failure of adults to remember their own childhood (in a complaint similar to that of Phylosarchus in *The Glasse of Governement*): 'I pray you, what is he that once boy hath not been?' He then grumbles about the unsympathetic attitude of his parents and complains that, after his lessons at the grammar school, he has to attend a song school, 'where my ears be set on the pillory.' His mother's servant, Ffenell, is sympathetic, but advises Dick to be patient. However, Dick can hardly

---

39. Folger Shakespeare Library, Washington, DC, MS 448.16.
40. Edited by Giles Dawson and published by the Malone Society, Oxford, in 1955.
41. Ibid., p. x.

wait for adulthood and he harbours dreams of revenge, albeit after accepting Ffenell's advice:

> So I will, but first handle all my masters then.
> I will pay them home for an old grudge. ...
> And he that my buttock for grammar hath slain,
> His body (if I live) I will slay again.[42]

One notable feature of *July and Julian* is the character of Dick's mother, Mawde, who is strict but fair and who values education. She insists that Dick gets up in the morning to go to school, threatening him with the birch if he doesn't, and then instructs Ffenell to accompany Dick to school, thereby ensuring that he doesn't play truant. She also reveals that she thinks too much physical activity can be bad for children: 'if boys should play too much they would be listless'.

Dick and Ffenell meet the grammar school master and the song school master on their way to school, and Dick is accused of loitering, and is punished, the schoolmaster indicating that he has heard groundless excuses from Dick before. Looking on while Dick is being beaten, Ffenell observes 'Schoolmasters be fiendish fellows, you may me believe.'

Overall, *July and Julian* paints a positive picture of motherhood (unlike *Nice Wanton*) and uses the mother to show that strict (but fair) parenting produces well balanced and well trained children. The servant Ffenell takes Dick's side in his disputes with his parents and his schoolmasters, but the audience will know that this is unfair, and that Dick's mother is fully deserving of their sympathy. In particular, she is seen as supporting the values of Dick's school and the authority of his schoolmasters.

The Schoolmaster in Early School Drama

The other main feature of early school drama was its treatment of schoolmasters, who were often portrayed in a negative light and were the object of scorn and ridicule. One of the first such portraits of a schoolmaster was in Philip Sidney's *The Lady of May*, written in 1578 as a short piece of court entertainment (performed by the boys of the

---

42. Ibid., p. 8.

Chapel Royal) for the visit of Queen Elizabeth I to Wanstead, the home of Sidney's uncle, the Earl of Leicester.[43]

Sidney, who was born in 1554, was educated at Shrewsbury School and Christ's College, Oxford. He was particularly noted for his *The Defence of Poetrie* (1595), the earliest work of English literary criticism. He spent much of his short life as a favoured member of Queen Elizabeth's court, before his death in 1586.

The Lady of May is set in Wanstead and centres on the conceit that the Queen is asked to judge between two suitors – a shepherd and a forester – who are wooing the pastoral May Queen. A schoolmaster, Rombus, is brought in to mediate.

Rombus is a village schoolmaster, and therefore a teacher of fairly lowly status, compared to a teacher at a grammar school. (R[h]ombus is also the term for an equilateral parallelogram – a reference to the science of arithmetic, which was, at the time, treated with a certain disdain by the aristocracy.) Nevertheless, the Queen, in introducing him to the audience, refers to him as a 'substantiall schoole-master', and Rombus himself is evidently proud of his status: 'I am *Potentissima Domina*, a schoole-maister, that is to say, a Pedagogue, one not a little versed in the disciplinating of the juventile frie wherein (to may laud I say it) I use such geometricall proportion, as neither wanted manuetude nor correction, for so it is described.'[44]

The rest of his opening speech emphasises his pompous and overbearing character – his language is ornate, obscure and peppered with Latin quotations (and the occasional misquotation), and his meaning is almost completely lost amongst his verbosity:

> Yet hath not the pulchitrude of my vertues protected me from the contaminating hands of these plebians; for comming, *solummodo* to have parted their sanguinolent fray, they yeelded me no more reverence, then if I had bin some *Pecorius Asinus* I, even I, that am, who am I? *Dixi verbus sapiento est*. But what sayd that Trojan Aeneas, when he sojourned in the

---

43. The extracts here are taken from the text printed in *The Countesse of Pembrokes Arcadia* (1605). (There is an online version of the text, transcribed, with an introduction, notes and bibliography, by Richard Bear of the University of Oregon, January 1992: https://www.luminarium.org/renascence-editions/may.html.).
44. *The Countesse of Pembrokes Arcadia* (1605), p. 571.

surging sulkes of the sandiferous seas, *Haec olim memonasse juvebit*.⁴⁵

In this, Rombus is demonstrating his elevated view of himself, dismissing his fellow villagers as plebians and decrying their lack of reverence for him. In particular, he highlights their opinion of him as nothing more than a *pecorius asinus* – i.e. a silly beast. An asinus, as John Brinsley pointed out in his *Ludus literarius*, was also the word used to describe a boy who had been appointed to oversee the behaviour of others and to report misbehaviour to the schoolmaster, although this was not a position to be proud of – as Brinsley explained, it is often the boy at the bottom of the class who was appointed.

The Lady of May is distinctly unimpressed by Rombus' rhetoric, as is Dorcas, an old shepherd who moans that, because he never went to school, he cannot understand a word of Rombus' 'mysterious speeches'. Nevertheless, Rombus perseveres ('first let me dilucidate the very intrinsicall maribone of the matter')⁴⁶ until the Lady of May has had enough, and Rombus is dismissed as someone who has neither the intelligence nor experience to arbitrate in affairs of the heart. Instead, it is left to the Queen herself to take this role. Rombus is, in effect, laughed off the stage, condemned by his contrived and bombastic language.

While Rombus is a schoolmaster, he appears outside a school environment, but he is an important figure in that he was the prototype for later portrayals of schoolmasters as bumbling buffoons.

Another pompous schoolmaster appears in *Pedantius*, a play first performed at Trinity College, Cambridge, in February 1581, and first published (by Robert Mylbourne) in 1631.⁴⁷ It was written by Edward Forsett,⁴⁸ who matriculated at Christ's College, Cambridge, in 1563 (at ten years of age), and later became a Fellow of Trinity College.

---

45. Ibid., p. 571. 'Haec olim memonasse juvebit' is a misquotation of 'haec olim meminisse juvabit' ('in time the memory of these will be pleasant') from Virgil's *Aeneid*.
46. Ibid., p. 575.
47. There appears to have been only one English translation (from the original Latin) of the play, by Dana F. Sutton, University of California, Irvine, and published online by the Philological Museum, University of Birmingham, in 1998 (last modified 18 November 2022): https://philological.cal.bham.ac.uk/forsett/).
48. Early sources credited it, erroneously, to Anthony Wingfield, a fellow of Trinity College.

Pedantius is a lengthy Romanesque comedy of manners, centring on the eponymous schoolmaster, thwarted in his love for a slave girl, Lydia, by a rival. Like Rombus (and Holofernes, see below), Pedantius peppers his speech with Latin quotations (and misquotations) and he is portrayed as a conceited buffoon. (The character of Pedantius is generally recognised as a satirical portrait of Gabriel Harvey, a colourful and controversial Cambridge academic.) The play is also about the use – and misuse – of language, exemplified by a series of verbal exchanges between Pedantius and his friend, Dromodotus, a philosopher, both of whom are aloof, proud and arrogant.

Pedantius is the schoolmaster of a village school some three miles outside Cambridge and three of his pupils appear throughout the play – Bletus (large but unintelligent), Ludio (who is obsequious when in the presence of Pedantius but disrespectful behind his back) and Parillus (who is clearly cleverer than his master and who derives a certain degree of ironic pleasure from observing his blunders).

Pedantius has ideas above his station, imagining himself becoming a man of letters and being elevated to a superior station in life, and he easily gets carried away by flights of fancy:

> **Ludio:** Here I am, most learned preceptor.
> **Pedantius:** Ah, see! Ludio, you sweetly eloquent lad, although I am in truth your most learned and most learning-dispensing preceptor, now, now I say, after I have been raised to higher and loftier station of dignity, you must henceforth address me in this wise: 'most honourable master, most worthy Maecenas', and 'if it please your highness'. These are the amplicative formulae of the rhetoricians. Procede.
> **Ludio:** Most honourable master, my most worthy Maecenas, I shall always satisfy my every duty, or rather my pious obligation, towards you, in which I can never do enough to satisfy myself.
> **Pedantius:** What a most Ciceronian young man! (One must employ a vocabulary of super-Latin superlatives, to keep the child happy.)[49]

In some dramas, Pedantius' apparent enthusiasm for learning would reflect his role of a schoolmaster, empowered to teach and prepare

---

49. Act III, Scene V.

boys for life beyond school. Here, however, it reflects his arrogance and inflated sense of his own importance. When he is later cheated out of a sum of money, his objection is not that he has been cheated *per se*, but that the act of misleading him was an affront to his professional standing: 'It does not grieve me that I am cheated out of my money because I am a man, but because I am learned.'

The nature of the relationship between his pupils, particularly Ludio, and Pedantius is one of tolerance above a barely-concealed contempt. Ludio appears to be an ally, but his words are dripping with sarcasm (which would have delighted an educated university audience). Parillus is equally as sarcastic, no more so than in a scene which reveals Pedantius as being wholly incompetent, with Parillus at one point saying to the audience: 'Listen for a wagonlaod of idiocies, and he'll surpass your expectations.'

However, while Pedantius is treated as a figure of fun, it is hard, ultimately, not to feel sorry for him. Towards the end of the play, he is misled into thinking that Lydia is dead, and his grief is clearly genuine and touching. At the same time, the audience learns that Pedantius was once thrown out of the university (Cambridge), although no reason is given. This gives added depth to the relationship between Pedantius and Dromodotus – the former an eccentric and incompetent schoolmaster, the latter an antiquated academic. When invited by Dromodotus to rejoin the university, Pedantius refuses, leaving the audience with an extra tinge of sympathy for this proud but flawed man.

Another comic figure appears in Joshua Cooke's romantic comedy, *How a Man May Choose a Good Wife from a Bad*, published by Mathew Lawe in 1602.[50] One of the characters who has a minor role in the play, but who is essential to the plot, is a schoolmaster, Aminadab – a figure of fun who is the butt of his pupils' humour. He is introduced at the opening of the second act, in a scene which illustrates the convention of the time that pupils, and masters, should converse in Latin rather than English, and which shows how difficult this was:

> **Aminadab:** Come, boys, come boys, rehearse your parts,
>   And then *ad prandium*; *jam, jam, incipe*!
> **1st boy:** Forsooth, my lesson's torn out of my book.
> **Aminadab:** *Quae caceris chartis deseruisse decet.*

---

50. Joshua Cooke, *A Pleasant conceited Comedie, Wherein is shewed how a man may chuse a good Wife from a bad* (London: Mathew Lawe, 1602). It was reprinted in Hazlitt (ed.), *A Select Collection of Old English Plays*, vol. 9.

> Torn from your book! I'll tear it from your breech …
> *Ubi est* Pipkin? where's that lazy knave?
> He plays the truant every Saturday;[51]

Pipkin, we later learn, is a 24-year-old servant, although intellectually he is much younger, or, perhaps, just cunning, as illustrated when he responds to a question as to when he last saw his master with 'when I last looked upon him'. He later grumbles about his earlier education, revealing that he took fifteen years, using a hornbook,[52] before he learnt to spell, and his slowness often led to him being beaten.

Aminadab goes on to play a vital role in the farce which unravels, although this is in his role as a thwarted lover rather than a schoolmaster.

Shakespeare's Schoolboys and Schoolmasters

Although none of William Shakespeare's plays are directly concerned with school life, schoolmasters (and the occasional schoolboy) make important sporadic appearances, and Shakespeare often used the concept of school, and the behaviour of schoolboys, in a figurative sense and by way of metaphor or comparison. For example, in *Romeo and Juliet* Romeo declares, when Juliet has bade him goodnight as he stands in Capulet's orchard:

> A thousand times the worse, to want thy light.
> Love goes towards love, as schoolboys from their books;
> But love from love, toward school with heavy looks. (ii.2)[53]

In *Coriolanus*, Volumnia responds to an enquiry as to her son: 'He had rather see the swords, and hear a drum, than look upon his schoolmaster' (i.3), and the Fool, in *King Lear*, disparages schoolmasters in a riposte to the King: 'Prithee, nuncle, keep a schoolmaster that can teach thy fool to lie: I would fain learn to lie' (i.4). Of course, most notably, in *As*

---

51. Hazlitt, p. 26.
52. Widely used in schools in the fifteenth to eighteenth centuries, a hornbook was a piece of paper or parchment containing the alphabet (in large and small letters), vowels, numbers and the Lord's Prayer, covered by a thin sheet of transparent horn and fixed in a frame with a handle.
53. This quote and all which follow are taken from *The Works of William Shakespeare: Gathered into One Volume* (Oxford: Oxford University Press, 1938).

You Like It, with its reference to the seven ages of man, we are reminded of 'the whining schoolboy, with his satchel and shining morning face, creeping like a snail unwillingly to school (ii.7)'.

Four schoolmasters make appearances in Shakespeare's plays: Pinch, in *A Comedy of Errors*; Holofernes in *Love's Labour's Lost*; Sir Hugh Evans in *The Merry Wives of Windsor*; and Gerrold in *The Two Noble Kinsmen*. (One can, possibly, add Artemidorus, a teacher of rhetoric in *Julius Caesar*, and Prospero in *The Tempest*, who describes himself as Miranda's schoolmaster.)

Pinch has only a minor role, and that as a conjuror, expected to exorcise Satan from Antipholus of Ephesus. Gerrold similarly has only a cameo role in one scene, arranging a morris-dancing entertainment. Only Holofernes and Sir Hugh Evans play anything approaching a major role in their respective plays, Sir Hugh in particular being a parson as well as a teacher.

Love's Labour's Lost

Written around 1593 and first performed for Queen Elizabeth I in 1597, *Love's Labour's Lost* focusses on the king of Navarre and three companions, who take an oath to devote themselves to three years of study, forsaking all bodily pleasures and the company of women. All four, despite this vow, fall in love with the princess of France and three of her companions.

Holofernes, who appears towards the end of the play, is the antithesis of the schoolmaster as he should be. He is rude, well educated yet ignorant, and a pedant of the highest order. In particular, his use of language is highly inappropriate – he frequently declines words he has just used, and provides synonyms which are quite superfluous in a vain attempt to demonstrate his learning.[54]

---

54. There has been much speculation as to who was the model for Holofernes. Darryll Grantley suggests Gabriel Harvey, the Cambridge academic who was also the model for Pedantius (Grantley, *Wit's Pilgrimage*, pp. 188–89); Richard L. DeMolen suggests it was Richard Mulcaster, the first headmaster of Merchant Taylors' School (founded in 1561) and then high master of St Paul's (from 1596 to 1608) (Richard L. DeMolen, *Richard Mulcaster and Educational Reform in the Renaissance* [Nieuwkoop: De Graaf, 1991], pp. 168–69). However, there is a hint in the play that the inspiration was Anthony Rate, the first headmaster of Harrow School:

His first appearance on the stage announces his verbosity. The schoolmaster, along with Sir Nathaniel, a curate, and Dull, a constable, have just left a shooting party:

> **Sir Nathaniel:** Very reverend sport, truly; and done in the testimony of a good conscience.
> **Holofernes:** The deer was, as you know, *sanguis*, – in blood; ripe as a pomewater, who now hangeth like a jewel in the ear of *coleo*, – the sky, the welkin, the heaven; and anon falleth like a crab on the face of *terra*, – the soil, the land, the earth. (iv.2)

In addition, Holofernes mixes English and Latin and, on occasion, French and Italian. These latter two languages were not taught in schools in Elizabethan England but were the preserve of the aristocracy who were tutored privately. This suggests that Holofernes either had a cultured background or picked up snatches of these languages in passing, evidenced, perhaps, by a disparaging remark (referring to both Holofernes and Sir Nathaniel) by Moth, a page: 'They have been at a great feast of languages, and stolen the scraps' (v.1).

Holofernes also belittles his listeners, pointing out their mistakes, but making even more mistakes himself – mispronouncing Latin words or making simple grammatical errors. A second slight at his character is made by the constable Dull:

> **Holofernes:** Via, goodman Dull! thou has spoken no word all this while.
> **Dull:** Nor understood none neither, sir;[55] (v.1)

> **Armado:** Do you not educate youth at the charge-house on the top of the mountain?
> **Holofernes:** Or *mons*, the hill.

Harrow, in 1593, was simply a village school for 30 boys held in the Church House at Harrow-on-the-Hill. Anthony Rate taught there from 1571 to 1611. He may also have been the inspiration for the pedant referred to in *Twelfth Night* as a person 'in yellow stockings ... and cross gartered most villanously; like a pedant that keeps a school i' the church' (iii.2).

55. See, also, Dorcas' response to Rombus in *The Lady of May*.

a comic but devastating comment on the verbal wordplay, riddles and abuse of language that typifies Holofernes' behaviour.

For all his apparent learning, however, Holofernes is merely an elementary school teacher – we quickly learn that he teaches the hornbook. This was only used in the teaching of very young children and, in keeping with other dramas of the period, gives Holofernes the character of someone with lofty ambitions, who tries to hide his true station in life. He thinks he belongs in a grammar school but, in reality, he is stuck in a school of lower status.

Holofernes receives his final, and most devastating, come-uppance in the final scene of the play, when he has assumed responsibility for laying on an entertainment for the king and his friends. He has suggested a play on the Nine Worthies (i.e. nine historical figures embodying chivalry). Holofernes' part in the entertainment is Judas Maccabaeus but he is mistaken by the audience for Judas Iscariot and is instantly heckled, and he is unable to defend himself against wild accuations. His exit from the play is an embarrassment, having been baited and abused. His final words ('This is not generous, not gentle, not humble' [v.2]) are a brave retaliation to the audience which has mocked him. Yet, for all that, he was brought down by the weapon he used himself – language. His fall from grace was typically Shakespearian poetic justice.

The Merry Wives of Windsor and *The Two Noble Kinsmen*

Shakespeare may well have included a younger version of himself in the cast of *The Merry Wives of Windsor* (written around 1596/97 and first performed in 1602) – as William Page, a schoolboy and the son of one of the women courted by Falstaff.

He takes part in a comic scene with Sir Hugh Evans, a schoolmaster, who bumps into William, along with William's mother, Mistress Page, and a friend, Mistress Quickly, in the street. Mistress Page asks Sir Hugh to test William's knowledge, which is the cue for a series of misunderstandings based on the womens' ignorance of Latin. William is asked a series of questions on grammar and vocabulary, with Miss Quickly indignantly interrupting, for example, misinterpreting the Latin 'hog' as meaning 'bacon', 'caret' as 'carrot', and 'horum' as 'whore'.

This scene would have had an important effect on an Elizabethan audience – some, who had been to school and learnt Latin, would fully understand the dialogue and would have found the questions posed by Sir Hugh easy. On the other hand, those members of the audience who knew little or no Latin would have remained in the dark, but been amused by Mistress Quickly's interjections – hearing the dialogue in English only, and mistaking Latin words for obscenities, for example, when Miss Quickly misinterprets the phrase 'genitive case' ('case' was slang for vagina) and she assumes it concerns a whore called Jenny. In many respects, this is bawdy schoolboy humour at its best.

The last schoolmaster to appear in a Shakespeare play was Gerrold, in *The Two Noble Kinsmen*, written in conjunction with John Fletcher in 1613.[56] This is a romantic tragi-comedy based on Chaucer's *The Knight's Tale* (from *The Canterbury Tales*) and centres on the competition between two cousins for the love of one woman.

Gerrold's appearance in the play is somewhat peripheral to the main plot and, like Holofernes and others before him, Gerrold is a poor advertisement for the teaching profession, being verbose and imperious. His role is to organise a morris dance, and he is horrified when he finds a member of the cast missing. As well as being a schoolmaster who misuses language (and who drops Latin quotations at the drop of a hat) Gerrold also reveals himself to be something of a tyrant, when he introduces himself to a hunting party led by the Duke of Athens:

> And I, that am the rectifier of all,
> By title Pedagogus, that let fall
> The Birch upon the breeches of the small ones,
> And humble with a ferula the tall ones. (iii.5)

An intriguing link between *Love's Labour's Lost* and *The Merry Wives of Windsor* is found in John Marston's play *What You Will*, published (by Thomas Thorpe) in 1607, but first performed in St Paul's Theatre in 1601.[57]

John Marston was born in October 1576 and studied at Brasenose College, Oxford, between 1592 and 1594. His writing career began with two collections of satirical verses, before he turned to plays, in particular for the boys' company at St Paul's. In 1603 he became a shareholder in the Children of Blackfriars Company, producing his most famous

---

56. It was first published in 1634. The text quoted here is from the edition edited by the Rev. Walter W. Skeat (Cambridge: Cambridge University Press, 1875).
57. It was reprinted in *Old English Plays: A Selection from the Early Dramatic Writers*, Volume II (London: Jhn Martin, 1814).

play, *The Malcontent*, for it in 1603. He was ordained a priest in 1609 and died in 1634.

What You Will is a romantic comedy, set in Venice, centring on a merchant, apparently drowned at sea, and his wife, subsequently pursued by several suitors until her husband reappears. Amongst the peripheral characters are a schoolmaster (unnamed and referred to as 'Pedant' in the text) and five pupils, who appear in a brief scene which has distinct Shakespearian echoes.

One of the pupils is called Holofernes Pippo and the lesson portrayed in the one schoolroom scene is similar to that of Sir Hugh Evans and William in *The Merry Wives of Windsor*, which had been written around 1596/97 but not published until 1602 (and, indeed, has similarities with the lesson given to Parillus by Pedantius). Pedant asks questions on Latin grammar and vocabulary, revealing his ignorance when he asks Slip, one of his pupils, why 'lingua' is feminine:

> **Slip:** Forsooth because it is the feminine gender.
> **Pedant:** Ha, thou ass! thou dolt! *idem per idem*, mark it: *lingua* is declined with *haec*, the feminine, because it is a household stuff, particularly belonging, and most commonly resident under the roof of women's mouths.[58]

The lesson continues, in a rather chaotic manner, until Holofernes Pippo catches the schoolmaster's eye and is obliged to reveal his ignorance, and Pedant orders him to be untrussed (i.e. his trousers undone) and to be held up by other pupils in preparation for a flogging. Holofernes' fear is so great that he soils himself:

> **Holofernes:** You know not what you ha' done now; all the syrup of my brain is run into my buttocks, and ye spill the juice of my wit; well, ah sweet, ah sweet honey Barbary sugar, sweet master.
> **Pedant:** Sans tricks, trifles, delays, demurs, procrastinations, or retardations, mount him! mount him![59]

Holofernes Pippo is saved from his beating by the intervention of a group of gentlemen, one of whom, Simplicius, chooses him as his page. After Holofernes been instructed to sing by his schoolmaster, Simplicius

---

58. Ibid., p. 230.
59. Ibid., p. 232.

observes that he is 'a very pretty child', and then that he has 'a good face' and 'a sweet face'. There are clear hints of sexual desire in this scene, made more potent by the fact that Simplicius first sees Holofernes when his trousers have been taken down preparatory to his beating.

* * *

Negative portraits of school and education continued throughout the seventeenth century. Scholarship, for example, was criticised in Thomas Nashe's satirical masque *Summer's Last Will and Testament*, published in 1600:[60]

> Young men, young boys, beware of schoolmasters;
> They will infect you, mar you, blear your eyes;
> They seek to lay the curse of God on you,
> Namely, confusion of languages,
> Wherewith those that the tower of Babel built,
> Accursed were in the world's infancy.[61]

The character of Will Summer agrees:

> Out upon it! who would be a scholar? Not I, I promise you; my mind always gave me this learning was such a filthy thing, which made me hate it so as I did. When I should have been at school, construing, *Batte, mi fili, mi fili, mi Batte*, I was close under a hedge, or under a barn wall, playing at span-counter, or jack-in-a-box. My master beat me, my father beat me, my mother gave me bread and butter, yet all this would not make me a squitter-book. ... O, in what a mighty vein am I now against horn-books! Here, before all this company, I profess myself an open enemy to ink and paper. ... Nouns and pronouns, I pronounce you as traitors to boys' buttocks; syntaxis and prosodia, you are tormentors of wit, and good for nothing but to get a schoolmaster twopence a week. Hang copies! Fly out, phrase books! Let pens be turned to pick-tooths! Bowls, cards, and dice, you are the true liberal sciences![62]

---

60. The text here is taken from Hazlitt (ed.), *A Select Collection of Old English Plays*, vol. 8.
61. Ibid., p. 74.
62. Ibid., pp. 74–75.

Similarly, in 1606, George Chapman mocked school education in *Monsieur D'Olive*, written for the children of the Blackfriars Company:

> When all is done, the Court is the only school of good education, especially for pages and waiting-women; Paris, or Padua, or the famous school of England called Winchester (famous, I mean, for the goose) where scholars wear petticoats so long, till their pen and inkhorns knock against their knees; all these, I say, are but belfries to the body or school of the Court.[63]

Grammar school education was satirised in Thomas Middleton's *A Chaste Maid in Cheapside*, written and first performed around 1611/13, and first published (by Francis Constable, London) in 1630.[64] This is an intricately plotted comedy centring on love and marriage, with one of the protagonists being Tim Yellowhammer, a fatuous student at Cambridge who, thanks to his monastic seclusion at the university, has a morbid fear of women. His mother, Maudlin, has a rather misguided view of youth and university life, at one point suggesting that his tutor should beat him in order to correct his flippancy. She also, like some previous characters, misunderstands Latin, for example when the tutor says, '*Non ideo sane*' (i.e. 'not for that reason'), she replies, 'True, he was an idiot indeed.' She reinforces this point, that Tim learned little, if anything, at school, when she encounters Tim and his tutor arguing (in Latin):

> **Maudlin:** How hard at first was learning to him! truly, sir, I thought he would never 'a took the Latin tongue: How many accidences[65] do you think he wore out Ere he came to his grammar?
> **Tutor:** Some three or four.
> **Maudlin:** Believe me, sir, some four and thirty.
> **Tim:** Pish, I made haberdines[66] of 'em in church porches.

---

63. Text taken from *The Plays of George Chapman: The Comedies*, ed. Allan Holaday (Illinois: University of Illinois, 1970), p. 442.
64. The extract here is taken from *The Works of Thomas Middleton* (London: Edward Lumley, 1840), vol. 4, p. 64.
65. I.e. books with rules for inflections, as opposed to 'grammars', which were books with rules for syntax.
66. I.e. red herrings, a reference to a tradition of creating effigies decorated with paper emblems during Lent.

> **Maudlin:** He was eight years in his grammar, and stuck horribly at a foolish place there called *as in presenti*.[67]

One of the last plays from this era with a school setting was *Apollo Shroving*, written by William Hawkins for the boys of Hadleigh Free School in Suffolk in 1626 (and published in 1627).[68] This is, in effect, a play-within-a-play, performed by schoolboys, the main play being a classical drama based on the legend of Apollo and the Nine Muses. Its characters include: Philoponus, a diligent scholar; Amphibious, a perplexed scholar; Novice, a young fresh scholar; and Ludio, a 'truantly' scholar. Its opening subverts the whole concept of school drama – the first boy on stage, Prologus (simply described as a young scholar), begins to introduce the play in Latin, only to be interrupted by Lala, a woman spectator, who demands that he speaks in English.

Lala continues to interrupt the Prologue, objecting to a reference to Terence's *Eunuchus* and then misunderstanding Prologus entirely:

> **Prologus:** But now we condescend with milde audacity in vulgar language unto low capacity.
> **Lala:** See you hold on your vulgar tongue, and bring not hither your latine vulgars, and lessons which you have chanted in the schools.[69]

After trying, and failing, to get rid of her, Prologus goes on to explain that the boys will be acting a play, and he gets Lala to spell out and read the title – *Apollo Shroving* – and points out that Apollo is the Lord and Master of the Muses. When Philoponus enters and speaks in Latin, Lala interrupts again, saying she has had enough and would rather be at home than listening to 'Barbarians' spouting Latin, unless someone translates.

There are echoes here of characters who are bemused by the verbosity of schoolmasters such as Rombus and Holofernes, although in this case the bemusement is based on a misunderstanding – the guilty party is a

---

67. I.e. 'as in the present tense' – but a common joke (on the theme of beating) in the drama of the period.
68. *Apollo Shroving composed for the Schollars of the Free-schoole of Hadleigh in Suffolk. And acted by them on Shrove Tuesday, being the Sixt of February 1626*, published by Robert Mylbourne in 1627.
69. Ibid., p. 4.

schoolboy, rather than a master, but, more importantly, his language is that of the play he is acting in, not that of his normal conversation.

Philoponus then proceeds, over seventeen lines, to describe daybreak – in flowery and overblown prose – to Lala's disgust:

> **Lala:** Trust you upon your word? Did not you promise to interprate? … I pray you what have you said all this while?
> **Philoponus:** I have said but one word – it is morning.
> **Lala:** And could you not have told me that in one word, by bidding me good morrow?[70]

Finally, after another brief soliloquy by Philoponus, Lala is reassured that the play will be in English, but determines to take part herself:

> Well, I see now it will bee English. It shall goe hard but I'le get a part amongst them. I'le into the tyreing house, and scamble and rangle for a mans part. Why should not women act men, as well as boyes act women? I will weare the breeches, so I will.[71]

The irony, of coure, is that Lala was being played by a boy.

Another comic tutor appears in Colley Cibber's *The School-Boy, or The Comical Rival: A Farce of Two Acts*, which was first performed at the Theatre Royal Drury Lane in 1702, with the script being first published by Benjamin Bragg in 1707.[72] Cibber (1671–1757) was an actor-manager, playwright and poet, who had a good reputation as a comic actor but was derided for his work as a tragic actor. The play's title is rather misleading, as the schoolboy of the title only has a minor role.

It begins with Young Rakish revealing to his friend that he is completely impoverished – although his father, Major Rakish, grants him £200 a year, he loses it playing his father at cards and backgammon. At the same time, Young Rakish is his father's rival for the affections of the affluent Lady Manlove, whose son, the schoolboy, Johnny, is pursuing Lettice, his mother's maid. His ambitions may, however, be thwarted by his mother's plans for him to go to St Omers, a Jesuit

---

70. Ibid., p. 8.
71. Ibid., p. 9.
72. The play was adapted from the farcical scenes in his earlier work, *Women's Wit; or, The Lady in Fashion*, which was badly received when it was first performed in 1697.

Academy, with the aim of him becoming a priest. When Lady Manlove comes across the young couple kissing, she strikes Lettice and promises that his governor, Father Benedict, will thrash him, a threat which Johnny treats with the utmost scorn.

When Father Benedict makes an appearance, he is exposed as something of a buffoon, talking in a strange mixture of English and cod-French (and apparently with a tortured accent), and revealed to be bald when Johnny knocks of his hat and wig. Much of what follows involves Major Rakish and Young Rakish arguing over money in front of Lady Manlove, with each trying to persuade her to marry him. As the two suitors continue to argue, and attempt to bribe each other, their fortunes ebb and flow, with Young Rakish eventually winning the day, and taking Johnny under his wing. The schoolboy, who at one point declares he has married Lettice only to discover that the ceremony was a sham, is therefore spared the prospect of studying at the Academy.

The Boys' School on Stage

The first appearance of a boys' school on the English stage in the eighteenth century appears to have been in *The School-Boy's Mask – Designed for the Diversion of Youth; and Their Excitement to Learning*, published anonymously (by J. Roberts) in 1742 but written by Thomas Spateman.[73] This is a play in five acts – the first act is set in a boys' school, the second largely at Cambridge and Oxford Universities, and so on, the whole play being, in effect, a treatise on education and, more importantly, the value of education.

In a preface, Spateman points out that the play was written specifically for use in schools – indeed, the second edition (J. Roberts, 1743) carries the subtitle, *A dramatic entertainment ... Acted with great applause, by some young gentlemen of distinction, in a boarding house at Westminster.* He adds that the first act, set initially in the playground of a boys' school, could be performed on its own. The characters mostly have allegorical

---

73. Thomas Spateman M.A., born in Yoxall, Staffordshire, in 1694, held several positions in the Church, with *The Gentleman's Magazine*, Vol. 31 (1761), recording him as dying, as vicar of Chiswick in 1761. David Erskine Baker's *Biographia Dramatica* (London: Rivingtons, 1782), identifies him as the author of *The School-Boy's Mask* and records him as being the rector of Wilton, Northamptonshire (presumably Whilton).

names, such as Stephen Goodwill, Sammy Bookish, Jo Rival, Ned Rakish, Charles Guzzle and Tommy Wild-rogue.

The first character to appear on stage is Time, who urges a group of schoolboys to honour and love their parents, not to lie, to be honest and, offering them books, to learn. If they follow these precepts, prizes such as wisdom, wealth, honour, esteem and fame will be there for the taking: 'Who knows, my Boys, if you no Labour grudge, But You may be a Bishop, – You a Judge?' Nonetheless, two of the boys, at least, are unimpressed:

> **Guzzle:** Be gone, Old Fellow, stand out of our Way:
> Don't talk to us, and interrupt our Play.
> **Wild-rogue:** We don't love Books; stand further, will you?
> Budge! I am to be a Captain, not a Judge.[74]

Another boy, Tinsel, also refuses the books offered by Time, explaining that he is a lord and has no need of learning. Some boys, however, are sympathetic, exiting the stage with Time and being followed by two others who have changed their minds.

Scene two paints an all-too-familiar picture of school life, with Jacky Fondler begging not to be sent back to school:

> Dear, dear Mamma! my Cause again espouse!
> Help, help me but this once; my Papa vows
> I shall this Hour be sent away to School,
> And not stay longer here to be a Fool.
> I hate my book, Mamma, and quake for Fear
> Whene'r I say't; my Master's so severe;
> He lugs my Ears and Hair, and with his Blows
> Oft fetches Crimson Currents from my Nose;
> Swindges my Back, and looks so furious! – And
> Oft with his Ferrule mauls my tender Hand.[75]

Jacky's mother makes it plain that she is on his side and, despite his father taking the opposite view, Jacky is allowed to stay at home.

In scene three, Rakish tries to persuade Bookish to do his Latin translation for him, offering him a penny. Bookish is, at first, reluctant,

---

74. *The School-Boy's Mask*, 1743, p. 2.
75. Ibid., p. 4.

citing the precept of honour, his fear of the Master, his reluctance to lie if he is found out, and his fear of God. However, after Goodwill has also refused, Bookish does agree to help. As the latter two boys are leaving the stage, to go and do their own exercises, Rival enters and makes a brief speech which initially suggests a bitter condemnation of the two boys, for being swots, but goes on to suggest that his envy will be overcome by effort:

> There they go! The Two I can hardly look at without Envy! My Master's favourites, whose Applauses I hear every Day! Whose Exercises, whose Construing, whose Diligence he is always commending to us, as if he thought he could never do them Honour enough! Whose Commendations and Improvements make such an Impression upon my Mind, that I am no sooner asleep, but I fall a-dreaming of some Applause or Honour, that Bookish or Goodwill receives; while I, methinks, am rated, or beaten, and threatened to be turn'd out of the School for a Blockhead! They are gone to make their Exercises, and strive to gain fresh Commendations; and shall I stay playing here? Will that make me like them, and procure me the Praise I desire? I will to my Exercise too, and try to be Third, if I cannot be First, or Second.[76]

In scene five, Wild-rogue is accosted by his father's servant, who reveals that he has been asked to leave the school:

> you will plague your poor Father into his Grave! ... This is the Fourth School you have been sent to: From two you have run away, and the other Two would keep you no longer; for my Master has received a Letter from Mr Birch here, complaining how intolerable you were, and desiring him to fetch you away, or else he should be obliged to turn you out of his School.[77]

The final scene of the first act sees Goodwill saying his goodbyes, as he is off to university. Time then reappears and stresses the importance of learning.

---

76. Ibid., p. 8.
77. Ibid., p. 9.

At the beginning of act two, the indulgent nature of Jacky Fondler's mother (who is now a widow) is made clear – she has to bribe Jacky with fruit and money to persuade him to read to her, and she reveals that he hasn't yet learnt to write. Yet we also learn that he is almost fifteen years old, and still sleeps in a room with his mother's maid. When he refuses to begin sleeping on his own, his mother loses her patience, acknowledging that her late husband's warnings as to the effects of mollycoddling her son were justified. She is finally reduced to chasing Jacky with a stick to beat him.

Meanwhile, Goodwill has proceeded to Cambridge and is visited in his room by Bookish, who is studying at Oxford. Both Goodwill and Bookish reveal themselves to be studying hard, but Guzzle, also at Cambridge, is said to have sold all his books and spent the proceeds on ale.

Another character, Grand-clerc, also at Cambridge, is visited by Tinsel, who reveals that he is about to travel, and is seeing both Oxford and Cambridge before he leaves. Tinsel sees the books that Grand-clerc is studying (including Plutarch's *Lives* and Perrault's *Lives of Illustrious Men*) and, when Grand-clerc points out that both he and Tinsel have it in them to become illustrious themselves, Tinsel replies: 'I am one of the first Barons in the Kingdom, and have Ten thousand a Year; Illustriousness enough, in my Opinion; I don't know what I need more.' Grand-clerc responds: 'Virtue, Knowledge, Wisdom, my Lord, to render you worthy of your Estate and Honour.'[78]

Grand-clerc insists that learning can be pleasurable but Tinsel will have none of it, insisting that only travel will make a man a gentleman.

Rakish and Guzzle are also shown arguing, although this time over the merits (or otherwise) of drinking – the message, that they are both ignoring their studies, is also clear. Time then reappears to stress the value of learning again, and to warn the students that time is running out.

The rest of the play takes us through the characters' adult lives. Bookish becomes a bishop, Rival a doctor, and Goodwill lord chancellor. Tinsel has become unspeakably rich, and even more arrogant, and refuses Lord Grand-clerc's request to subscribe to a hospital. Guzzle is a drunkard and, eventually, after becoming ill and unable to afford medical treatment, dies an early death, as does Rakish – after Goodwill and Bookish have given them both money, and they also paid for their

---

78. Ibid., p. 22.

funerals. Fondler, who had had a child by his mother's maid, had later married, mistreated his wife to such an extent that she died, and was similarly mistreating his children when he died.

Lord Tinsel ends up in debt and turns to Grand-clerc for help, eventually acknowledging that his problems are the result of him neglecting his education, although he still manages to be slightly disingenuous in recognising this: 'I fell into all this Misconduct for want of a better Education, and of improving my Understanding.'

The last word is left to the character who played Guzzle, who, in an epilogue, points out that what the audience has just witnessed was, like life itself, simply a diversion – although the play still had an important message:

> You see, my Friends, I'm sober, as before:
> Guzzle I mean to represent no more.
> Ambitious to be good, I quite detest
> To act a shameful Part, although in Jest;
> – Be Guzzle, Rakish, Fondler, Fool, or Knave!
> Much rather let me hasten to my Grave!
> Opprobious Life much more than Death I dread.
> The Worthless I lament, and not the Dead.[79]

Like many of the dramas that preceded it, *The School-Boy's Mask* is a clear plea for education, and a dire warning of what can happen if learning is neglected. Interestingly, it is yet another play which features an indulgent mother, laying the blame for her son's dissolute life at her doorstep – little, it seems, had changed in the previous hundred or so years.

Dramatic Portrayals of Girls' Schools

Girls' schools seem to have featured rarely in seventeenth- and eighteenth-century drama. Thomas d'Urfey's 1691 comedy *Love for Money, or The Boarding School*,[80] centres partly on Mirtilla, an orphan and heiress to £3,000 a year, who has been secretly placed in a boarding school by Old Merriton, a religious and pleasant gentleman. The only other pupils in the play are Miss Molly and Miss Jenny, described as a rowdy, boisterous romps. Old Merriton would like his son to marry Mirtilla and, while describing her to his father as 'the brightest Jewel of her Sex' (Act II,

---

79. Ibid., p. 56.
80. First published by Abel Roper and J. Hindmarsh, 1691.

Scene I), Young Merriton fears that he is not worthy of her. For her part, she is unaware of her impending wealth, and so thinks she is not worthy of him. Needless to say, things turn out as they should, despite the efforts of three teachers, a singing master, dancing master and French master, who try to take advantage of the absence of parental guidance and protection, and try to impose themselves on the girls. The play was so successful that in 1733 Charles Coffey adapted it into an opera, with the title, *The Boarding School, or The Sham Captain*,[81] although the plot was substantially different, and it was a comparative failure.

While there is no evidence that *The Governess; or, The Boarding School Dissected*[82] was ever performed on the London stage, it is a landmark drama in that it is a very early plea for a rounded education for girls, suggesting that parental pressure on the providers of girls' boarding schools meant that intellectual education was too often sacrificed on the altar of 'polite education' and the desire to prepare girls for marriage.

The script was published (anonymously, and printed for the author) in 1785. Set in a country boarding school for girls, it is staffed by a cast of largely symbolic characters: the governess is Mrs Teachwell; her assistant is Miss Wisely; and her pupils include Miss Witty, Miss Friendly, Miss Simple, Miss Fullgold, Miss Fiere, Miss Maline and Miss Captious. (Such allegorical names were a common feature of eighteenth-century school stories.) The drama's basic premise is set out in the opening speech by Mrs Teachwell (one of several direct addresses to the audience), in which she criticises the type of education offered by some schools:

> How few do we find of our sex, whose education surpasses a minuet, cotillon, talking a little French, playing a few airs on the harpsichord, and an easy deportment. Mental knowledge, and fashioning the soul, are esteemed as trivial and unnecessary. Do but speak of a young lady at school (the reply is) Oh! How well she dances; how she excels in all sorts of needlework; and I'm sure you would be charmed to see how gracefully she enters a room, and retires. As if forms and ceremonies, needlework

---

81. First published by J. Watts, 1733.
82. *The Governess, or, The Boarding School Dissected, a Dramatic Original in Three Acts, wherein are exposed, in Dramatic Order, the Errors in the present Mode of Female Education, and a Method of Correcting them, in order to form the Mind and improve the Understanding*, (London: Printed for the Author, and sold by Appointment at the Female Academy, No. 103, Hatton Street, 1785).

> and a genteel carriage, added to gross and barbarous corruption in their own language, as well as in others, incapable to write two lines correct in either, was, as is now called, a finished Education.[83]

Also later:

> so many, what are called well bred young ladies, brought up at boarding schools for several years, fall into all vulgar habits and opinions, and very often terminate in their future ruin: they become the favourites of coxcombs and an easy prey to the artful and designing. And then it is that Education is calumniated, and Boarding Schools condemned.[84]

Nevertheless, Mrs Teachwell, while providing an all-round education, is still concerned with manners and deportment: 'pay strict attention that they walk properly, and hold up their heads; for there is Miss Dowdy, and Miss Downcast, who are very remiss; indeed, they are a disgrace to a genteel school.'[85]

The school's maid, Betty, is avaricious and open to bribery, which is freely offered by some of the girls, who themselves fall into two camps – the lazy, dilettante and snobbish, and the hardworking, polite and obedient. One of the many dilemmas faced by governesses and teachers is highlighted shortly after the play's opening, when Miss Wisely urges Mrs Teachwell to expel a girl, Miss Maline, who is constantly undermining her authority. The governess is unable to agree, for purely selfish reasons: 'you know not why I bear so many inconveniences from Miss Maline. Miss Maline pays me fifty guineas per annum, and the rest of the ladies thirty only; that I have frequent and valuable presents from her family.'[86]

The theme of indulgent parents crops up from time to time, most notably, when Miss Wisely is talking to a new girl, Miss Enteté:

> **Miss Wisely:** [A]s I have not had an opportunity of speaking to you since you have been at school, pray tell me how you like it?

---

83. Ibid., p. 2.
84. Ibid., p. 27.
85. Ibid., p. 25.
86. Ibid., p. 8.

> **Miss Enteté:** Not at all!
> **Miss Wisely:** Why so?
> **Miss Enteté:** Because you won't let me do as I like!
> **Miss Wisely:** Why, my dear, it is not fit it should be so; you are very young, and not capable of judging yet what is good for your present or future advantage; besides, you are sent here to learn what is right.
> **Miss Enteté:** Why I used to do as I pleased at home; and if I wanted any thing I always had it.
> **Miss Wisely:** Oh that is very strange! And pray tell me what methods you employed to procure all your wishes? ...
> **Miss Enteté:** Suppose I wanted to go abroad with any young lady of my acquaintance, or to pay a visit, and I asked my mamma permission, and was refused; I immediately began to cry violently; and my mamma, because she was fearful of my going into fits, would grant me my request.[87]

Miss Enteté goes on to reveal that she never stayed at any one school long enough to learn anything, telling Miss Wisely that she had been to at least 20 schools in the past and was always accommodated whenever she asked her parents to take her away.

Another girl, Miss Fullgold, is shown as aloof and snobbish, refusing to be civil to those girls she sees as lower in rank ('tradesmen's sons'), and dismissive of the notion that humility, politeness and friendship are the bedrocks of virtue – 'all your learning, sense, and judgement, will ever counterbalance two thousand pounds a year, and a title at the death of my mother'.

The scene which opens with the above dialogue is surprisingly intense, with Miss Fullgold arguing at length with Miss Wisely, until she slowly comes round to Miss Wisely's point of view, albeit after expressing her distaste for the curriculum on offer:

> It was not so at my former schools. There dancing, dressing for advantage, playing at cards, and haughty aim, were looked upon as the Haut Ton of education. But here it is nothing but books and grammar rules till one is stupid, and dispossessed of one's five natural senses.[88]

---

87. Ibid., pp. 20–21.
88. Ibid., p. 37.

Miss Wisely (who is disliked by some because of her comparative poverty) has similar conversations with several other pupils, not all of which end on a positive note, leaving her to remark:

> What a disagreeable office is a teacher in a boarding school! So many tempers to please; so much anxiety for children's improvement; so much malevolence from the disobedient and refractory, because you are obliged by duty to compel them to perform those things, that the practice of mild means will not produce. So much fatigue, and so little profit, that a menial domestic (except the respectability of the occupation) is far preferable.[89]

Mrs Teachwell later makes a plea for some sort of teacher training:

> if boarding schools were to be examined into, there would be found a great number, whose governesses are decayed tradesmen's wives, and not possessed of more education than is necessary to provide for a family, and manage a kitchen. ... I could wish a plan was adopted by Parliament to restrain all such persons from the business of teachers, unless examined by proper persons that the Legislature should appoint; and those persons qualified, should have a certificate from such great authority. This would be the effectual means of rewarding persons of real merit.[90]

She goes on to condemn schools that use their pupils as skivvies, the poor pay offered to some teachers (especially French teachers) and the influence of parents, who see subjects such as needlework and dancing as of overarching importance.[91]

The play ends with Miss Wisely, having unexpectedly come into a fortune, leaving the school, with the girls, who had earlier maligned and despised her for her poverty, expressing guilt and shame, and promising to reform – although their motives for this are unclear: is it genuine

---

89. Ibid., p. 45.
90. Ibid., pp. 58–59.
91. Charles Dickens later made a similar complaint about men, wholly unsuited to the role, setting up private schools, exemplified by the character of Wackford Squeers, the headmaster of Dotheboys Hall, in *The Life and Adventures of Nicholas Nickleby*, published in 1839.

remorse or is it simply because Miss Wisely is now rich and 'one of them'?

The play was published anonymously, and the identity of its author remains unknown, although one clue lies on its title page, which reads: "Printed for the author, and sold by appointment at the Female Academy, No. 103 Hatton Street." Arden Hegele has shown, in 'Identifying Jane Austen's "Boarding-School"', that, at the time of publication, 103 Hatton Street (by which Hatton Garden was sometimes known) was occupied by a Miss Paxton, who offered classes for 'Ladies' in 'Drawing and Painting'. When the lease of the property was sold in 1788 the contents included a 'double-key'd Harpsichord, a Piano Forte … Bookcases and Books … ' – which would have been found in the sort of girls' school the play describes. Miss Paxton later turned up at 20 Greville Street, Hatton Garden, where she taught 'Drawing, Painting and Music'.[92] The irony, of course, is that even Miss Paxton, if, indeed, she was the author, was obliged to teach these accomplishments in order to attract pupils, despite her apparent distaste.

The play may also have been familiar to Jane Austen, who wrote, in a letter to her sister, Cassandra, in January 1801, 'Fanny shall have the Boarding-school as soon as her Papa gives me an opportunity of sending it.'[93] This was clearly a reference to reading material, and while, at that time, a number of girls' school stories had been published, the likeliest candidate, as put forward by Vivien Jones, in *Jane Austen: Selected Letters*, is *The Governess; or, The Boarding School Dissected*, the only text of this type published during Austen's childhood (in fact, it was published whilst she was at school in Reading).[94]

---

92. Arden Hegele, 'Identifying Jane Austen's "Boarding-School": A Proposed Author for *The Governess; or, The Boarding School Dissected*', in *Persuasions: The Jane Austen Journal* 31 (2009), pp. 175–79.
93. Edward, Lord Brabourne (ed.), *The Letters of Jane Austen*, 2 vols (London: Richard Bentley & Son, 1884), vol. 1, p. 271.
94. Jane Austen, *Selected Letters*, ed. Vivien Jones (Oxford: Oxford University Press, 2004), p. 234.

A Forerunner of *If* .... ?

One final piece worth drawing attention to is *Hornbyes Hornbook*, a lengthy poem, or rather two poems, written by William Hornbye and published in 1622.[95] This opens with a poem in praise of the hornbook, and is followed by *A Tale* in verse which purports to be autobiographical, which describes the narrator's schooldays, first, at a Free School and then at a school in Peterborough, where the master destroys his love of learning and drives the boys to revolt:

> Before a Chrstmasse time, we did conspire
> Against our Master, for to have desire
> Of libertie, for double paines we tooke
> All the yeare long by toyling at our booke,
> With many a wofull smarting lash beside,
> Which our poore buttocks patient did abide.
> So with a generall and free consent,
> We shut him forth of dores incontinent;
> For this did strongly for our reason stand,
> And since that others did attempt the same,
> If we should not do so, it was a shame.

This suggests that rebellions such as this were not uncommon at the time. The boys, sleeping on the floor, keep the master locked up for four days, but by then only six of the original 60 boys have maintained their vigil. They then release the master on what turns out to be a false promise of mercy, and they are severely beaten:

> There was prepared Rods a large elne long,
> Of tuffe-red-willowes binded very strong;
> Pepper and salt he did together blend,
> Full halfe a pecke he on our tayles did spend.
> Twixt every fower yerkes, we a handfull had
> On our bare bumbs, which almost made us mad.

The verse finishes with a series of bawdy exercises involving hornbooks and young maidens.

---

95. *Hornbyes Hornbook*, published by Thomas Bayly. The text here is taken from *Early English Books Online Creation Partnership*: http://name.umdl.umich.edu/A03687.0001.001.

Like several of the plays which preceded this work, there is an emphasis on harsh punishment, although it might be argued that, on this occasion, at least, the punishment was deserved.

* * *

The portrayal of education in fifteenth-, sixteenth- and seventeenth-century drama was, on the whole, a negative one – while education was shown to be an essential prerequisite for life, schools and, in particular, schoolmasters were easy targets for scorn, satire and condemnation.

Schools were generally portrayed as harsh, demeaning places, where the standard of education was poor and discipline was harsh, and schoolmasters were caricatures – brutal, or foolish, conceited and ignorant. They abused both the English and Latin tongues, had delusions of grandeur and were set up by dramatists to be mocked and laughed at, a trait that was largely ignored by later writers of school fiction (except the writers of the 'penny dreadful' school story in the mid to late nineteenth century). School fiction in the late eighteenth and early nineteenth centuries had a different purpose from the drama of the sixteenth and seventeenth centuries; stress was placed on the importance of school in religious and moral terms, and school was a place where the authority of the master was rarely questioned. In Tudor and Jacobean drama school was a place where rebels flourished, and where schoolmasters flogged with unparalleled brutality.

Nevertheless, underlying this, at least in the earlier dramas, was the concept that school was important in terms of the future – boys who neglected their education were likely to meet untimely deaths or, at the very least, have an unhappy adulthood. This was echoed in later school fiction, with many stories having an identical plot to that of *The Rebels* or *The Glasse of Governement*.

5

The First School Novel: *Dobsons Drie Bobbes*

It may come as a surprise to learn that the first, full-length school story pre-dates *Tom Brown's Schooldays* by exactly 250 years. In 1607 the London printer Valentine Simmes, who had earlier printed editions of several of Shakespeare's plays, issued the first and only edition of *Dobsons Drie Bobbes*, an anonymous comic tale of a Durham schoolboy (and later a student at Cambridge). The story followed the sixteenth-century tradition of 'jest books' – collections of jokes and quips, comic biographies and comic short stories – and, with its series of practical jokes played by its fictional hero, it fits firmly within the jest book pattern.[1] However, it is also a continuous narrative, one which follows its hero's school career, set against a real background and using real people and places and, as such, is a genuine novel.

The story is set largely in Durham and begins with its hero, George Dobson, being adopted by his uncle and sent first to a church school and then to the song school, before he secures a place at Christ's College, Cambridge. Most of his school life is concerned with playing tricks and practical jokes on his usher and schoolfellows and this continues at university, resulting in his expulsion. He spends some time as an ostler

---

1. This is also evidenced by the story's title – a 'dry bob' means an ironical jest or trick – and by its style, much of it comprising extremely long and rambling sentences. It has no relation to the Eton term 'dry bob', meaning a boy who plays cricket during the summer term, as opposed to a 'wet bob' who rows or swims.

until he is caught stealing a horse, and narrowly escapes the gallows by the intervention of his uncle. He ends up with a position in the Church and reforms into a respectable and respected member of the clergy.

Unfortunately, the story has remained almost wholly neglected. Only two copies of the original volume are known to exist, one in the Capell Collection at Trinity College, Cambridge, and the other in the Folger Shakespeare Library, Washington, DC. It was first seriously studied by Ernst Schulz in 1912.[2] This was followed in 1951 by a detailed analysis by Bertram Colgrave,[3] which identified many of the story's characters and places as well as summarising the plot. Most importantly, the text was reprinted by the Oxford University Press in 1955, along with an introduction by E.A. Horsman.[4] However, while it has received a modicum of critical attention, it has never before been linked to the origins of the school story.

* * *

The story opens with a portrait of Sir Thomas Pentley, vicar of St Giles' Church, Durham. His sister, who acts as his housekeeper, becomes concerned when he starts spending his money rather too liberally, and fears that there will be nothing left for her and his other sister to inherit on his death. She therefore writes to her sister and urges her to bring her entire family to Durham with the aim of settling there and sharing his money while he is still alive. Sir Thomas is subsequently somewhat taken aback to see not only his extended family but all their possessions arriving in the vicarage courtyard. When all has been explained, Sir Thomas promises that, if they return home, he will adopt their eldest son, George Dobson, which is agreed. Recognising almost immediately that his nephew is 'knavish', he enrols him into a church school. Within three days, George has broken his hornbook over a schoolfellow's head, causing severe bleeding. The injured boy's mother ensures that George is beaten by the schoolmaster and also extracts a promise from Sir Thomas

---

2. 'Die englischen Schwankbücher bis herab zu 'Dobson's Drie Bobs (1607)', in the Berlin-based German journal, *Palaestra* 117 (1912).
3. Bertram Colgrave, 'Dobson's Drie Bobs' (*sic*), *Durham University Journal* 43, no. 3 (New Series 12, no. 3) (June 1951), pp. 77–85. For a discussion of the text as a novel, see Avril S. O'Brien, '*Dobsons Drie Bobbes*: A Significant Contribution to the Development of Prose Fiction', *Studies in English Literature, 1500–1900* 12, no. 1 (Winter 1972), pp. 55–70.
4. E.A. Horsman (ed.), *Dobsons Drie Bobbes: A Story of Sixteenth Century Durham* (Oxford: Oxford University Press, 1955).

that he will beat the boy as well, otherwise 'shee would have him debarred of comming any more to schoole there'. When the unsuspecting George arrives home, 'as blithe as Bird on briar', his uncle, who clearly has some sympathy with his nephew, asks to see his hornbook, and George is obliged to confess what happened, claiming it was in self-defence, and adding that he has already been punished. However, Sir Thomas, remembering his early promise, 'caused poore Dobson to untrusse, and to offer his breech to the blocke, which hee soundly lashed'.

Sir Thomas sends George back to school with both a warning and a promise:

> that if hee so ill carried himselfe, hee would for ever eject and turne him out of the doores, whereas otherwise, if as a duetifull boy he would apply his booke, and would also conforme himselfe to the disposition of his fellowes, and with them live in unitie and concord, hee should not then want any manner of thing convenient to his estate and calling, but that after his death hee would make him his sole haire, and possesse him of all his landes, leases, farmes, and hereditaments.[5]

So George, on returning to school, tries his best to do his uncle's bidding, but fails miserably:

> so many blockes were set for him to stumble upon, for naturally he was of a crabbed and untoward disposition, and so rustike like, that he could not cover his clownish and wayward manners with the habite of civility, and in regard of his rude and ill favoured gestures, antique trickes, and apish toyes, his Schoolefellowes many times took occasion to deride, scorne, and laugh at him.[6]

In addition, in the evenings on their way home from school his schoolfellows played a multitude of tricks, for which George received the blame, such as: 'bursting glasen windowes, overthrowing Milke Maides pailes, pulling down stalles, and crushing out the linckes which were hung foorth to give light to the Passengers in the streetes'.

George is caught between a thirst for revenge and the desire to stay on the right side of his uncle. The last straw comes when some boys

---

5. *Dobsons Drie Bobbes* (1955), p. 12.
6. Ibid., p. 13.

post a libellous verse, signed with George's name, above the entrance to a haberdasher's. The enraged shopkeeper reports this to the dean and chapter – although happily George is able to prove his innocence. After this, he throws caution to the wind and fights with his schoolfellows at every opportunity, 'wherein fortune so much favoured him, as shee always granted him victory'.

Eventually, his uncle arranges for him to be entered into the song school of the cathedral, from where he soon proceeds to be beneficed as a chorister, under the master, Mr Bromeley. Nonetheless, this elevation does nothing to curb Dobson's mischievous instincts – indeed, he finds an immediate ally in another pupil, James Raikebaines, 'whom Dobson highly loved, and more esteemed of, than of all other fellowes, both in regard hee was borne in the country, and also for that his manners and conditions were more correspondent to his humour than any others'.

Their first joint enterprise is to frighten the usher by shooting an arrow in his direction, for which Raikebaines is subsequently beaten. This annoys Dobson, who decides to play another trick on the usher. He steals one of the dean's turkeys from the cathedral garden and implicates the usher by using a pair of his shoes to make incriminating footprints in the snow. Dobson and his friends have a splendid feast in a neighbouring cook's house. The following morning, when the turkey's disappearance is discovered, the unfortunate usher is accused of theft – although he manages to convince the dean of his innocence.

Dobson's next trick, aided by his friends, is to kill and steal a deer from the prior's park in the middle of the night. He later arouses the keeper and tells him that he has seen four men, one of whom was the usher, carrying the deer towards the usher's room. The keeper hurries to the dean and demands that the usher's room is searched. However, instead of finding the deer, they find a young girl, the daughter of a local merchant, who was a regular night-time visitor and who was hiding under the bed. The usher is subsequently told that he must marry the girl, but otherwise remains unpunished.

Dobson's subsequent pranks lead to a degree of local fame: 'he spared no persons but as occasion was offered, he played the wagge, sometime in the city, otherwise in the countrey, by meanes whereof his fame spread it selfe all over: and all pleasantly disposed humourists, sought to be acquainted with him, although he were yet a scholler'.

He next turns his attention to his friend, Raikebaines, who has received a meat pudding from his father. Putting it close to the schoolroom fire so that it will warm through, he asks Dobson to help him keep an eye on it and to keep other pupils away with a promise that they will share it for breakfast. Nevertheless, Dobson has other ideas and, having distracted Raikebaines, he makes off with the pudding and shuts himself in the canon's hall. Raikebaines follows him and hammers on the door, to no avail, until Sir Thomas comes along and orders his nephew to come out. Dobson patiently listens to the accusations of his friend, and then tells his uncle that the pudding he has just eaten was sent to him by his aunt and, while he had promised Raikebaines a share, he was afraid that his friend would deceive him, either by eating it all if Dobson was called away, or by helping himself to more than half.

Raikebaines realises that he is beaten and, afraid of losing Dobson's friendship, says nothing further. This does not stop Dobson from playing yet another trick. His uncle has recently been appointed 'Choraster', one of his duties being to light the candles in the cathedral at six o'clock in the morning. Reluctant to rise at such an early hour, he arranges for Dobson to do this for him, promising him the short ends of the candles and tapers as a reward. Raikebaines offers to help, but one morning Dobson lures him into the cupboard where the candles are kept and locks him in. He is forced to stay there from half past six until ten o'clock, when he is rescued by Sir Thomas and the other canons who have arrived for the morning service. On being told what happened, Sir Thomas seeks out Dobson and demands an explanation – Dobson offers up an excuse based on the lie that Raikebaines entered the cupboard of his own accord, intent on stealing a whole candle. Sir Thomas, for once, sees through Dobson and, after giving Raikebaines two whole candles, strikes Dobson on the mouth, drawing blood. Not surprisingly, Dobson vows revenge on his uncle, while at the same time promising Raikebaines he will play no more tricks on him.

What happens next is a little out of keeping with the earlier, comic tenor of the story. Dobson arranges for a few friends to break into the vicarage orchard and to overpower and tie up not only his uncle but also his aunt and their two servants, while Dobson himself arranges to be somewhere else. The four victims are left trussed up all night, to be 'rescued' by Dobson the following morning. However, all four are ill for some time afterwards, Sir Thomas, in particular, and, after they have recovered, Dobson vows to be more circumspect in future. Nevertheless, he still remains wedded to his propensity for practical jokes and misbehaviour. He lends his uncle's horse to a friend, without permission and the horse ends up six miles away in the pound at Chester-le-Street; he later tricks his aunt into providing him with a large quantity of beer which he shares with his friends, after which he fills the now empty casks with water. The beer was actually meant for a party being given by his uncle and, when the substitution is discovered, Dobson is naturally suspected. He flees to the hen house and refuses to emerge unless he is forgiven. His uncle, urged on by his guests, has little choice but to agree.

However, by way of revenge, Sir Thomas:

> purposed to hold his nose to the grindstone, and to keepe him at hard meat, he spared his purse, and made him go thinly apparelled, and scarcely sometimes did he allow whole cloathes, but forced him to weare his old rags for want of newe, till they hung in totters about his taile.[7]

Dobson, not to be beaten, 'enrolled his uncle's name in the Drapers booke, for a sute and a cloake, which his uncle was constrained to discharge for his credite sake'. Sir Thomas is obliged to visit all the clothiers and milliners in Durham to urge them not to grant him any more credit. In desperation, Dobson steals the manuscript of a song written by one of his schoolfellows and presents it to some of his music-loving cousins, claiming it is his own work. In return, he receives a new suit.

Dobson's next trick is prompted by an old school custom: 'It hath bin a custome of olde, and it is yet to this day in the schools of Durham, for three Schollers every Satterday to be marshaled forth to the woods in the countrey, to provide birchen roddes for the correction of the disordered and negligent.'

Dobson, having avoided this task in the winter, chooses to go in May. Afterwards, he dresses in a fine suit belonging to Raikebaines, complete with a cloak and rapier, while his two friends are dressed as servants. As they make their way to the nearby village of Witton Gilbert, they make it known that Dobson is the son of the chancellor of Durham. At Witton, they go into an alehouse where they order a large breakfast, at a cost of two pence each. They actually only have three pence between them, a problem solved by Dobson ordering another breakfast, after which the hostess tells them that the total cost is twenty pence. Dobson flies into a rage, accusing her of gross overcharging and orders her to appear at the chancery on the following Friday, where he will apply to have her licence to sell ale revoked. Despite the hostess' desperate pleading, Dobson remains unmoved, and the three boys then hurry away, leaving just their three pence.

When the hostess does attend the chancery, the chancellor, of course, is wholly ignorant of the matter and, after hearing her account and

---

7. Ibid., p. 64.

reading a petition she has raised from the Witton Gilbert parishioners, concludes that she has been duped. He gives her a French crown for her troubles, although everyone remains none the wiser as to who the imposters were.

Dobson's penultimate escapade is to steal a goose from a poultry yard and cook it in one of the school cellars. Mr Bromeley smells the cooking but, on trying to investigate, finds the cellar door locked. When he cries out, Dobson begs him not to enter:

> for Gods sake come not heere sir, for you are not able to indure the stinch of this place, it is so mighty, that it will hazard your strangling: for this last night, in the raine which fel, there are come downe such a multitude of frogs and other vermine into this house, that no man is able to set foote upon any ground for them: and therefore, lest they should be the cause of any infection in this house, if they should continue untill Summer, wee have made a fire to burne them, whereof proceedes this terrible stinch which you taste, and from which we pray you to absent your selfe.[8]

Mr Bromeley promptly withdraws, and Dobson and his friends are able to eat the goose in peace.

At long last, Dobson is so proficient in music and Latin that he is considered ready for university but before he leaves he is anxious to play one last trick. One day around Midsummer he persuades all the scholars that they need not attend school because it is a Feast Day. So, while they go off to enjoy themselves, Dobson returns to school and waits for the arrival of Mr Bromeley. When the master arrives, he demands to know where his pupils are. Dobson replies that they have insisted that it is a feast day on which the school is due a holiday. Mr Bromeley tells Dobson to fetch them but Dobson has one more trick up his sleeve; he tells his schoolfellows that they are wanted at the school to sing to a company of gentlemen who have travelled from London and that, if they comply, Mr Bromeley will give them another holiday at a later date. When they are all assembled in the schoolroom, Mr Bromeley enters and bolts the door, demanding an explanation for their absence. All the boys turn against Dobson and, in the face of their angry testimony, Mr Bromeley concludes that Dobson is the guilty party. However, when he commands him to 'prepare his breech for the strappado', Dobson dashes off and finds refuge in an 'old Jakes in the Schoole, wherein they used to throwe

---

8. Ibid., pp. 78–79.

all their filthy dust and sweepings'. He refuses to come out until Mr Bromeley agrees to pardon both him and his fellow pupils and, of course, he emerges triumphant yet again.

Within a week he is at Cambridge, where he manages to curb his playful inclinations and becomes a highly respected scholar. After three years he is an expert in Logic and Philosophy, and is called to 'the publike schooles' to debate with other students. He falls foul of some of them and, eventually, of the university authorities and, shortly before he is due to take his degree, he is expelled. Too ashamed to return to Durham, he finds a job as an under-ostler at an inn in Huntingdon and later becomes a servant to a rich gentleman. Although he is highly regarded, a series of incidents leads him to suddenly leave his employment, stealing his master's best horse and then selling it. He is eventually tracked down, arrested and imprisoned in York Castle. Fortunately, his uncle secures his release and, after promising to reform, he is:

> beneficed in the Abbey, as he requested. Whereupon entring into consideration how much Almighty God and his frindes had helped him, he mortified all his irregular passions and spent the residue of his course in an admirable course of civility. For the which he was generally respected of all the people and the whole Cleargie, and after the death of his Unkell, possessed of all his substance and beneficed with his Vicarige, in which estate he ended and finished his life.[9]

* * *

There are several aspects to *Dobsons Drie Bobbes* which mark it out as a significant, albeit wholly overlooked, contribution to the development of the English novel and, of course, to the development of the school story. Although it tells us little about school life in the late sixteenth and early seventeenth centuries, what it does reveal is undoubtedly authentic. While the identity of the author is unknown, it is quite clear that he knew Durham and the cathedral intimately. The details of the cathedral and its school timetables have been shown to be accurate, as has the topography of both the cathedral and the surrounding area.[10] In addition, most of the characters in the story actually existed. A George Dobson is recorded in the cathedral treasurer's book as a chorister in 1558, although, interestingly, in 1568 the records suggest that he ran away, the entry for him for that year having had the word 'fugitive'

---

9. Ibid., p. 100.
10. See Colgrave, 'Dobson's Drie Bobs'.

added. Whilst he was at the cathedral school, his salary was paid by a Thomas Pentland, who was, for a time, a vicar of St Oswald's in Durham, although in his will he described himself as being 'of the parishe of Sainct Gyles'.[11] A Thomas Raikebaines joined the song school in 1564. The master, Mr Bromeley, is based on John Brimley, who was the organist and master of the choristers between 1557 and 1576. His gravestone is in the Galilee Chapel at the west end of Durham Cathedral. The only imaginary character associated with the cathedral and the school is the usher, whose name is occasionally given as 'Sir William'.

The story is also notable for the way in which the character of its hero is developed and the way that motive is explored. To begin with, George Dobson pays heed to his uncle's warning to behave himself otherwise he will be turned out of his home. Yet he finds it very difficult to control his passions – after the author has told us that his schoolfellows 'deride, scorne, and laugh at him', he goes on:

> whereof hee being very impatient, and not daring with clubbe and fist to revenge it, lest thereby hee should procure his unckles indignation, for excessive griefe, anger and sorrow, he would wrinckle his browes, whet his teeth, and pull the haires from his head, which hee would scatter and throw abroad in franticke manner. And if it had not beene more for the feare hee had to loose his unckles favour, than the whipping hee assured himselfe would ensue the combate, the most part of them had felt the weight of his fists.[12]

Even after he is falsely accused of causing havoc in the streets:

> hee uppon every such occasion suffered alwayes the punishment that others had deserved: and these contrivings of his felows were so continuall, that they made him almost wearie of his life, and so desperate in the end, that he became in respect thereof, that he resolved rather than any further to tollerate this mis-usage, either to runne his countrey, or to forsake his friendes and their company.[13]

There follows a long passage in which Dobson explores all his options, until the trick played on the haberdasher is one trick too many and,

---

11. Horsman, *Dobsons Drie Bobbes*, p. x.
12. *Dobsons Drie Bobbes,* pp. 13–14.
13. Ibid., p. 15.

after being unjustly punished, he confronts the real culprits, fights them and forces them to confess in front of his uncle. Not only is Sir Thomas delighted to learn that Dobson was innocent, he refuses to listen to further complaints, and treats Dobson so favourably that the boy 'plaid the wagge with more libertie than before'.

Dobson then becomes a shrewd and calculating prankster, plotting revenge on the usher on two occasions and exhibiting an excess of cunning. When he turns his attention to his friend, Raikebaines, he shows himself to be a skilled liar. Later, having experienced his uncle's temper after locking Raikebaines in the candle cupboard, he shows some remorse, by promising that he will not play any more tricks on his friend, a promise that he keeps: 'Raikebaines being of a gentle and good nature easily pardoned the offence, and joyning hands, they protested to continue perfit Friends each to other during their lives, and so returned to the Schoole wel satisfied.'

Dobson also promises to be more circumspect after the incident in the orchard, or at least he decides to 'no more hazard his uncles life and welfare', although Sir Thomas continues to be a victim of Dobson's pranks.

The major fault of the story is its sudden ending. While Dobson's schooldays take up 84 pages (in the Oxford University Press edition), his time at Cambridge is covered in only ten pages, and his subsequent career in only five. His sudden and total transformation into a respectable member of the clergy is simply stated as fact, with no elaboration. However, as Avril O'Brien has pointed out in her article on *Dobsons Drie Bobbes*, this 'rapid conversion' was a Renaissance convention.[14] Otherwise, Dobson as a schoolboy is a well-rounded and believable character, even if his antics are occasionally outrageous. As such, he is a precursor of numerous later fictional schoolboys, in particular, those who appeared in the late nineteenth century in penny dreadfuls and boys' story papers, such as Jack Harkaway, Ned Nimble, Tom Wildrake and Dick Lightheart, some of whose exploits were equally as disingenuous. With the episode of the meat pudding there are even shades of Billy Bunter, although Dobson is a rather more accomplished liar.

Certainly, the author of *Dobsons Drie Bobbes* invented a character who has echoed down through the centuries, and for that he merits more than just a footnote in literary history.

---

14. O'Brien, '*Dobsons Drie Bobbes*', p. 69.

6

Defoe's Quarrelling Schoolboys

Daniel Defoe, while generally considered to be one of the founders of the English novel, is not usually associated with the school story. Yet in 1717 he wrote the second work of English fiction to be set in a school – albeit as a satire on the Parliament of the day. Now, like *Dobsons Drie Bobbes*, completely forgotten, the story – *The Quarrel of the School-Boys at Athens* – nevertheless established a pattern for future school stories, in that it featured some of the themes that were later to become common, particularly those of popularity and unpopularity, favouritism and disunity amongst the boys.

Defoe, born in 1660 or 1661 (sources differ) in the parish of St Giles, Cripplegate, London, was educated at a private dissenting school in Dorking and then, from the age of around fourteen onwards, at a dissenting academy in Stoke Newington. After a brief and generally unsuccessful career as a merchant, he became a close associate of King William III, and later the governing Tory Party. He began his writing career in 1697 and wrote many political pamphlets, although he was best-known for his novels, most notably, *The Life and Strange Surprizing Adventures of Robinson Crusoe of York*, published in 1719, and *Moll Flanders* (1722). He died in 1731.

His place in the history of the school story is merited by a pamphlet (of 38 pages), published anonymously in 1717 (by J. Roberts), entitled *The Quarrel of the School-Boys at Athens, As Lately Acted at a School near Westminster*. Ostensibly, this is the story of a school in Greece, but in reality it is a satire on the Parliament of King George I.

George, the first of the Hanoverian kings, had succeeded to the throne in August 1714, on the death of his second cousin, Queen Anne. The early years of his reign were marked by strong divisions in Parliament. On his succession, the Tories had been the dominant political party, but the new King soon sided with the Whigs, with key ministerial posts being given to prominent Whig politicians.

On the surface, the Whigs became a powerful and united force, although there were divisions, and there was, in early 1716, no clear leader:

> Four men stood out: Stanhope, Sunderland, Townshend and Walpole. In the Commons both Stanhope and Walpole were in the van, the former very much the King's favourite. ... If he had a weakness it was ... that his oratorical and parliamentary skills were limited. Such abilities came much more naturally to Walpole. ... In the House of Lords the 3rd Earl of Sunderland acted as a close ally of Stanhope, being noted for his 'great knowledge of foreign affairs' which endeared him to the King. ... His rival in the Lords was Townshend, Walpole's brother-in-law.[1]

It was two of the four men who 'stood out', along with two others, whom Defoe caricatured in his pamphlet.

Robert Walpole was born in Norfolk in 1676 and educated at Eton and Cambridge. Having entered Parliament in 1701, he had become one of the Tories' most outspoken opponents and in 1712 was expelled from Parliament and imprisoned in the Tower of London on trumped-up charges of corruption. After his return, he was appointed Paymaster of the Forces and in 1715 he was promoted to First Lord of the Treasury. In Defoe's words:

> He was a Native of the Country, and one the Schoolmaster had heard much of, though he had no Knowledge of him. ... [H]e had signalised himself by his extraordinary Conduct, and early appearing in the Interest of the present Schoolmaster, as much as any Boy in the School; also in the Case of some Privileges of the School, which were invaded during the Government of former Schoolmasters and Ushers; he had appeared very boldly, and indeed had been ill used by them for it; for they had him soundly whipp'd, put into *Dunce's Hole*, and at last expell'd the School. ... [H]e stood stoutly up

---

1. Julian Hoppit, *A Land of Liberty? England 1689–1727* (Oxford: Oxford University Press, 2000), p. 397.

to them, and never flinched; nay, when he was turned out of the School, he came up to the very School Door, and insulted them all; and thus he continued to behave until the last, till the Vacancy came, and the new Schoolmaster took Possession, and then it was his Turn; for as the new Schoolmaster embraced him with a great deal of Affection. ... The Schoolmaster did not make him Captain of one of the ordinary Classes ... but made him Head of those selected Boys, who he employed for the greatest Trust, viz. to keep, receive, and direct the common Cash of the School, as well the ordinary Salary or Revenue of the Teachers, Usher, and Master, as the extraordinary Money for the Incidents of the School-Government: In this Employ he was very faithful, as to the Money; but as this Post furnished him with extraordinary Power and Influence over the rest of the Scholars, so it raised him many Enemies.[2]

Charles Townshend, born in Norfolk in 1674 and educated at Eton and Cambridge, had succeeded to his peerage in 1687 and, while initially a Tory sympathiser, he began to support the Whigs. (Walpole and Townshend were brothers-in-law by virtue of his second marriage sometime before 1713 to Walpole's sister, Dorothy.) In 1714 he was appointed Secretary of State for the Northern Department, serving alongside James Stanhope (who was the Secretary of State for the Southern Department) – although he was sacked in 1716 and he briefly served as Lord Lieutenant of Ireland. Defoe described him as being:

> of a better Family, and of a higher Rank than the other, though a Degree lower in his Station in the School, being one of the chief Clerks of the School: He was a Youth of admirable Integrity, had great and just Ideas of things, and a most clear and penetrating Judgment; he was a steady Friend to the Master, and had always espoused his Interest in the Time of the greatest Opposition to it, and was deservedly therefore placed in a Post of as great Trust as any in the School.[3]

The other two protagonists were John Churchill, the first Duke of Marlborough, and John Campbell, the second Duke of Argyll. Churchill

---

2. *The Quarrel of the School-boys at Athens* (1717), pp. 16–19.
3. Ibid., pp. 20–21.

(1650–1722) was educated at St Paul's School, London, and in 1667, aged seventeen, was apppointed to the household of James, the Duke of York and Lord High Admiral, and the second in line to the throne. He served in both the navy and the army, although he was later accused of embezzlement, and exiled to France. He returned to England after the succession of George I and was appointed Commander-in-Chief. Defoe gave him the title of 'the Captain of the Mathematical Form', which, being the school's top class, led to him being known as 'Captain General of all the Boys'. Defoe described him as:

> a sprightly, vigorous Youth, of a wonderful Vivacity and Spirit; he had a Genius for great things, and his peculiar study was in those parts of the Mathematicks, which relate to the *Art of War*. ... [H]e had a cool *Head*, and a warm *Heart*; and in a Word, as he delighted in great Actions, so he discharged himself in the greatest Affairs of the School with such Dexterity, that he kept all the tumultuous, clamouring Classes that were under him in great Awe. ... [H]e had with great Applause been entertain'd by the new Schoolmaster, not as an inferior, and a Pupil, or Scholar, but rather as a Friend, an Intimate or Confident, and one on whose Counsel and Fidelity the Master might depend in Matters of the greatest Consequence.[4]

Campbell (1678–1743), born in Petersham, Surrey, succeeded as Duke of Argyll in 1703. He fought under Marlborough, and in 1711 he was appointed Commander-in-Chief of the British Forces in Spain. However, by 1713 he had become critical of the Tory administration and he joined the Whig opposition in the House of Lords. He became an intimate of the Prince of Wales after George I had succeeded to the throne and, as such, was regarded with suspicion by other Whigs. Defoe wrote that he was:

> ambitious and avaritious, but managed both with more Policy than he did his Passion: He had long envy'd the Captain of the Mathematick Class, and aspired to be *Captain General* of all the School; nay, in a Word, he had upon many Occasions given to understand, that nothing less would content him. ... To allay the good Qualifications he was Master of, he had

---

4. Ibid., pp. 11–12.

some dark Ways with him, which very much exposed him; for he very early drank in wicked Principles, and gave himself over to all manner of Vice; in a Word, he was lewd enough to have debauch'd the whole School.[5]

Three other parliamentarians featured in the turmoil, which followed a year or so after the succession of George I, also featured briefly in Defoe's pamphlet. These were: James Stanhope, first Earl Stanhope; Charles Spencer, third Earl of Sunderland; and Henry St John, first Viscount Bolingbroke.

Stanhope (1673–1721), educated at Eton and Oxford, entered the House of Commons in 1701, although he was still an active soldier. In 1712 he abandoned the army to concentrate on politics. Following the succession of King George I, he was appointed as Secretary of State for the Southern Department, and in 1717 he was made First Lord of the Treasury, although a year later he returned to his former office of Secretary of State. He was made Lord Stanhope in 1718.

Sunderland (1674–1722) succeeded to his peerage in 1702, and joined the cabinet in 1715 as Lord Privy Seal, after having initially been appointed by the new king as Lord Lieutenant of Ireland. In 1717 he took over as Secretary of State for the Northern Department, and he became First Lord of the Treasury in 1718.

Finally, Bolingbroke (1678–1751), educated at Eton and Oxford, entered Parliament in 1701 as a Tory, and was the prime mover of the Bill which secured the Protestant succession to the throne (the Act of Settlement). However, his time in parliament was turbulent and he was suspected of being sympathetic to the claims of James Edward Stuart, the Pretender to the throne. After the succession of George I, he fled to France and, while he tried to gain reconciliation with the government, after abandoning his support for James, he was only pardoned in 1723. Defoe caricatured Bolingbroke as:

> a very scandalous, unhappy Wretch, Captain of his Form; a Boy he was, whose principal Merit lay in those Things which wise Men reject, and who was advanced to be Captain of that Class, rather because he had servile, base Principles, which would prostitute him to any Drudgery that was imposed upon him, than for any Respect those who placed him there really entertained for him.[6]

---

5. Ibid., pp. 13–14.
6. Ibid., pp. 21–22.

Towards the end of 1716, King George left London to return to Hanover, leaving his son, the Prince of Wales, in nominal charge of the country. For a while, there were arguments as to the nature of the authority the prince was to exercise – the prince was made Guardian and Lieutenant of the Realm rather than Prince Regent, which restricted his powers – although, on this occasion, a serious split (between the king and his son and between members of the Government) was avoided. However, splits eventually arose as a result of foreign policy, in particular, a treaty between Britain and France signed in November 1716, which was expanded into a triple alliance with the Dutch in December of that year.

This especially worried Townshend, but the king, then in Hanover, supported by Stanhope and Sunderland, turned against him, with accusations that he was a little Englander, and he was sacked in 1716:

> Townshend did not hesitate to tell his master of his worries but his voice now carried too little weight. The King was in Hanover, from where he had negotiated the alliance with France, and where he had the constant advice and support of Stanhope. There, the King and Stanhope, encouraged by Sunderland, the Lord Privy seal ... turned decisively against the absent Townshend. They accused him of being a little Englander, indeed of being a Tory, and of obstructing the conclusion of the Treaty with France. Given the primacy of foreign affairs to George's ambitions it was impossible that he could continue with Townshend in office and in December he was dismissed.[7]

It was against this background that Defoe wrote his satire, in which the Houses of Parliament became a rumbustious and anarchic public school.[8] The narrative portrays the school during the schoolmaster's absence, with the boys shown as a fractious and divided bunch, squabbling and fighting, until the schoolmaster returns and restores peace (albeit, as later events showed, only temporarily).

The story opens by introducing the reader to a Grecian schoolmaster (i.e. King George himself) in 'the days of ancient Philosophers', describing him as: 'a Person of great Excellency in himself, famed for his

---

7. Hoppit, p. 400.
8. For a further discussion of the events described by Defoe, see *The Works of Daniel Defoe: Satire, Fantasy and Writings on the Supernatural*, Volume 3, edited by Geoffrey Sill (London: Pickering & Chatto, 2003), pp 22–25.

Wisdom and for his Experience, and especially for his Dexterity in the Government of his School, and for his exquisite Skill in Instructing his Scholars'.

His fame had spread to a 'Neighbouring Commonwealth' and, when there was a vacancy in 'the greatest and most famous School in those parts of the World', he was the only candidate. However, his appointment was opposed:

> by some of the idlest, and most ignorant of the Scholars,[9] who were apprehensive of being kept under a stricter Discipline, than they had been used to in the former Time; and who loving their Vices, and especially Indulging their Neglect of Learning, were loth to submit to such a regular Government of the School, as they expected from him; These laid several Plots, got together into Parties, and form'd several Designs, to have prevented the new School-master's taking Possession of the School; nay, so far had they carried on their Projects, that, after his Coming, they offered great Disturbance to him, insomuch, that contrary to his inclination, which was to have taught them Obedience by Precepts and Persuasions, rather than by Coercion and Discipline; he was obliged to take the Rod and the Ferula in his Hand, almost as soon as he came into the School; and first, whereas at his very Entrance, he found some Dunces and illiterate Youths,[10] and who, he thought, were placed too high in the School, beyond the Proficiency they had arriv'd to; These he began with, and immediately displacing them caused them to go back to the lower Classes, from whence they had been too hastily raised by the Favour, rather than Judgement, of the former Pedagogues.[11]

However, even those who were demoted to lower classes continued to misbehave, until they were eventually expelled.

Having purged the school of troublemakers, the new schoolmaster was left with a senior school full of 'VERY GOOD BOYS' and, after

---

9. That is, Jacobites, who supported the recognition of James Edward Stuart (1688–1766), the 'Old Pretender' and son of James II, as the legitimate heir to the throne.
10. A reference to the Tories and some Whigs, whose loyalty to the king was uncertain.
11. Defoe, pp. 4–5.

appointing his only son as usher, was able to return to his native country. The new usher is described as 'a Person of some Proficiency in learning', but inexperienced in running a school. The inevitable consequence of this was that the school:

> became a Scene of Confusion and Disorder; not that the conduct of the USHER can be reflected on, who did his best, according to the utmost of his Skill and Capacity, to have preserv'd the Harmony and good Understanding of the Senior Boys. But alas! they despised his Youth, and his want of Authority to punish them; they also said some very ill-natured Things of him, with Respect to his Judgment, in teaching and instructing the Boys; Tho' this was very disobliging, and the USHER was not quite destitute of good Intelligence in the Case, yet he concealed his Resentment for the present, and from time to time laid it all before his Father, resolving to receive all his Instructions from his own Hand.[12]

The king was being kept informed of events at Westminster, which were turned by Stanhope and Sunderland, who were with him in Hanover, into evidence of either a conspiracy or mismanagement by Walpole and Townshend.

The narrative goes on to point out that those responsible for the disorder were chiefly those who had initially welcomed the new schoolmaster, and who had been promoted to responsible positions, with the narrative plunging into a description of the school following the schoolmaster's departure:

> The Master being thus gone Abroad, and the Conduct of the School being left too much in the Power of these three or four upper Boys, it was not long, but not only all the Harmony and Affection, good Understanding and Unanimity, which at the Deparure of their Master appeared among them, was lost; but they, as *Boys will*, and as indeed *none but Boys would*, fell all to wrangling, quarrelling, and disputing with one another, till the Concern for the publick Good of the School, which was their Duty, and ought to have been their disinterested Care, was quite forgot, or turned almost wholly to the forming of Parties and Interests to supplant and to undermine one

---

12. Ibid., p. 8.

another, to the great endangering the Peace of the *School*, perplexing the good Humour'd USHER; and, in a Word, to the putting the inferior *Scholars* and *Classes* into the utmost Confusion.[13]

Defoe then identifies the main cause of the chaos as lying: 'between the said Captain General, and his Interest on one Hand, and the other Favourite Boy who kept the School Cash, and his Friends and Dependents on the other'.

In other words, the main protagonists were Marlborough and Walpole. As Defoe saw it, Marlborough considered Walpole and his brother-in-law to be a threat to his power and position, and reckoned that the removal of Townshend was the key:

> The Captain General of the Boys ... found that the Captain of the Cashkeepers, supported by the extraordinary Assistance of his Brother in Law, began to be formidable, and therefore found, that if he expected to carry his Point, this Supporter must be removed; not that he had either any Room to form an Accusation against him, or any malicious Desire to hurt or defame him, but he found he stood in the Way of his Interest, and would, perhaps, in Time, be fatal to it: and therefore, as it is said, he resolv'd he must be removed.[14]

Defoe then describes the way Townshend was ousted by the machinations of Stanhope and Sunderland:

> Historians differ in the Manner how this Blow was given. Some relate that it was done purely by Defamation and Slander, representing him to the *Schoolmaster* as turbulent and quarrelsome in the *School*, haughty and fierce, affronting his *Schoolfellows*, presuming on the Merit of his Services, and his Interest with the Master, and such like; Others relate, that they got a Proposal craftily made to him, about bringing in some *Foreign Boys* into the *School*, which the Master had a Kindness for; and that, on the other Hand, they as craftily brought him to oppose it; and then accused him of Disrespect to the Master: Others relate it otherwise; so the Matter is

---

13. Ibid., p. 24.
14. Ibid., p. 29.

left doubtful in History; but this they all agree in, (*viz.*) that without any Reproof, or the least Hint from the Schoolmaster, that he was displeased with him, his Quietus was brought over, and presented him, and he was immediately removed from the Class.[15]

Not surprisingly, this divided the school and there was a fear that, with the boys behaving as badly as they had before the new schoolmaster took over, the reputation of the school would be ruined. Word is sent over to the schoolmaster that he should return as soon as possible, 'that by his Presence and Authority, and the Majesty of his Office, he might quiet the School, and bring things into some better Order'. However, he is unable to conclude his affairs in his own country quickly and:

> In the Mean Time, the School was a meer *Bedlam*, Books and Business seem'd all laid aside, every mean Scholar, that had scarce entred into Verges of Philosophy, was over Head and Ears in Politicks, and attach'd to his Party. The Forms were all up in Arms against one another, as the Heads or Captains guided them, they fell into the warmest Disputes imaginable; nay, sometimes they were so hot, that they were ready to throw their Books at one anothers Heads.[16]

Eventually, the schoolmaster returns:

> he went directly to the School: He found by the Noise, there was no Room for Words, Perswasions, Expostulations etc. wherefore with an awful Frown upon his Brow, and holding up his Rod in his Hand, he enters the *School*, and being just within the Door, looked sternly round him, not speaking a Word. The Boys no sooner saw the Master and the Rod, but they all sat down as quiet and as still, as if nothing had happened at all; not a Word was spoken, not the least Noise heard, all was perfectly calm and quiet in a Moment; the Master went peacably up to his Chair of Instruction, and laid down his Rod; the *Scholars* fell very lovingly to their Books, and have been very good Boys ever since.[17]

---

15. Ibid., pp. 29–30.
16. Ibid., p. 36.
17. Ibid., pp. 37–38.

Defoe wrote his pamphlet in December 1716/January 1717 and published it in January 1717, after Townshend's dismissal but before he had agreed to accept the post in Ireland. Defoe announced its forthcoming publication in the December issue of *Mercurius Politicus*, a journal which he edited from 1716 to 1720. In it, he quoted some verses which were to have appeared on the title page of the pamphlet, and which succinctly summarise the story he was telling, but which were, inexplicably, omitted when the pamphlet appeared:

> *A Master kept a Grammar School,*
>   *From Foreign countries brought,*
> *The Boys learnt well, and liv'd by Rule,*
> *And very seldom play'd the Fool,*
>   *But did as they were Taught.*
>
> *But he no sooner stept* a-wry
>   *On Business of his Own,*
> *But they fell out,* they knew not why,
> *And carried* Classic Feud *so high,*
>   *The School's a* Bedlam *Grown.*
>
> *But soon as* Master Pedagogue
>   *Came back with* Rod *in Hand,*
> *Good Manners came again in Vogue,*
> *They all left off to play the Rogue,*
>   *And mute as Fishes stand.*[18]

It is, perhaps, a shame that Defoe published his satire when he did, as later events in Parliament were even more dramatic – a bitter quarrel between the king and the prince of Wales, and a later reconciliation between Stanhope/Sunderland and Walpole/Townshend – which would have made for a more intriguing story.

Nevertheless, *The Quarrel of the School-Boys at Athens* remains an integral, if neglected, step in the development of the school story, an example of how life in a school can echo life in the wider world (or, in this case, vice versa) and a demonstration of the potential this offered for storytellers.

---

18. *Mercurius Politicus: Being Monthly Observations on the affairs of Great Britain*....(London: J. Morphew), January 1717, p. 43.

7

School Life in the Early English Novel

The English novel, or rather the English novel of character, was, in the view of most literary historians, born in 1740 with the publication of Samuel Richardson's *Pamela; or, Virtue Rewarded*. This was followed a year later by Henry Fielding's satirical riposte, *Shamela*, but, more importantly, in 1742, by Fielding's *The History of the Adventures of Joseph Andrews and of His Friend, Mr Abraham Adams*, initially another parody of *Pamela* but which develops into a ribald and comic novel in its own right. Fielding followed this in 1743 with his satire, *Jonathan Wild, the Great*, another early picaresque English novel, and, most famously, in 1749 with *The History of Tom Jones, A Foundling*.

Both *Jonathan Wild* and *Tom Jones* feature vignettes of their heroes' education, which puts their adulthood into context and explains, to some extent at least, how their characters were forged. The same is true of two other great picaresque novels of the mid-eighteenth century – Tobias Smollett's *The Adventures of Roderick Random* (1748) and *The Adventures of Peregrine Pickle* (1751). A few other mid-eighteenth-century novels also merit a small footnote in the history of the school story for their brief snapshots of school life.

These stories, like the plays which preceded them, have been mostly overlooked in previous historical studies of school fiction. While the school episodes, or references to school life, are short and take up only a small part of the whole narrative, they are important for establishing character, as well as revealing something of the authors' attitudes to schooling and education and for being, in some cases, vivid pictures of eighteenth-century school life. A somewhat different picture of school life was painted by Jonathan Swift in *Gulliver's Travels*, first published in 1726, which satirised the early eighteenth-century school system. However, before considering these novels, it is worth going back to the seventeenth century, to one of the first European novels to include a portrait of a tutor and his pupil.

François l'Hermite and *The Disgraced Page*

The English picaresque novel had its roots in earlier novels from Europe, notably Spain and France – and the novels listed above had their own precursor in *Le Page disgracié*, or *The Disgraced Page*, by François l'Hermite (under his pseudonym, Tristan l'Hermite), first published in France in 1642.[1] As well as being one of the very first picaresque novels, this was almost certainly the first novel to feature a young boy's relationship with his tutor.[2]

François l'Hermite was born around 1601 and at the age of eleven he became a page to the marquise of Verneuil. Two years later he was exiled to England after a duel, in which his opponent was killed. It was this period of his life – as a page, and his later vagabond existence in England – which he described in his novel.

The Disgraced Page, written in the first person, tells the story of a young man born into a rich and aristocratic family. He is sent to school to learn Latin, as a way of weaning him off the romances he has become fond of; but he only learns because he fears corporal punishment if he does not, and then he forgets much of what he has been taught. He is then taken in by a prince to be a companion and page to one of his sons. The two boys immediately forge a close bond and they are both taught by a highly-regarded tutor. However, the tutor gives more of his attention to the prince's son than to the page, who instead begins to follow the bad example set by 'the many young libertines' he sees in the house.

The page subsequently becomes a close friend of another young boy in the same position in the household, who teaches him to play cards and dice and who drives the page into debt. The tutor soon discovers the page's predilection for gambling but, despite constant punishment, and the realisation that what he is doing is wrong, the page cannot

---

1. The only English translation appears to be that by Robert Levine, which can be found online at http://people.bu.edu/bobl/tristan.htm.
2. The only reference to this novel in the context of it being (partly) school fiction appears to be in Ascott R. Hope (real name Robert Hope Moncrieff), *A Book about Schools, Schoolboys, Schoolmasters and Schoolbooks* (London: A. & C. Black, 1925), pp. 107–15, in which it is described, inaccurately, as 'the first made-up story, at any length, of schoolboy life'.

mend his ways, and he often escapes being punished by virtue of his acquaintance with 'powerful people' who intercede on his behalf. This strategy is not, however, always successful, and the tutor continues to whip him whenever circumstances merit it and the opportunity arises. On one occasion, the tutor gives the page a letter to be delivered to a visiting monk. In turn, the page, having been distracted from his task by gambling, gives the letter to another page to deliver, only for the monk to mistake him for the boy the tutor had sent and thrash him for being late. The second page subsequently takes it out on the first with his fists.

The page is later punished for trying to reproduce magic tricks from a book he has bought, which causes chaos in the household. One of the servants, by way of revenge, plays a trick on the page; he appears in the page's bedchamber disguised as a ghost and the page reacts by attacking him with a sword. When the page realises what has happened, and fearing that he may have killed the servant, he panics and runs away. He soon returns, vowing to reform and, for a while, succeeds, becoming 'more attentive than ever to reading and to principles, and [he] no longer gambled, and hardly ever mingled with gamblers or debauchees'.

After his old tutor leaves, his replacement is far less tolerant and the page falls into low spirits. His downfall comes when he is accidentally jostled by a royal bodyguard – they exchange words, draw swords and the bodyguard is seriously wounded. Panicking again, the page runs away for a second time, eventually making his way to England.

The character of the page, in these early chapters of the novel, is a clear forerunner of many later fictional schoolboys – an incorrigible troublemaker but with little if any malice. His rebelliousness is not against authority but rather born out of a sense of mischief and, while he is astute enough to recognise this as a fault in himself, he is powerless to do anything about it. Such characters abound in school fiction – loveable rogues who, despite their misdemeanours, retain the reader's sympathy. Similar characters also appeared in the novels of Henry Fielding and Tobias Smollett.

Jonathan Swift and *Gulliver's Travels*

In 1726 the English educational system was satirised by Jonathan Swift in *Gulliver's Travels*.[3] Swift (1667-1745) had a strongly conventional education, attending Kilkenny College from the age of six to fourteen. He then went on to study at Trinity College, Dublin, before becoming

---

3. Originally titled, *Travels into Several Remote Nations of the World, in Four Parts. By Lemuel Gulliver, First a Surgeon, and then a Captain of Several*

an essayist, poet and novelist. In 1713 he became Dean of St Patrick's Cathedral, Dublin.

Gulliver's Travels, a satire on human nature and a parody of the novel of exploration, features the adventures of Lemuel Gulliver, educated at Emmanuel College, Cambridge, who later becomes a surgeon. His main interest, however, is travel, and the novel portrays his voyages to and adventures in fantastical places such as Lilliput, Brobdingnag, Glubbdubdrib, Luggnagg and the country of the Houyhnhnms.

During his first voyage, Gulliver is shipwrecked and washed ashore on the island of Lilliput, inhabited by a race of tiny people less than six inches tall. Initially held prisoner, he gives assurances of good behaviour and becomes a respected visitor, allowed to roam at will, with much of the story consisting of his observations on Lilliputian society. In some respects, this is similar to Swift's own early eighteenth-century English society, although Swift is skilful at making it appear radically different. This is exemplified in his description of Lilliputian education, which is founded on the premise that 'parents are the last of all others to be trusted with the education of their own children'. Accordingly, at the age of 'twenty moons' (i.e. just under two years) all children, except those of 'cottagers and labourers', are sent to 'public nurseries', of which several kinds exist, 'suited to different qualities, and both sexes':

> The nurseries for males of noble or eminent birth, are provided with grave and learned professors, and their several deputies. The clothes and food of the children are plain and simple. They are bred up in the principles of honour, justice, courage, modesty, clemency, religion, and love of their country; they are always employed in some business, except in the times of eating and sleeping, which are very short, and two hours for diversions consisting of bodily exercises. They are dressed by men till four years of age, and then are obliged to dress themselves. ... They are never suffered to converse with servants, but go together in smaller or greater numbers to take their diversions, and always in the presence of a professor, or one of his deputies; whereby they avoid those early bad impressions of folly and vice, to which our children are subject. Their parents are suffered to see them only twice a year; the visit is to last but an hour; they are allowed to kiss

---

Ships, 2 vols (London: Benjamin Motte, 1726). The extracts here are taken from the 1826 edition published by Jones & Co.

the child at meeting and parting; but a professor, who always stands by on those occasions, will not suffer them to whisper, or use any fondling expressions, or bring any presents of toys, sweetmeats, and the like.[4]

Children of lesser rank are treated more or less the same until they reach the age of eleven, when they are apprenticed, or, if they are 'persons of quality', they remain at school for a further four years.

Girls are treated differently:

In the female nurseries, the young girls of quality are educated much like the males, only they are dressed by orderly servants of their own sex; but always in the presence of a professor or deputy, till they come to dress themselves, which is at five years old. ... [N]either did I perceive any difference in their education made by their difference of sex, only that the exercises of the females were not altogether so robust; and that some rules were given them relating to domestic life, and a smaller compass of learning was enjoined them: for their maxim is, that among peoples of quality, a wife should be always a reasonable and agreeable companion, because she cannot always be young. When the girls are twelve years old, which among them is the marriageable age, their parents or guardians take them home, with great expressions of gratitude to the professors, and seldom without tears of the young lady and her companions.[5]

Finally, children of the lowest rank are denied education: 'The cottagers and labourers keep their children at home, their business being only to till and cultivate the earth, and therefore their education is of little consequence to the public.'[6]

Therefore, in Lilliputian society, children of rank are brought up in a strictly regimented and institutionalised manner, with minimal parental contact. This, of course, echoed the English boarding school system at the time, although Swift is presents its virtues differently. Furthermore, Swift is satirising the educational philosophies of John

---

4. Defoe, *Gulliver's Travels* (London: Jones & Company, 1862), Volume 1, pp. 67–68.
5. Ibid., pp. 68–69.
6. Ibid., p. 70.

Locke as espoused in his treatise *Some Thoughts Concerning Education*, published some 33 years earlier.[7] While some of the Lilliputian methods echo those put forward by Locke – plain and simple clothing and food, and children being kept busy – others are a rejection, with the Lilliputian system depending on a harsh, institutionalised environment that forbids parental affection.

Henry Fielding

Henry Fielding (1707–54) was the older brother of Sarah Fielding, born in 1710, who went on to write *The Governess; or, Little Female Academy* (see chapter nine). He was educated at Eton between 1719 and 1724. Little is known of his time there, although it is known that he was an Oppidan, rather than a Colleger,[8] and that he felt he owed his literary style to the classics he studied there. After a period in the 1730s as a playwright and political writer, he turned to novel writing in 1741, with *Shamela*. He would write a further five novels before his death.

Joseph Andrews

Fielding's first major novel, *The History of the Adventures of Joseph Andrews and of His Friend, Mr Abraham Adams*, was published in two volumes by A. Millar in 1742. It centres on a young footman, Joseph Andrews, who is, purportedly, the brother of Pamela, the heroine of Samuel Richardson's novel of the same name, published in 1740. Sacked from his post because of his refusal to be seduced by his late employer's widow, Lady Booby, and her servant, Mrs Slipslop, he is cast out and alone in London. He decides to return to his home and seek out Fanny Goodwill, his childhood sweetheart, who is a maid at Lady Booby's country house. On his journey he meets up with Fanny and with Abraham Adams, a curate he has known since childhood and from whose lessons in morality he had drawn strength while resisting Lady Booby's amorous advances.

Most of the novel is taken up with the narrative of their journey and the events which happen when they arrive at Booby Hall. However, in chapter three of volume one we learn that Joseph was taught to read by

---

7. John Locke, *Some Thoughts Concerning Education* (London: A. & J. Churchill, 1693).
8. An Oppidan boarded in the town, and a Colleger boarded in the school itself.

and write by his father and, then, during his leisure hours, after being apprenticed to Sir Thomas Booby, he 'read the Bible, the Whole Duty of Man, and Thomas à Kempis'.

It is in volume two, chapter five that Fielding refers to his schooldays at Eton, in a conversation between Joseph and Parson Adams after they had spent the night at the house of a gentleman who had told them his life story. Adams, after concluding that the gentleman had had an unhappy childhood, declares:

> I have found it; I have discovered the cause of all the misfortunes which befel him: a public school, Joseph, was the cause of all the calamities which he afterwards suffered. Public schools are the nurseries of all vice and immorality. All the wicked fellows whom I remember at the university were bred at them. Ah, Lord! I can remember as well as if it was but yesterday, a knot of them; they called them King's scholars, I forget why – very wicked fellows![9]

This appears to be the first written criticism – or certainly the first fictionalised criticism – of Eton's Long Chamber, the notorious barn-like room, 172 feet long, 27 feet wide and 15 feet high, unheated until 1784, which was home to the 52 King's Scholars, or Collegers. It achieved notoriety as a place of anarchy, brutality and vice and, whilst its reputation was sealed in a variety of memoirs, especially in the nineteenth century, fictional portrayals were very thin on the ground.

Fielding, through Parson Adams, goes on to express other concerns about the effects of a public school education:

> Joseph, you may thank the Lord you were not bred at a public school; you would never have preserved your virtue as you have. The first care I always take is of a boy's morals; I had rather he should be a blockhead than an atheist or a presbyterian. What is all the learning in the world compared to his immortal soul? But the masters of great schools trouble themselves about no such thing. I have known a lad of eighteen at the university, who hath not been able to say his catechism; but for my own part, I always scourged a lad sooner for missing that than any other lesson. Believe me, child, all

---

9. *The History of the Adventures of Joseph Andrews and His Friend Mr Abraham Adams* (London: George Bell & Sons, 1889), p. 224.

that gentleman's misfortunes arose from his being educated at a public school.[10]

However, Joseph disagrees:

> you know my late master, Sir Thomas Booby, was bred at a public school, and he was the finest gentleman in all the neighbourhood. And I have often heard him say, if he had a hundred boys he would breed them all at the same place. It was his opinion, and I have often heard him deliver it, that a boy taken from a public school and carried into the world, will learn more in one year there than one of a private education will in five. He used to say the school itself initiated him a great way (I remember that was his very expression), for great schools are little societies, where a boy of any observation may see in epitome what he will afterwards find in the world at large.[11]

He goes on to argue that the discipline in public schools is more effective, only for Parson Adams to hit back: 'Discipline indeed! Because one man scourges twenty or thirty boys more in a morning than another, is he therefore a better disciplinarian?'

Fielding's arguments on public versus private schools are inconclusive, but an indication of his attitude to private schools is found in his second novel, *Jonathan Wild*.

Jonathan Wild

The History of the Life of the Late Mr Jonathan Wild, the Great was published as volume three of *Miscellanies* by A. Millar in 1743. The novel is a satirical exploration of the parallels between the political elite and the criminal underworld, with hints that the character of Jonathan Wild was a caricature of Sir Robert Walpole. Wild, was a real (and notorious) highwayman who had been executed at Tyburn in 1725, although most of the fictional Wild's adventures, or misadventures, were figments of Fielding's imagination.

For the first time in the English novel, a character's adult personality is shown as being forged by his experiences at school. In chapter three,

---

10. Ibid., pp. 224–225.
11. Ibid., pp. 225.

we learn that Wild, even as an infant, was cunning and devious, and could be bribed to do anything ('which made many say he was certainly born to be a great man'). The narrative goes on to reveal more of his cunning and artifice, this time at school:

> He was scarce settled at school before he gave marks of his lofty and aspiring temper. … If an orchard was to be robbed Wild was consulted, and, though he was himself seldom concerned in the execution of the design, yet was he always concerter of it, and treasurer of the booty, some little part of which he would now and then, with wonderful generosity, bestow on those who took it. He was generally very secret on these occasions; but if any offered to plunder of his own head, without acquainting master Wild, and making a deposit of the booty, he was sure to have an information against him lodged with the schoolmaster, and to be severely punished for his pains.[12]

Fielding then reveals Wild's schoolmaster as being complicit in his pupil's attitude towards learning:

> He discovered so little attention to school-learning that his master, who was a very wise and worthy man, soon gave over all care and trouble on that account, and, acquainting his parents that their son proceeded extremely well in his studies, he permitted his pupil to follow his own inclinations, perceiving they led him to nobler pursuits than the sciences, which are generally acknowledged to be a very unprofitable study, and indeed greatly to hinder the advancement of men in the world: but though master Wild was not esteemed the readiest at making his exercise, he was universally allowed to be the most dexterous at stealing it of all his schoolfellows, being never detected in such furtive compositions, nor indeed in any other exercitations of his great talents, which all inclined the same way, but once, when he had laid violent hands on a book called *Gradus ad Parnassum*, i.e. *A step towards Parnassus*, on which account his master, who was a man of most wonderful wit and sagacity, is said to have told

---

12. *The History of the Life of the Late Mr Jonathan Wild, the Great* (London: J.M. Dent & Co., 1893), pp. 9–10.

him he wished it might not prove in the event *Gradus ad Patibulum*, i.e. *A step towards the gallows.*[13]

Wild is removed from the school at the age of seventeen and taught by his father, who tried to 'inculcate principles of honour and gentility into his son'. It goes without saying that his father's efforts were, ultimately, in vain, and his schoolmaster's fear were realised.

Tom Jones

Fielding's most famous novel, *The History of Tom Jones, A Foundling*, was published by A. Millar in four volumes in 1749. A long and complex novel, it begins with the discovery of a baby in the bed of the wealthy Squire Allworthy, who takes it upon himself to raise the child in his household. Christened Tom Jones, the boy becomes a vigorous, kind-hearted youth although frequently in trouble. He makes an enemy of Blifil, the son of Allworthy's sister, who is a year younger and, outwardly, pious and dull but inwardly devious, discrediting Tom at every opportunity. Tom falls in love with Sophie Western, the daughter of a wealthy neighbour, but his love is thwarted by Allworthy's desire that she should marry Blifil. Tom is eventually expelled from Allworthy's house after he has an affair with a gamekeeper's daughter and much of the novel is taken up with his adventures on the road to London, which culminate in him being sentenced to hang. Ultimately, Blifil's duplicity is revealed (after Sophie has fled to London to escape her marriage to him) and the various threads, including the identity of Tom's mother, are brought together in a satisfyingly happy ending.

As a teenager, Tom also makes an enemy of Mr Thwackum, tutor to Tom and Blifil. Squire Allworthy appointed Thwackum because of his antipathy towards public schools, which he saw as places where boys were exposed to vice and too easily corrupted.

The foundation for much of what follows in the novel is an incident in which Tom is severely punished by Thwackum after he and a gamekeeper, known as Black George, shoot a partridge on neighbouring land. Tom, caught in possession of the dead bird, promises to protect the gamekeeper by insisting that he was solely responsible and, even while being whipped by Thwackum, refuses to deviate from his position: 'The consequence of this was, so severe a whipping, that it possibly fell

---

13. Ibid., p. 10.

little short of the torture with which confessions are in some countries extorted from criminals.'[14]

Allworthy, impressed with the way Tom took his punishment, believes him to be innocent, and apologises, presenting Tom with a horse by way of making amends. The tutor is unimpressed by Allworthy's leniency, telling him that 'to remit the punishment of such crimes was ... to encourage them'. The truth later emerges after Tom has given a Blifil a bloody nose following a petty argument, and Blifil tells the whole story to Thwackum. Tom begs forgiveness for the gamekeeper and his family and for himself from Allworthy, who, secretly admiring the boy's spirit, agrees to forgive Tom, but dismisses the gamekeeper, pointing out that he had unjustly suffered Tom to be severely beaten when he should have owned up. This only serves to raise Tom to the status of a hero:

> When this story became public ... Master Blifil was generally called a sneaking rascal, a poor-spirited wretch, with other epithets of the like kind; whilst Tom was honoured with the appellations of a brave lad, a jolly dog, and an honest fellow. Indeed, his behaviour to Black George much ingratiated him with all the servants; for though that fellow was before universally disliked, yet he was no sooner turned away than he was as universally pitied; and the friendship and gallantry of Tom Jones was celebrated by them all with the highest applause.[15]

The antipathy between Tom and his tutor gains momentum. Blifil is seen by the tutor as polite, pious and hard-working, whereas Tom is disrespectful and oblivious to Thwackum's 'precepts and example'.

After Tom has sold the horse that Squire Allworthy had given him, in order to provide for the gamekeeper, Allworthy: 'stood silent for some moments, and before he spoke the tears started from his eyes. He at length dismissed Tom with a gentle rebuke, advising him for the future to apply to him in cases of distress, rather than to use extraordinary means of relieving them himself.'

Squire Allworthy also begins to see through Thwackum, although he accepts that Thwackum's negative qualities are outweighed by more positive ones. Tom is then discovered to have sold a Bible, given to

---

14. *The History of Tom Jones, A Foundling* (London: J.M. Dent & Co,, 1893), p. 101.
15. Ibid., p. 112.

him by Squire Allworthy, to Blifil, again to raise money to give to the gamekeeper. Blifil sneakily, and deliberately, brings this to the attention of Mr Thwackum, who:

> resolved a crime of this kind, which he called sacrilege, should not go unpunished. He therefore proceeded immediately to castigation: and not contented with that he acquainted Mr Allworthy, at their next meeting, with this monstrous crime, as it appeared to him: inveighing against Tom in the most bitter terms, and likening him to the buyers and sellers who were driven out of the temple.[16]

Tom is eventually banished from the house after two romantic entanglements and more machinations by Blifil.

Although Tom is not educated at a public school, the themes in this part of the book are identical to some of those explored in later school fiction: a tyrannical master/tutor; schoolboy honour; unjust punishment, brought about by the duplicity of a third party; and the recognition of something good in a boy's character that is all too often hidden by misbehaviour or high spirits. Tom is undoubtedly a rascal and a troublemaker, but the reader's sympathy is always with him.

Sarah Fielding and *The Adventures of David Simple*

Sarah Fielding, born in 1710 and the sister of Henry Fielding, was educated at a private boarding school in Salisbury, and spent much of her life in London. She died in Bath in 1768.

Her first novel was a picaresque story, *The Adventures of David Simple*, published (as by 'A Lady') by A. Millar in 1744, which portrays the eponymous hero's lengthy search through London for friendship, and his eventual happiness in marriage and a rural life away from the corrupting influence of a big city.

The opening two chapters of the novel paint a somewhat idyllic picture of public school life and, in particular, a picture of brotherly affection. David Simple is the eldest son of Mr Daniel Simple, who keeps a mercer's shop in London. He has a younger brother, and:

> as soon as they were capable of learning were sent to a public school. ... The strict friendship they kept up was remarked by

---

16. Ibid., p. 126.

the whole school; whoever affronted the one, made an enemy of the other; and while there was any money in either of their pockets, the other was sure never to want it: the notion of whose property it was, being the last thing that ever entered into their heads. The eldest, who was of a sober prudent disposition, had always enough to supply his brother, who was much more profuse in his manner of spending. ... On the other hand, Daniel ... had more cunning, and consequently being more suspicious, would often keep his brother from being imposed on; who, as he was too young to have had much experience, never had any ill designs on others, never thought of them having any upon him. He paid a perfect deference to his brother's wisdom, from finding, that whenever he marked out a boy as one that would behave ill, it always proved so in the end. He was sometimes indeed quite amazed how Daniel came by so much knowledge; but then his great love and partiality to him easily made him impute it to his uncommon sagacity; and he often pleased himself with the thoughts of having such a brother. Thus these two brothers lived together at school in the most perfect unity and friendship, till the eldest was seventeen.[17]

At this point both boys are obliged to leave school after their father has become dangerously ill. Daniel is then revealed as being two-faced and duplicitous; he had taken advantage of his brother's generosity at school and, after their father's death, he forges a new will in which he is the principal beneficiary. When David discovers this, he sets out on his journey to see whether he can find a true and honest friend.

In *David Simple*, Fielding launches a theme that was to appear in many later school stories – that of two brothers at the same school, who are either the closest of friends, sworn enemies, or who simply ignore each other. Even in cases where brothers are friends, there are often tensions bubbling underneath: the respective roles of brothers at the same school were never easy to reconcile, the older generally being somewhat aloof and overt signs of familial friendship being beneath his dignity, and the younger brother either in awe of his sibling or contemptuous of him.

---

17. *The Adventures of David Simple Containing an Account of His Travels Through the Cities of London and Westminster in the Searcg of a Real Froend* (London: George Routledge & Sons Ltd., 1904), pp. 1–2.

Tobias Smollett

Tobias Smollett, born in Scotland in 1721, was educated at Dumbarton Grammar School (where he boarded in lodgings in the town) under John Love, a noted schoolmaster and educationalist, who helped to instil in Smollett a love of Latin and classical literature. Smollett's earliest writings stemmed from this period, in particular, satirical verses about his fellow pupils and more serious verses centring on Scottish history. After studying at Glasgow University, he became a surgeon, before becoming a full-time writer in the mid-1750s. He died in Tuscany in 1771, the year of publication of his last, and what is often considered to be his best, novel, *The Expedition of Humphrey Clinker.*

The Adventures of Roderick Random

Smollett's first novel, *The Adventures of Roderick Random*, was first published, anonymously, by J. Osborn in two volumes in 1748. Like many first novels, it has elements of autobiography, in its early chapters at least.

The story is narrated in the first person and begins with Roderick Random's birth in Scotland, and the subsequent death of his mother (his grandfather's housekeeper) and the disappearance of his father. Roderick therefore grows up in his grandfather's house alongside several cousins, all of whom have an implacable hatred towards him. Roderick is sent to school in a nearby village, although his grandfather refuses to pay for his board, or supply him with books and clothes, and consequently:

> my condition was very ragged and contemptible, and the schoolmaster, who, through fear of my grandfather, taught me *gratis*, gave himself no concern about the progress I made under his instruction. In spite of all these difficulties and disgraces, I became a good proficient in the Latin tongue; and, as soon as I could write tolerably, pestered my grandfather with letters to such a degree that he sent for my master, and chid him severely for bestowing such pains on my education, telling him that, if ever I should be brought to the gallows for forgery, which he had taught me to commit, my blood would lie on his head.[18]

---

18. *The Adventures of Roderick Random* (London: George Routledge & Sons, 1895), p. 22.

The schoolmaster therefore agrees to try to prevent any further improvement in Roderick's learning and goes so far as to stop him writing:

> on pretence that I had written impertinent letters to my grandfather, he caused a board to be made with five holes in it, through which he thrust the fingers and thumb of my right hand, and fastened it by whipcord to my wrist, in such a manner as effectually debarred me the use of my pen.[19]

When Roderick hits a boy who has insulted him, the wooden board causes serious injury, and he is consequently severely punished. In what, in school fiction, was to become a familiar complaint, Roderick goes on to reveal:

> I was often inhumanly scourged for crimes I did not commit, because, having the character of a vagabond in the village, every piece of mischief, whose author lay unknown, was charged upon me. I have been found guilty of robbing orchards I never entered, of killing cats I never hunted, of stealing gingerbread I never touched, and of abusing old women I never saw. Nay, a stammering carpenter had eloquence enough to persuade my master that I fired a pistol loaded with small shot into his window; though my landlady and the whole family bore witness that I was abed fast asleep at the time when this outrage was committed. I was once flogged for having narrowly escaped drowning, by the sinking of a ferry boat in which I was passenger. ... In short, whether I was guilty or unfortunate, the correction and sympathy of this arbitrary pedagogue were the same.[20]

However, Roderick has a friend in the usher, who had known his father, and, as a result of his encouragement, he becomes, by the age of twelve, the best scholar in the school. By this time, he has also gathered together a cabal of thirty boys with a view to defying the headmaster, although they spend most of their time in combat with boys from the village.

---

19. Ibid., p. 23.
20. Ibid., p. 23.

Roderick's uncle, Tom Bowling, then returns from overseas (he is a lieutenant of a man-o'-war) and, on visiting Roderick and seeing his pitiful condition, buys him clothes and other necessities of school life, despite his own slender resources, and promises not to leave the country again until he has persuaded Roderick's grandfather to make future provision for him. When Roderick's grandfather dies, leaving him nothing in his will, Bowling suggests he take Roderick to sea with him, but this is not at all to Roderick's fancy and, fortunately for him, not to his usher's fancy either – he thinks Roderick has the potential to make his fortune on land. Bowling therefore agrees to send Roderick to university. Before he leaves, Roderick has one last brush with authority, when the master accused him of being 'a wicked, profligate, dull, beggarly miscreant'.

Roderick has no difficulty in persuading some of his schoolfellows to join him in a plot to turn the tables on the master on the afternoon of his departure, by flogging him with his own birch while the usher is out of the room. When Bowling is appraised of this, he fully endorses the idea and offers to help, both in thrashing the master (with a home-made cat-o'-nine-tails) and in helping Roderick and his colleagues, two of whom are leaving the school on the same day, to escape.

At the appointed time, when the usher has left the room, the master is seized. His shouts, and those of the boys, send the usher rushing back, only to find himself locked out of the schoolroom:

> My uncle bade him have a little patience, and he would let him in presently. ... By this time we had dragged the criminal to a post, to which Bowling tied him with a rope he had provided on purpose; after having secured his hands and stripped his back. In this ludicrous posture he stood (to the no small entertainment of the boys, who crowded about him, and shouted with great exultation at the novelty of the sight), venting bitter imprecations against the lieutenant, and reproaching his scholars with treachery and rebellion; when the usher was admitted ... he allowed himself to be bound to his own desk, where he sat a spectator of the punishment inflicted on his principal. My uncle, having upbraided this arbitrary wretch with his inhumanity to me, told him, that he proposed to give him a little discipline for the good of his soul, which he immediately put in practice, with great vigour and dexterity. This smart application to the pedant's withered posteriors gave him such exquisite pain that he roared like

a mad bull, danced, cursed, and blasphemed, like a frantic bedlamite.[21]

Bowling tells the master that he hopes the flogging he has just received will teach him to have more sympathy in the future, and then invites all the boys to accompany him to a nearby inn, where he will treat them all.

Roderick therefore leaves school with a feeling of triumph, having fully avenged the barbarous treatment he received from his schoolmaster and having led his schoolfellows in their joint rebellion. While later school fiction featured the occasional rebellion, it was not until the penny dreadful school story of the mid to late nineteenth century that schoolmasters were treated with such disrespect and brutality.[22] There had been nothing like this in earlier fiction or drama – even though it must have been a common dream amongst generations of schoolboys. Roderick's actions were wish fulfilment writ large, although, given the way the school story was to develop – along moral and didactic lines initially – it was a theme that more or less vanished, at least for a hundred years, as quickly as it had appeared.

The Adventures of Peregrine Pickle

A similar, dark and dramatic picture of school life is painted in Smollett's second novel, *The Adventures of Peregrine Pickle*, first published (privately) in four volumes in 1751. Like his earlier novel, this is a picaresque tale, this time narrated in the third person, and again involves its hero in a number of comic and dramatic adventures. Again, the hero's character is forged by his early years and his experiences at school – in this instance two village schools, a private boarding school and, finally, Winchester.

Peregrine has effectively been disowned by his mother shortly after his birth and, as a very young child, finds an ally in his uncle, Commodore

---

21. Ibid., pp. 32–33.
22. A tutor does suffer a similar fate in the first part of Henry Brooke's *The Fool of Quality*, published in 1766 (see next chapter), although the most famous acts of insubordination appear in Charles Dickens's *The Life and Adventures of Nicholas Nickleby* (1839), when Nickleby, an assistant master, thrashes Wackford Squeers, the tyrannical headmaster of Dotheboys Hall, after he has taken his brutality on a pupil too far, and when the boys later revolt on learning that Squeers is to be transported, and attack his wife and children.

Hawser Trunnion, despite Peregrine's propensity for playing practical jokes on him. At the age of four, Peregrine is sent to a local day school under a schoolmistress who, despite his misbehaviour, is reluctant to punish him for fear of upsetting his mother. However, Mrs Pickle is not impressed with this indulgence and sends Peregrine to another school under a master who is a keen advocate of corporal punishment. Peregrine is regularly flogged twice a day, which has the effect of making him obstinate and resentful, and 'hardened and confirmed in his vicious inclinations'.

At the age of six, Peregrine is sent to a boarding school, whose reputation is due entirely to the efforts of the usher rather than the headmaster:

> the assistant was actually a man of learning, probity, and good sense; and though obliged by the scandalous administration of fortune to act in the character of an inferior teacher, had, by his sole capacity and application, brought the school to that degree of reputation, which it never could have obtained from the talents of its superior. He had established an economy, which, though regular, was not at all severe, by enacting a body of laws suited to the age and comprehension of every individual; and each transgressor was fairly tried by his peers, and punished according to the verdict of the jury. No boy was scourged for want of apprehension, but a spirit of emulation was raised by well-timed praise and artful comparison, and maintained by a distribution of small prizes, which were adjudged to those who signalized themselves either by their industry, sobriety, or genius.[23]

(This hints at the method of control and discipline – by a transgressor's peers – adopted 21 years later in Richard Johnson's *Juvenile Trials for Robbing Orchards, Telling Fibs and Other High Misdemeanours* [see chapter nine].)

The usher, Jennings, having studied Peregrine for a brief while, decides that the best way to change his behaviour is to ignore him, which has the effect of spurring Peregrine into applying himself to his work:

> he exerted himself with surprising alacrity, by which he soon acquitted himself of the imputation of dullness, and obtained

---

23. *The Adventures of Peregrine Oickle* (London: George Routledge & Sons, 1857), p. 45.

> sundry honorary silver pennies, as acknowledgments of his application; his school-fellows now solicited his friendship as eagerly as they had avoided it before; and in less than a twelvemonth after his arrival, this supposed dunce was remarkable for the brightness of his parts; having in that short period learnt to read English perfectly well, made great progress in writing, enabled himself to speak the French language without hesitation, and acquired some knowledge in the rudiments of the Latin tongue. The usher did not fail to transmit an account of his proficiency to the commodore, who received it with transport, and forthwith communicated the happy tidings to the parents.[24]

However, having achieved academic success, Peregrine decides to exercise physical as well as intellectual power, gradually subduing the rest of the school by the use of his fists, although he remained good-natured and was liked by many of the boys.

The reader then learns something of the history of the school, which is owned by a Mr Keypstick,

> an old illiterate German quack, who had formerly practised corn-cutting among the quality, and sold cosmetic washes to the ladies, together with teeth-powders, hair-dyeing liquors, prolific elixirs, and tinctures to sweeten the breath. These nostrums, recommended by the art of cringing, in which he was consummate, ingratiated him so much with people of fashion, that he was enabled to set up school with five-and-twenty boys of the best families, whom he boarded on his own terms and undertook to instruct in the French and Latin languages, so as to qualify them for the colleges of Westminster and Eton. While this plan was in its infancy, he was so fortunate as to meet with Jennings, who, for the paltry consideration of thirty pounds a year, which his necessities compelled him to accept, took the whole trouble of educating the children upon himself.[25]

Keypstick becomes the target of satire and jokes from Peregrine and his schoolfellows, and suspects that these are being encouraged

---

24. Ibid., p. 46.
25. Ibid., p. 47.

by Jennings. This leads to Jennings' resignation, as a consequence of which the school descends into anarchy, with parents withdrawing their children and Peregrine successfully begging his uncle to allow him to leave.

Peregrine is later despatched to Winchester, with Tom Pipes, Commodore Trunnion's retainer, as his footman, and under the care of a governor, Mr Jacob Jolter. This does not, however, mark any turning point in Peregrine's behaviour and within a year, having defied 'the laws and regulations of the place', he has become the leader of a large group of his contemporaries. When Jolter is asked by the headmaster to curb Peregrine's high spirits, he tries to instil in him a love of mathematics but, while Peregrine initially approaches this new branch of learning with enthusiasm, he soon tires of it and returns to his old ways:

> His behaviour was now no other than a series of license and effrontery; prank succeeded prank, and outrage followed outrage with surprising velocity. Complaints were every day preferred against him; in vain were admonitions bestowed by the governor in private, and menaces discharged by the masters in public; he disregarded the first, despised the latter, divested himself of all manner of restraint, and proceeded in his career to such a pitch of audacity, that a consultation was held upon the subject, in which it was determined that this untoward spirit should be humbled by a severe and ignominious flogging for the very next offence he should commit.[26]

In the meantime, Pipes has become the life and soul of the school:

> He mingled in all their parties, and superintended the diversions, deciding between boy and boy, as if he acted by commission under the great seal. He regulated their motions by his whistle, instructed the young boys in the games of hustle-cap, leap-frog, and chuck-farthing; imparted to those of a more advanced age the sciences of cribbage and all-fours, together with the method of storming the castle, acting the comedy of Prince Arthur, and other pantomimes, as they

---

26. Ibid., p. 65.

commonly exhibited at sea; and instructed the seniors, who were distinguished by the appellation of bloods, in cudgel-playing, dancing the St. Giles's hornpipe, drinking flip, and smoking tobacco.[27]

Peregrine, now aged fourteen, and Pipes are then involved in a dispute with a gardener, which culminates in a bloody fight and the death of the gardener's dog. As the ringleader, Peregrine is sentenced to be thrashed before the whole school, a punishment which takes place after his schoolfellows, who had vowed to stand by him and either have the beating rescinded or share in it with him, are cowed into submission by the master.

As a result of this, Peregrine abandons his friends and falls in with a group of older boys, who introduce him to more adult society which includes girls, who are attracted to him by virtue of his engaging personality, self-assurance, generosity, sense of humour and learning. One such girl is Emilia Gauntlet, with whom Peregrine is so enamoured that he absents himself from school to be with her. Their relationship ends after a series of events concerning a poem Peregrine has written, which, thanks to Pipes' misguided actions, is replaced by a verbose and flowery effusion written by the parish clerk. This is so unintelligible that Emilia, on reading and rereading it, assumes that Peregrine has either taken leave of his senses or is ridiculing his passion for her. Emilia refuses to reply to the letter; and Peregrine, initially hurt by her rejection of him, eventually recovers his equanimity, and acts as if Emilia's disdain for him was neither here nor there.

In the meantime, Trunnion has decided, with the agreement of Peregrine's father, to withdraw the boy from Winchester and place him at Oxford, which he does before Peregrine can get into any more trouble, with his school or with members of the opposite sex. After taking his degree, he travels to Paris, where he lives a life of debauchery and criminality, which is replicated on his subsequent return to England, swindling money from wealthy people and posing as a doctor. In turn, he is swindled out of all his money and ends up in the Fllet Debtors' Prison. His story ends when he unexpectedly inherits £80,000 from his father, and he is able to repay his debts and marry.

---

27. Ibid., p. 65. This appears to be the first use of the word 'bloods' to describe certain senior boys at a public school.

Robert Paltock and *The Life and Adventures of Peter Wilkins*

At least Peregrine did not, as a schoolboy, get a girl pregnant, unlike the eponymous hero of Robert Paltock's *The Life and Adventures of Peter Wilkins*, published by J. Robinson and R. Dodsley in 1751.[28]

Paltock (1697–1767) was born in Westminster, but little is known of his life other than that he was an attorney practising in London. He owes his fame to his one novel, which has sometimes been referred to as the first-ever science fiction story. Initially, a straightforward adventure story, which owed something to Daniel Defoe's *Robinson Crusoe* (1719), it develops a life of its own when the hero discovers a race of people who can fly, and whom he tries to transform into a progressive, Europeanised society. As such, the novel is an investigation into the processes and consequences of colonisation.

The early chapters of the novel are not of any relevance to the main plot, and serve only to introduce the hero and establish his reason for leaving England in search of adventure.

Peter Wilkins was born in Cornwall in 1685, shortly after his father's death. Kept at home by his mother, he is befriended by a 'country gentleman' (who also has designs on his mother), who, when Peter is sixteen, arranges for him to go to 'an Academy, kept by a very worthy and judicious gentleman, about thirty or more miles from us, in Somersetshire'.

On his departure he is given a large sum of money, which helps to establish him in his new environment, although this was scant consolation for his ignorance, which left him learning elementary Latin grammar whilst his fellow pupils were reading classic texts. After three months or so, Peter is still making little progress in his education. A maid, Patty, coming across him in a melancholy state in his room, suggests that he must be in love, as he looks so sad. He explains the real reason for his unhappiness:

> I fairly opened my heart to her; and for fear my master should know it, gave her half a crown to be silent. This last engagement fixed her my devotee, and from that time, we had frequent conferences, in confidence together; till at length, inclination,

---

28. An abridged edition was published by Joseph Thomas in 1839 for a juvenile market – the publisher stated: 'In the present edition care has been taken to expunge such incidents, only, as are unsuited to the perusal of children, for whom alone the book was not originally written.'

framed by opportunity, produced that date of a world of concern to me; for, about six months after my arrival at the Academy, instead of proving my parts by my scholarship, I had proved my manhood, by being the destined father of an infant, which my female correspondent then assured me would soon be my own.[29]

Peter is initially nonplussed by this news, but is eventually stirred into action when Patty points out that, as a mere servant, she has no money with which to prepare for the birth of her child. Peter, whose own money has long run out, writes to his mother, but receives short shrift in a reply which also reveals that his mother has a new husband. Patty's answer to this is to suggest marriage, which Peter consents to, and Patty leaves her post to live with an aunt while Peter stays on at the school. By now aged nineteen, Peter has vastly improved in academic terms, thanks in no small part to his affair with Patty, and the fact that she was someone he could talk to openly and honestly, and thus he becomes a favourite of the master, a result of his willingness to do extra work.

Peter eventually discovers that his mother has died and that his father's estate has now passed to his stepfather, who offers to pay for Peter's education for a further year. The master offers to take Peter on as an usher, but Peter has no desires in that direction, and, despite his master's efforts to persuade him to stay, Peter walks out of the school (and on Patty, who had had one child by Peter and was expecting a second) early one morning, determined to leave England at the earliest opportunity. The story subsequently develops into the realms of science fiction. Peter goes to sea, is captured by a French privateer and is sold into slavery, but manages to escape and spends several months alone on a small island (hence the novel's frequent comparison to *Robinson Crusoe*). He is then sucked into a subterranean cave and falls in with a group of people who can fly. He eventually returns to England, yearning for Patty, only to die on his arrival in Plymouth.

Oliver Goldsmith

Oliver Goldsmith (1728–74) was born in Ireland to English parents. After a near-fatal attack of smallpox he went to a series of schools, at the first two of which he was bullied and mistreated because of his

---

29. *The Life and Adventures of Peter Wilkins* (London: Reeves & Turner), pp. 16–17.

smallpox scars and other physical deformities. He found a much more amenable environment at his third school. He went on to spend two years at Trinity College, Dublin, and then briefly studied medicine at Edinbugh University. He moved to London in 1756, where he had two brief spells as a schoolmaster, before eventually making his reputation as a writer. He became particularly associated with John Newbery, a noted publisher of books for children, for whom he wrote several books including, it is often alleged, *The History of Little Goody Two-Shoes* (see chapter nine).

His first teaching role was at Thornhill Grammar School in Yorkshire, which was not, from Goldsmith's point of view, a success. In his essay, 'On Education', first published in 1749, he painted a rather sardonic picture of a schoolmaster:

> [The usher] is the laughingstock of the school. Every trick is played upon him; the oddity of his manner, his dress, or his language, is a fund of eternal ridicule; the master himself now and then cannot avoid joining in the laugh; and the poor wretch, eternally resenting this ill-usage, lives in a state of war with all the family. ... He is obliged, perhaps, to sleep in the same bed with the French teacher, who disturbs him for an hour every night in papering and filleting his hair, and stinks worse than a carrion with his rancid pomatums, when he lays his head beside him on the bolster.[30]

He returned to this view of schoolmasters in his novel, *The Vicar of Wakefield*. In the meantime, he had a rather more enjoyable time in his second teaching role, as a temporary headmaster of a Presbyterian boys' school in Peckham, then part of Surrey. The headmaster, a dissenting minister by the name of Dr Milner, had fallen ill and Goldsmith was encouraged to step into his shoes by Milner's son, who had known Goldsmith during their time at Edinburgh. According to his biographer, Washington Irving, he

> acquitted himself to the satisfaction of Dr Milner. He was a favourite, too, with the scholars, from his easy, indulgent good-nature; he mingled in their sports; spent his money in treating them to schoolboy dainties, told them froll stories,

---

30. From 'On Education', *The Bee*, 10 November 1749. Reproduced in Washington Irving, *Oliver Goldsmith: A Biography* (London: John Murray, 1849), p. 80.

and played on the flute for their entertainment. His familiarity was sometimes carried too far; he indulged in boyish pranks and practical jokes, and drew upon himself retorts in kind.[31]

The Vicar of Wakefield was first published in 1766 by Francis Newbery (nephew of John Newbery) in London (and by at least two publishers in Ireland in the same year). In general, it is simply a comical account of eighteenth-century country life, although its second half develops into something of a melodrama, and it can also be seen as a gentle satire on sentimentalism. Its place here is merited only by a short passage, in which George Primrose, the son of the vicar of the book's title, is quizzed by a Mr Arnold, with whom he is staying, as to his suitability for the role of a schoolmaster:

> My first scheme, you know, Sir, was to be usher at an academy, and I asked his advice on the affair. Our cousin received the proposal with a true Sardonic grin. Aye, cried he, this is indeed a very pretty career, that has been chalked out for you. I have been an usher at a boarding school myself; and may I die by an anodyne necklace, but I had rather be an under turnkey in Newgate. I was up early and late: I was brow-beat by the master, hated for my ugly face by the mistress, worried by the boys within, and never permitted to stir out to meet civility abroad. But are you sure you are fit for a school? Let me examine you a little. Have you been bred apprentice to the business? No. Then you won't do for a school. Can you dress the boys hair? No. Then you won't do for a school. Have you had the small-pox? No. Then you won't do for a school. Can you lie three in a bed? No. Then you will never do for a school. Have you got a good stomach? Yes. Then you will by no means do for a school. No, Sir, if you are for a genteel easy profession, bind yourself seven years as an apprentice to turn a cutler's wheel; but avoid a school by any means.[32]

* * *

Most of these early fictional snapshots of school life have one thing in common – a characteristic also shared by most of the dramas which

---

31. Washington Irving, *The Life of Oliver Goldsmith* (New York, NY: Harper & Brothers, 1840), p. 57.
32. *The Vicar of Wakefield* (London: George Routledge & Sons, 1886), pp. 169–170.

preceded them: the image they present is a negative one. In *Joseph Andrews*, Henry Fielding has one of his characters condemning public schools, describing them as 'the nurseries of all vice and immorality', drawing particular attention to the King's Scholars at Eton. Whilst Fielding had been an Oppidan, the activities and reputation of this small group of Eton boys must have been well-known to him and also, presumably, sufficiently well-known beyond Eton for any further explanation to be considered unnecessary.

The objections of Parson Adams to public schools is based largely, it seems, on their size, and the inability of the authorities to supervise and control the boys, which leads to moral depravity – hence his preference for smaller private schools, 'where boys may be kept in innocence and ignorance'. In fairness, Fielding has Joseph Andrews defending the public schools, having him point out that such establishments were the world in miniature and, as such, an ideal preparation for adulthood. Fielding's Jonathan Wild, at a private school, is allowed to go his own way by the master, who has his own slightly cynical view of education. A similar dichotomy was apparent in late eighteenth- and early nineteenth-century school stories, with some authors comparing private schools unfavourably with public schools, and other authors doing the opposite.

Similarly, there are vivid portrayals of excessive discipline and the brutality of schoolmasters, a theme which echoes that of the plays written and performed in the sixteenth and seventeenth centuries. This is exemplified in Smollett's *Roderick Random*, with Roderick's complaint that he was often beaten for crimes he had not committed, and for which he exacts sweet revenge on the day he leaves the school. Again, Peregrine, in *Peregrine Pickle*, is frequently beaten by his village schoolmaster and is subject to a public flogging whilst at Winchester; and Fielding's Tom Jones is frequently, and unjustly, beaten by his tutor.

Overall, however, the most notable feature of these depictions of mid eighteenth-century school life is that the role of schools as places of education is secondary to that of being places for high jinks, misbehaviour and, on one occasion, rebellion. Of course, this fits in with the nature of the stories, for the most part narratives of adventure and misadventure, and boys who behaved demurely at school, obeyed all the rules and worked hard, would not have embarked on such adventurous and, at times, dissolute adulthoods.

Secondary to this depiction of horseplay and rule-breaking is the appearance of characters, in particular, Jonathan Wild and Peregrine Pickle, who were later to become familiar in the school story – best-known as 'bloods', boys who were ringleaders and looked up to because of their disdain for authority and school rules. They were clear forerunners of penny dreadful schoolboys' heroes such as Jack Harkaway, Ned Nimble and Tom Wildrake.

Having said that, there are some positive aspects to these early fictional school episodes, most notably, the portraits of sympathetic masters, who saw their role as educators rather than disciplinarians and who tried to understand the boys in their care. This is especially the case with the usher in Roderick Random's school, the usher, Jennings, in Peregrine Pickle's private school and the master who takes in Peter Wilkins and who comes to treat his pupil as a friend.

The principal novels highlighted in this chapter spanned a period of just under ten years – from 1742 to 1751. However, their role in the development of the school story as a distinct literary genre should not be underestimated – to some extent, they followed a tradition of portraying schools and schoolmasters in a generally negative light that went back to the mid-1500s, but they also paved the way for longer, and more considered, stories about school life and education.

* * *

Footnote: Yorkshire Schools before Charles Dickens

In his 1839 novel, *The Life and Adventures of Nicholas Nickleby*, Charles Dickens was strongly critical of boarding schools, in which children were mistreated, poorly fed and clothed, and often left for years without ever going home. Such schools, many of which were in Yorkshire, formed the basis for Dickens' fictional Dotheboys Hall, run by the tyrannical Wackford Squeers, and such was the impact of the novel it is claimed, erroneously, that many of the Yorkshire schools were forced to close.[33] Such schools had existed for at least a hundred years before Dickens launched his attack, and were familiar enough to merit the occasional brief reference in late eighteenth-century fiction and drama.

In Samuel Foote's play, *The Lyar: A Comedy in Three Acts* (first performed in 1762 and first published in 1764), one of the characters reveals that he 'had sustained the dignity of sub-preceptor to one of those

---

33. See Robert J. Kirkpatrick, *Charles Dickens, Nicholas Nickleby and the Yorkshire Schools: Fact v Fiction*, (Snaisgill: Mosaic (Teesdale) Ltd, 2017).

cheap rural academies with which our county of York is so plentifully stocked'.[34]

In Charles Jenner's 1770 novel, *The Placid Man, or Memoirs of Sir Charles Beville*, one of the characters:

> was accordingly sent to a school ... the master of which took a journey on foot, or in the waggon, to London, every Whitsuntide-hollidays, on purpose to advertise, that 'At Stonelands, in Yorkshire, youth are boarded, educated and cloathed, at twelve pounds a year, by Zachary Birch, and proper assistants (his wife and a parish apprentice). N.B. Mr Birch is in town, and will take the care of any young gentlemen down;' by which means, he sometimes contrived to get his own passage gratis. To this gentleman's care I was committed, and underwent the usual discipline of the school, namely, cold, hunger, and beating, where I learned too, in the most complete manner, one science more than my father bargained for, which was patience; for what I know, of more use to me than any other thing that I learned there.[35]
> [Parentheses Jenner's.]

A similar picture was painted in the anonymous author's *The History of the Curate of Craman*, published in 1777.[36] The hero is sent to a school run by a Mr John Conjugate at *B–es* in Yorkshire (i.e. Bowes, the centre of the Dotheboys Hall controversy and where several schools were established):

> With what frugality we lived passes all credulity. ... Our dinner consisted of a very coarse hard pudding, made chiefly of rye, peas, and broken pieces of bread, which was succeeded

---

34. *Samuel Foote*, The Lyar: A Comedy in Three Acts (Dublin: G. Faulkner, 1764), p. 8.
35. *The Placid Man, or Memoirs of Sir Charles Beville* (London, J. Wilkie, 1770), pp. 44–45. The practice of a Yorkshire schoolmaster staying in London during holiday periods in order to recruit new pupils and then to take them with him to his school existed for several decades, with London newspapers carrying similar advertisements up until the 1840s. It is, of course, vividly illustrated in *Nicholas Nickleby*.
36. *The History of the Curate of Craman: Taken from Real Life, in Two Volumes. By an Unbeneficed Clergyman of the Church of England* (London: J. Johnson & F. Blyth, 1777).

by nearly half a pound of mutton that had died a natural death, or was in danger of dying of some disease. ... We were sent to a common at a considerable distance, to fetch bundles of furze for the use of the house. ... My department generally was, with another boy, to milk two cows, clean the vessels of the dairy, and conduct the cows from and to the field.[37]

It was also apparent that the practice of schools taking in boarders for indefinite periods, with no holidays (adverts for such schools declared 'No Vacations') was common, as shown in Vicesimus Knox's 1788 book of essays, *Winter Evenings*:[38]

> She declared in all companies that she thought it the first of a mother's duties to take care that her children were well-educated. She therefore sent them outside passengers by the stage coach to an academy in Yorkshire, where she stipulated that they should not come home in the holidays, and indeed not till her husband arrived from abroad.[39]

Whether or not Charles Dickens was aware of these brief references to Yorkshire boarding schools when he came to write *Nicholas Nickleby* is not known, but it suggests that the reputation of such schools had been established some 70 years previously.

---

37. Quoted in *Notes and Queries* (London), Eleventh Series, Volume VIII, 5 July 1913, p. 4.
38. Vicesimus Knox, *Winter Evenings: or, Lucubrations on Life and Letters, in Three Volumes* (London: Charles Dilly, 1788).
39. Ibid., p. 247.

8

Education outside School: *Émile, The Fool of Quality* and *Sandford and Merton*

Private tutors had a particularly important role in the eighteenth century. Evidence suggests that, in this period, over a quarter of university entrants were taught at home or prepared by private tutors, rather than having attended school.[1] The proportion of children educated at home in this way would actually have been much higher – many would not have gone on to university, especially those who were expected to work in their family business, to inherit large estates or to go into the army, and girls were not to be admitted into universities until 1868.

However, private tutors were not always seen in a positive light, as shown in Henry Fielding's *Tom Jones*. A rather different tutor was portrayed in Francis Coventry's groundbreaking novel, *The History of Pompey the Little; or, The Life and Adventures of a Lap-Dog*, published by M. Cooper and George Faulkner of Dublin in 1751. This was a satirical novel, targetting contemporary notable people and events, and being told from the point of view of a Bolognese, a small breed of toy dog. In chapter nine of the book, the dog has been acquired by a rich family who had moved out of London to the country. The father suffers from gout, the mother from consumption, and their four children (three girls and a boy) are 'ricketty, scrophulous, sallow in their Complexions,

---

1. Nicholas Hans, *New Trends in Education in the Eighteenth Century* (London: Routledge & Kegan Paul, 1951), p. 23. (Hans' study looked at the educational careers of 3,500 men taken from the *Dictionary of National Biography*.)

and distorted in their Limbs'. They are also 'proud, selfish, obstinate and cross-humoured'. Instead of being sent to school, 'where they would have been whipt out of many of their Ill-tempers, and perhaps by Conversation with other Children, might have learnt a more open generous Disposition', they are being taught at home. The boy, described as his mother's darling, is 'put into the care of a domestic Tutor, partly because [the mother] could not endure to have him at a Distance from her sight, and partly because she had heard it was genteel to educate young Gentlemen at home'.

The author's description of the tutor is devastating. Described as 'impertinent and a Coxcomb', he had left university and adopted a new persona:

> He soon grew to despise the Books he had read at the University, and affected a Taste for polite Literature – that is, for no Literature at all; by which he endeared himself so much to the Family he lived in, by reading Plays to them, bringing home Stories from the Coffee-house, and other Arts, that they gave him the Character of the *entertainingest, most facetious, best-humoured Creature that ever came into a House*. As his Temper led him by any means to flatter his Benefactors, he never failed to cry up the Parts and Genius of his Pupil as a Miracle of Nature; which the fond Mother, understanding nothing of the Matter, very easily believed.[2]

The tutor is far more interested in gaining the approval of the boys' parents than he is of actually educating the child. Unlike some tutors, however, he is full of flattery rather than violence, the end result presumably being a deeply obnoxious and self-centred adult.

Later in the novel, the dog is acquired by a student at Cambridge, who had:

> received the first part of his education at *Westminster* school, where he had acquired what is usually called, *a very pretty knowledge of the town*; that is to say, he had been introduced, at the age of thirteen, into the most noted bagnios [i.e. brothels], was acquainted with the most celebrated women of pleasure, and could drink his two bottles of claret in an evening, without being greatly disordered in his understanding. At the age of

---

2. *The History of Pompey the Little* (1751) pp. 80–81.

seventeen, it was judged proper for him, merely out of fashion, and to be like other young gentlemen of his acquaintance, to take lodgings at a university; whither he went with a hearty contempt of the place, and a determined resolution never to receive any profit from it.[3]

This was the first appearance of Westminster School in English fiction, although it was not, it must be said, a very flattering image of the school.

Two eighteenth century novels which had a particular focus on the role of private tutors were Henry Brooke's *The Fool of Quality* and Thomas Day's *The History of Sandford and Merton*. These were richly-detailed portrayals of the education of boys outside school, and they were both heavily influenced by the philosophy of Jean-Jacques Rousseau, who had earlier espoused his ideals in his novel *Émile*.

Jean-Jacques Rousseau and *Émile*

Émile, ou de l'éducation was first published in France in 1762 and translated into English (by William Kenrick) the same year.[4] Rousseau (1712–78) was born in Geneva, although he is far better known as a 'French' educationalist and philosopher. He first moved to France in 1732, establishing himself as a music teacher, moving to Lyon in 1740 to serve as a private tutor, and then to Paris in 1742, where he again worked as a music teacher (and began a relationship with a chambermaid at the hotel where he was living and with whom he subsequently had five children, all of whom were sent to a foundling hospital shortly after they were born). (He later claimed that this was because he could not afford to bring them up properly, that he thought they would get a better upbringing in an institution and that he wanted them to avoid the deviousness of Parisian high society. He also said that he regretted his actions.) Despite his failure raise his own children, he became famous when his treatise on education, *Émile*, was published. It was initially condemned by the French government, and banned in parts of France, for its attack on religion and Rousseau was obliged to return to Switzerland. However, *Émile* and some of his other works (including *Du contrat social* – translated as *The Social Contract*, with its famous opening line, 'Man is born free and everywhere he is in chains', published

---

3. Ibid., p. 231.
4. William Kenrick, *Emilius and Sophia: or, A New System of Education*, 4 vols (London: R. Griffiths, T. Becket and P.A. de Hondt, 1762).

shortly before *Émile*) were also unpopular there and after only two years Rousseau fled to England. He returned to France, under a false name, in 1767 and was eventually officially allowed to stay, where he wrote several more books, including his posthumously published *Confessions*. He died in July 1778 and was buried in Ermenonville. In 1794 his remains were removed to Paris and re-interred in the Panthéon, close to the remains of Voltaire.

Émile was a lengthy fictional espousal of Rousseau's idea that human beings are good by nature, but become corrupted by society.[5] It describes the upbringing and education of a boy, Émile, from birth to adulthood, in the company of a tutor. Rousseau divides the boy's development into five stages: birth to infancy; aged two to twelve (the 'age of nature'); twelve to fifteen; fifteen to 20; and 20 to 25. Most importantly, during the second stage, Rousseau argues that a child should only receive a 'negative education', being allowed to learn for himself, with no moral or verbal instruction from above. Children, he argues, have a right to happiness and freedom, and in experiencing these, especially by being close to nature, they will develop physical strength. Mental strength can then be developed during the third stage, when a child learns by experience. This is exemplified by the fact that the only book that Émile is allowed to read is *Robinson Crusoe*, a personification of the self-sufficient man that Rousseau is trying to develop.

However, despite the tenet that a child must learn for himself, he still needs, in the absence of a mother, a nurse to teach him during his early years. In particular, a young child must learn to fear nothing, a lesson which can only be learnt from guided experience. Similarly, a child needs to learn to accept pain, for example, as a result of falling over, as a small pain experienced during childhood will prepare him for the greater pains of adulthood. Later on, a child needs a tutor, not only to guide him but also to punish him, if necessary, with any punishment being fitted to the crime.

By the age of fifteen, Émile is both physically and mentally strong enough to deal with the emotions of adolescence, and with religion and moral issues. This allows for a gradual entry into society, while still letting the child go with his natural inclinations without undue interference. This is also the period during which a child should learn a

---

5. For a fuller discussion of *Émile* and some of the children's books which were influenced by it, see Sylvia W. Patterson, *Rousseau's* Émile *and Early Children's Literature* (Metuchen, NJ: The Scarecrow Press, 1971).

trade. In the final stage, Émile is introduced to Sophie, his ideal partner, and learns about love.

The philosophy behind this final stage, in particular, the idea that women should be weak and passive, and that female education should encourage feminity and the learning of domestic skills, did not meet with universal approval. Mary Wollstonecraft was one writer who, although accepting many of Rousseau's ideas, and incorporating them in her 1788 book, *Original Stories, from Real Life*,[6] attacked his approach to female education in her 1792 book, *A Vindication of the Rights of Woman*.[7]

Rousseau's ideas were enthusiastically taken up by Richard Lovell Edgeworth (an Anglo-Irish politician and writer, and the father of Maria Edgeworth, who wrote numerous books for children and adults), who brought up his own son by Rousseau's principles. However, the results were, to Edgeworth, disappointing and he abandoned Rousseau and developed his own ideas, which culminated in the publication in 1798 of *Practical Education*,[8] written in conjunction with his daughter. Similarly, Thomas Day sought to follow Rousseau's philosophy in the education of two girls he adopted, with the aim of moulding a perfect wife for himself. Again, this was not a success, one eventually being apprenticed and the other sent away to boarding school. This did not, however, dent Day's faith in Rousseau, and this found its apogee in his novel *Sandford and Merton*, an exploration of some, although by no means all, of Rousseau's ideas transposed to the English countryside and written as a book for boys.

Day was also influenced by another Rousseau-inspired novel, *The Fool of Quality* by Henry Brooke, although this was less of an English version of *Émile* and more of an attack on the aristocracy and an expression of the author's distaste for the way that some institutions of British society had become corrupted by the people who ran them.

Formal education, in school, was not part of Rousseau's philosophy and, hence, not part of that followed by either Day or Brooke. However, the novels of both Day and, to a smaller extent, Brooke, are important

---

6. *Original Stories, from Real Life; with Conversations, Calculated to Regulate the Affections, and Form the Mind to Truth and Goodness* (London: J. Johnson, 1788).
7. *A Vindication of the Rights of Woman: with Strictures on Political and Moral Subjects* (London: J. Johnson, 1792).
8. *Practical Education* (London: J. Johnson, 1798).

for their depictions of education, and they also had their own influence on the later development of the school story.

Henry Brooke and *The Fool of Quality*

Henry Brooke (1703–83) was born in Ireland and studied Law at Trinity College, Dublin. After a career as a playwright (curtailed when one of his plays was banned by the Lord Chamberlain), he found some commercial success with his two novels, the first of which was *The Fool of Quality; or, The History of Henry Earl of Moreland*, first published in five volumes between 1765 and 1770.[9]

Like *Sandford and Merton*, which is far better-known, *The Fool of Quality* focusses on the education of two boys, although it is also a celebration of the middle-class values of hard work, self-reliance and benevolence. In particular, Brooke is highly critical of the aristocracy and the way they traditionally bring up their children, teaching them to be – or rather failing to prevent them becoming – callous, mean, self-centred and unthinking. This is illustrated, at the beginning of the novel, by the comparison between the two sons of the aristocratic Richard Clinton, Earl of Moreland. Clinton's older son, also called Richard, has been kept at home during his childhood and is thereby thoroughly spoiled. (He would finish his education abroad and die there of the pox.) The younger son, Harry, is, in contrast, put out to nurse as an infant and does not even visit his parents until he is five years old. Even then, he is soon taken away by a Mr Fenton, a successful merchant who it later transpires is also Harry's uncle. Fenton raises Harry to adulthood, and in doing so teaches him to be a useful, rather than a parasitic, member of society.

The early part of *The Fool of Quality* is dripping with satire – for example, in its description of a dinner party held at Richard Moreland's mansion, which includes guests such as Sir Christopher Cloudy, Sir Standish Stately, Lady Childish, Squire Sulky, Lord Prim and Lord Flippant, all with characteristics appropriate to their names. The novel

---

9. *The Fool of Quality; or, The History of Henry Earl of Moreland*, 5 vols, printed for the author by Dillon Chamberlaine of Dublin, 1765–70. It was reprinted in London, again in five volumes, by W. Johnston between 1766 and 1770, with a revised edition published by Edward Johnston in 1777, and an abridged version in two volumes (abridgement by John Wesley) published by J. Paramore in 1781. The extracts here are taken from the 1859 edition (in two volumes) published by Smith, Elder & Co.

also quickly establishes where the fault in the family's bringing up of its children lay, a point made by some earlier dramatists and, with no small degree of force, by later writers of school stories – that is, with the mother (as, indeed, is the case in *Sandford and Merton*). It is the mother who takes the side of Harry's older brother when he and his friends play tricks on him, Harry bearing these with fortitude, which leaves his mother regarding him as a simpleton. Harry's father, on the other hand, recognises that Harry is misunderstood and maligned, although the constraints of aristocratic society render him unable to intervene.

A second strand to Brooke's criticism of the aristocracy is his attitude to trade, personified in the character of Mr Fenton. This theme had previously been taken up by John Newbery (see the next chapter) and Brooke echoes Newbery's view that the merchant classes are equally as valuable to society as the aristocracy, illustrating his point in a lively debate between Moreland and Fenton. He goes on to point out that the land-owning classes see themselves as aloof and separate from the rest of the economy, although they are more dependant on trade than any other class. The merchant does not need land to trade, but the landowner depends on the merchant to raise the value of his land. Brooke goes on to argue that the landowner's particular social function is to use his wealth to help others. This is illustrated in Mr Fenton's habit of inviting the heads of deserving local families to dinner every Sunday, after which he makes them gifts of money, thereby helping them to pay their debts or buy necessities. (A similar benevolence occurs in *Sandford and Merton*, dispensed by a local clergyman, although in this case the dinner is held only once a year.)

The education of Harry in *The Fool of Quality* is portrayed in a series of lessons, far removed from the classroom, each of which is designed to teach virtue, on the basis that Harry, like anyone else and despite his aristocratic background, needs to learn the precepts of responsibility, compassion and so on, as these are not inherent. Brooke sets out to show that the values of appearance and rank are worthless, and that a man should rather be judged on his contribution to society.

The Fool of Quality comes close to the school story in narrative terms when Harry and Ned, an orphan whom Harry has earlier befriended and who is now living with Mr Fenton, are placed with a tutor, Mr Vindex, who visits daily to give the two boys Latin lessons. When Mr Fenton goes away for a few weeks, Vindex becomes something of a tyrant. Ned, after being reproved for some misdemeanour, looks at Vindex with contempt and the tutor responds by bringing a birch rod and a ferule to the house, and uses the latter to beat Ned. The boy plots revenge and enrols a servant (described as Ned's 'bedfellow') to help him to construct an ingenious contraption beneath the tutor's chair, which causes a hidden needle to rise suddenly upwards when pulled by a thin piece of thread, held by Ned who is sitting some distance away.

The trick works perfectly, Vindex initially is unable to determine the cause of the sharp shock he receives whenever he sits down, until he turns the chair over and discovers the truth. Correctly identifying Ned as the culprit:

> Vindex at length looked smilingly about him, with much fun in his face, but more vengeance in his heart – Mr Edward, said he, perhaps you are not yet apprised of the justice of the Jewish laws, that claim an eye for an eye, and a breach for a breach; but I, my child, will fully instruct you in the fitness and propriety of them. Then, reaching at the rod, he seized his shrinking prey as a kite trusses a robin; he laid him, like a little sack, across his own stool; off go the trousers, and with the left hand he holds him down, while the right is laid at him with the application of a woodman, who resolves to clear part of the forest before noon.[10]

Harry, who was totally unaware of Ned's plot, tries, unsuccessfully, to intercede on Ned's behalf and, when Ned is confined to bed as a direct result of his beating, Harry offers to help in seeking revenge on the tutor. This is later effected by the boys attaching a thread to the knocker on the front door of the tutor's house and, from the safety of a house opposite, knocking on the door. The more frequently this happens, with no one actually outside when the door is opened, the more the tutor's servants panic, believing it to be the work of ghosts.

Unfortunately, flushed with the success of this latest trick, Ned cannot help boasting about it and inevitably Vindex learns the truth. The first person Vindex questions is Harry, who immediately acknowledges that he was aware of the trick that had been played. Vindex, who has been accompanied by one of the pupils who boards with him, is swift to exact retribution:

> Here, Jacky, down with his trousers, and horse him for me directly. Jack was a lusty lubberly boy, about ten years of age, and stooping to unbutton Harry, according to order, our hero

---

10. *The Fool of Quality* (1859), volume 1, p. 99.

> gave him such a sudden fist in the mouth, as dashed in two of his teeth that then happened to be moulting, and set him a crying and bleeding in a piteous manner. Vindex then rose into tenfold fury, and took our hero in hand himself; and notwithstanding that he cuffed, and kicked, and fought it most manfully, Vindex at length unbuttoned his trousers, and set him in due form on the back of his boarder. The pedagogue, at first, gave him the three accustomed strokes, as hard as he could draw.[11]

When Vindex demands that Harry reveals who else was behind the trick with the door-knocker, Harry refuses to say and suffers further violent punishment.

Again, this time supported by members of Mr Fenton's household, revenge is plotted, which culminates in Vindex being stripped and flogged in a darkened room (a fate similar to that previously suffered by the schoolmaster in Smollett's *Roderick Random*).

When Mr Fenton returns from his trip and is appraised of all the events that have taken place during his absence – notably by one of his servants, who 'set forth, in due contrast, the baseness and barbarity of Vindex on the one part, and the unassailable worthiness of his Harry on the other', he visits Vindex and, after apologising for the treatment meted out to him, tempers this by adding that he fully deserved it, and proceeds to lecture him on the inappropriateness of using fear and brutality to bring up and educate children. He goes on to point out that some schoolmasters apply corporal punishment to disguise their own weaknesses and to gratify their 'naughty passions'.

Brooke is astute enough, however, to recognise that the opposite of fear and tyranny is not the answer and he has Mr Fenton continue:

> There are, I admit, some parents and preceptors, who annex other motives to that of the rod; they promise money, gaudy clothes, and sweetmeats, to children: and, in their manner of expatiating on the use and value of such articles, they often excite, in their little minds, the appetites of avarice, of vanity, and sensuality; they also sometimes add the motive of what they call emulation, but which, in fact, is rank envy, by telling

---

11. Ibid., pp. 104–105.

one boy how much happier, or richer, or finer, another is than himself.[12]

Mr Fenton's final condemnation succinctly sums up the dilemma that has always faced tutors and schoolmasters:

> When you, Mr Vindex, iniquitously took upon you to chastise my most noble and most incomparable boy, you first whipped him for his gallant and generous avowal of the truth; and next, you barbarously flayed him because he refused to betray those who had confided in his integrity.[13]

In fact, there have been few fictional schoolmasters who have adopted such a double standard and in later school stories it is common to find a master who will punish a boy for an offence, but who will also respect him for not revealing his co-offenders. Mr Fenton is left bemoaning the fact that, thanks to tutors such as Vindex, there are too many 'scoundrels walking openly throughout the land who are styled your honour' and who wholly lack the most important of all characteristics – that of 'a gentleman'.

Thomas Day and *The History of Sandford and Merton*

Thomas Day (1748–89) was born in London. His father, a collector of customs at the Port of London, died within a year of Thomas' birth, leaving him with a large fortune in trust until he came of age. He was educated at a small private school in Stoke Newington and then as a boarder at Charterhouse, after which he studied Classics at Corpus Christi College, Oxford, although he left in 1767 without a degree.

Later, whilst living with his mother at Barehill in Berkshire, he met Richard Lovell Edgeworth, who introduced him to the works of Rousseau. Day would later declare that, if all the books in the world were to be destroyed, the two he would save would be the Bible and *Émile*.

In 1769, after unsuccessfully looking for marriage (his love for Edgeworth's sister being unrequited), Day decided to groom the perfect wife by following Rousseau's philosophy. He adopted two young girls (aged eleven and twelve), one from an orphanage in Shrewsbury and one from the Foundling Hospital in London, named them Sabrina

---

12. Ibid., p. 110.
13. Ibid., p. 111.

and Lucretia, and took them to France to educate them according to Rousseau's principles. The experiment, for that was what it was, turned out to be a failure and Day eventually married Esther Milnes, an heiress from Chesterfield, in 1778.

Ironically, whilst one of his strongest moral principles was his opposition to cruelty to animals, he died after being thrown from an unbroken horse he was trying to train by kindness. His wife promptly shut herself away, and died two years later.

Although his experiment in bringing up children according to Rousseau's philosophy had failed, Day never lost his faith in the ideals he had adopted, and these were expansively expressed in his story *The History of Sandford and Merton*.[14] This started life as a short story intended for insertion in Richard and Honora Edgeworth's *Harry and Lucy*, although domestic circumstances led to Richard Edgeworth abandoning the project and the book was eventually completed by his daughter, Maria, in 1801. In the meantime, Day expanded his original story into what became the first volume of *The History of Sandford and Merton*, published anonymously in 1783, with two further volumes appearing in 1786 and 1789. It was an immediate success, thanks more to its intimate and affectionate portrayal of the relationship between the two main characters, Harry Sandford and Tommy Merton, than its didactic intent, signalled by the inclusion of numerous inset stories, lessons, lectures and asides.

Superficially, the story shows how Tommy, initially aged six and the spoilt son of a wealthy plantation owner from Jamaica, and Harry, the son of a poor farmer, are educated by a local curate, with Tommy learning by example and, through self-discovery and, in particular, from the example set by honest and down-to-earth Harry, developing into a virtuous gentleman. Tommy's character is established from the outset:

> While he lived in Jamaica he had several black servants to wait upon him, who were forbidden to contradict him upon any account. If he walked, he was always accompanied by two negroes; one of whom carried a large umbrella to keep the sun from him, and the other was to carry him in his arms

---

14. *The History of Sandford and Merton: A Work Intended for the Use of Children*, printed by J. Stockdale, in three volumes, 1783, 1786 and 1789. The extracts here are taken from the 1860 edition published by Ward & Lock.

whenever he was tired. Besides this, he was always dressed in silk or laced clothes, and had a fine gilded carriage borne upon men's shoulders, in which he made visits to his playfellows. His mother was so excessively fond of him, that she gave him everything he cried for, and would never let him learn to read because he complained that it made his head ache. ... He was so delicately brought up, that he was perpetually ill; the least wind or rain gave him a cold, and the least sun was sure to throw him into a fever ... when Master Merton came over to England, he could neither read, write, nor cipher; he could use none of his limbs with ease, nor bear any degree of fatigue; yet he was very proud, fretful, and impatient.[15]

Harry, on the other hand, is described as: 'active, strong, hardy, and fresh-coloured. He was neither so fair nor so delicately shaped as Master Merton, but he had an honest, good-natured countenance, which made everybody love him; was never out of humour, and took the greatest pleasure in obliging everybody.'[16] He is also described as being kind to animals and insects, keen to learn, self-restrained and scrupulously honest.

This immediately sets the tone for the story, by contrasting the effete aristocratic upbringing of Tommy (aided by his over-indulgent mother) with the wholesome and worthy background of Harry. Like Brooke, Day is dismissive of aristocratic values, the story frequently contrasting ostentation and power with simplicity and the values of the working class. The rich, he is saying, have much to learn from the poor.

The two boys first meet when Harry rescues Tommy from a snake which has wound itself around his leg. Harry is immediately invited to dinner by Tommy's mother, but is unimpressed by the luxury of the Merton family home and the flamboyant nature of the meal, and makes no bones about it. Mrs Merton, while acknowledging Harry's 'openness of temper ... general good-nature and benevolence of his character', dislikes his attitude towards rich people.

Mr Merton then declares that he and his wife have both been guilty of over-indulging their son, and he proposes sending him to live with Mr Barlow, a local clergyman who taught Harry to read and write and who has continued to tutor him. Mr Barlow agrees to take Tommy, while insisting that he should be seen as a friend rather than a pedagogue.

---

15. *The History of Sandford and Merton* (1860), p. 2.
16. Ibid., p. 3.

Tommy's introduction to Mr Barlow's methods comes as something of a shock. On his first morning at the vicarage, Mr Barlow and Harry start digging in the garden, Mr Barlow explaining to Tommy that 'everyone who eats ought to assist in procuring food' – but when he offers Tommy a piece of ground of his own he is rebuffed: 'I am a gentleman, and don't choose to slave like a ploughboy.' Two hours later Mr Barlow and Harry share a plate of cherries, ignoring Tommy, who subsequently bursts into tears. He learns his lesson in the evening, when, denied any dinner, he finds Harry willing to share his with him, with Mr Barlow sardonically remarking, 'I see ... that though gentlemen are above being of any use themselves, they are not above taking the bread that other people have been working hard for.'[17] The following day, Tommy asks for a hoe and starts preparing his part of the garden.

Later, Harry begins to teach Tommy to read, which enables Day to expand his pedagogical purpose by inserting numerous tales and fables into the narrative, narrated by the three main characters. Almost all of these either have a moral lesson or illustrate a particular precept that Mr Barlow wishes to get across, or form part of a general education, covering history, geography, natural history, exploration, medicine, science and astronomy, although not, despite Mr Barlow being a clergyman, religion or theology. Day uses many of these stories to promulgate the (basically Christian and socialist) ideals that, first, people should not only be kind to and respect each other, irrespective of status or race, but be kind to animals as well and, second, they should labour to the best of their ability, thereby contributing to the common good. The idle rich are to be condemned and despised.

Many of the later editions of the book omitted several of Day's stories and fables, leaving the focus as the relationship between the two boys and Mr Barlow.[18] Tommy is shown as learning from experience and observation – for example, how cider is made, the physics of levers and magnetism, and lessons in astronomy and optics. He learns how

---

17. Ibid., pp. 13 and 18.
18. The first abridgement, by Richard Johnson and published by E. Newbery, appeared in 1790, just a year after the publication of the third and final volume of the original. Even Day himself helped in condensing later editions, admitting that those sections on educational theory would not be understood by children. This was a recognition that the book, originally subtitled by Day as *A Work Intended for the Use of Children*, had become something else, with later editions subtitled *For the Amusement and Instruction of Children* or *A Moral and Instructive Lesson for Young People*.

poor people can be generous and he also learns the value of philanthropy, persuading his father to give him £40 which he in turn uses to pay the debts of a farmer's family.

Halfway through the story Tommy returns home, in the company of Harry, and immediately reverts to his old self, re-adopting the worst mannerisms of his class and ignoring Harry in favour of the aristocratic boys to whom he is introduced. Day again uses this episode to excoriate the upper classes and, in particular, their attitudes to education. An acquaintance of Mrs Merton, Mrs Compton, observes that Harry has 'a plebeian look and vulgar air' and asks Mrs Merton why she:

> 'will suffer your son, who, without flattery, is one of the most accomplished children I ever saw in my life, with quite the air of fashion, to keep such company. Are you not afraid that Master Merton should insensibly contract bad habits, and a grovelling way of thinking? For my own part, as I think a good education is a thing of the utmost consequence in life, I have spared no pains to give my dear Matilda every possible advantage.' 'Indeed,' replied Mrs Merton, 'one may see the excellence of her education in everything that Miss Matilda does. She plays most divinely upon the pianoforte, talks French even better than she does English, and draws in the style of a master.'[19]

Mrs Compton later suggests that:

> 'it would be infinitely better to remove Master Merton, and place him in some polite seminary, where he might acquire a knowledge of the world, and make genteel connections. This will be always of the utmost advantage to a young gentleman, and will prove of the most essential service to him in life. For, though a person may have all the merit in the world, without such acquaintance it will never push him forward, or enable him to make a figure. This is the plan I have always pursued with Augustus and Matilda: I think I may say, not entirely without success; for they have both the good fortune to have formed the most brilliant connections. As to Augustus, he is

---

19. Ibid., pp. 225–26. This, of course, was one of the pointed criticisms of girls' education levelled in *The Governess; or The Boarding School Dissected* – see chapter four above.

so intimate with Lord Squander, who, you know, is possessed of the greatest parliamentary interest, that I think his fortune is as good as made.'[20]

However, she is overheard by the only member of the party who has any sympathy with Harry – Miss Simmons, a young woman who, having been born into a rich family, had been orphaned and brought up by an uncle, who had educated her almost as if she had been a boy: cold baths, early rising, long walks and lessons in the rudiments of geometry and the laws of nature. She is baited by Mrs Compton, and feels obliged to 'speak the truth' about Augustus:

> 'I have a cousin, a very good boy, who is at the same public school with his lordship; and he has given me such a character of him as does not much prepossess me in his favour ... he is one of the worst boys in the whole school; that he has neither genius, nor application for anything that becomes his rank and situation; that he has no taste for anything but gaming, horse-racing, and the most contemptible amusements; that though his allowance is large, he is incessantly running in debt with everybody that will trust him; and that he has broken his word so often, that nobody has the least confidence in what he says. Added to this, I have heard that he is so haughty, tyrannical, and overbearing, that nobody can long preserve his friendship, without the meanest flattery and subservience to all his vicious inclinations; and, to finish all, that he is of so ungrateful a temper, that he was never known to do an act of kindness to any one, or to care about any person or thing but himself.'[21]

This is not, at first glance, an attack on the public schools, but rather an expression of distaste for a certain type of boy, who enjoys and abuses all the privileges a public school education has to offer, although Day later refers to Master Compton as having 'almost finished his education at a public school, where he had learned every vice and folly that are usually taught at such places'.

Despite the solicitousness of Miss Simmons, Harry feels isolated and out of place. The first evening's dinner is a particular trial, with its variety

---

20. Ibid., p. 230.
21. Ibid., p. 231.

of courses, servants and etiquette, which Harry mentally compares with the meals enjoyed by his father's labourers, 'who, when they are hungry, can sit at their ease under a hedge, and make a dinner without plates, table-cloths or compliments'.

Harry is soon ostracised by Tommy and his friends, most of whom are much older and regale Tommy with stories of bad behaviour that Tommy longs to emulate. He gets his chance when they go to see a play, at which they criticise the actors and the audience and generally disrupt the proceedings, until a farmer puts a stop to their activities.[22] While this episode shows the aristocracy at its worst, Day then uses a ball, thrown by Mrs Merton in honour of Tommy, to show the aristocracy at its most pretentious, overly concerned with appearance and obsequiousness. The day after the ball, when walking in the country, Harry is struck by Tommy after an argument and is then drawn into a fight with one of Tommy's friends – thanks to his hardiness and courage, he wins. Immediately following this, he is instrumental in saving Tommy from being gored by a bull, after which he takes himself off to his own home. However, this marks a turning point in Tommy's attitude, as he subsequently paints Harry in a positive light, although Mr Merton is far from impressed with his son. When Mr Barlow makes a surprise visit, he is made aware of Tommy's behaviour, for which Mr Merton blames himself for not regulating him better. Mr Barlow, however, is not too dismayed and remains optimistic that Tommy can still grow out of his old ways. He stays with the Mertons and Tommy is slowly educated by way of stories, lectures and discussions. For his part, Tommy comes to recognise his faults, and those of his acquaintances, admitting to Mr Barlow that he loves Harry 'better than any other boy in the world' and that he is desperate for Harry's forgiveness. This is, of course, forthcoming, but before their reconciliation Tommy takes it upon himself to renounce his past and he effects a sudden transformation: 'Tommy now entered the room, but with a remarkable change in his dress and manner; he had demolished the elegance of his curls; he had divested his dress of every appearance of finery; every article of his attire was plain and simple.'

Finally, after staying with Harry for a while and learning the life of a farmer, he presents Mr Sandford with a team of horses by way of gratitude for everything Harry has done for him (Mr Sandford having

---

22. Later, when Harry is asked what he thought of the play, he replies: 'It seemed to me to be full of nothing but cheating and dissimulation; and the people that came in and out did nothing but impose upon each other, and lie, and trick, and deceive.' The play was *The Marriage of Figaro*.

earlier turned down a gift of hundreds of pounds from Mr Merton). When it is time for Tommy and Mr Merton to return home, Tommy acknowledges his debt to Harry:

> 'to your example I owe most of the little good that I can boast; you have taught me how much better it is to be useful than rich or fine – how much more amiable to be good than to be great. Should I ever be tempted to relapse, even for an instant, into any of my former habits, I will return hither for instruction, and I hope you will again receive me.' Saying this, he shook his friend Harry affectionately by the hand, and, with watery eyes, accompanied his father home.[23]

* * *

Émile had a huge influence on both the rearing of children and on children's literature. One of the most immediate contradictions it presents is that, while Rousseau argued that children should not read anything until they had reached the age of fifteen, many writers influenced by him wrote books targeted at much younger children. Amongst these were Anna Laetitia Barbauld and her brother John Aikin, Maria Edgeworth, Lady Ellenor Fenn and Hannah More, all of whom wrote children's books which leaned heavily on the ideas that Rousseau had put forward. In particular, a common theme was that of children learning from experience, being allowed to go their own way and suffering the consequences, exemplified, for example, by Maria Edgeworth's story *The Purple Jar*.[24] In this, a young girl, Rosamund, chooses to spend her money on an attractive jar in which she hopes to put flowers, rather than on a much-needed pair of shoes. The jar turns out to be a deceit and, in the absence of a pair of serviceable shoes, Rosamund is unable to go out with her father. A variation on this theme appears in Mary Wollstonecraft's *Original Stories, from Real Life*, in which a governess allows one of her pupils to spend all her money on toys, leaving her unable to help a poor woman – the girl consequently learning that 'prodigality and generosity are incompatible'.

---

23. Ibid., p. 388.
24. Originally published in *The Parent's Assistant* (1796) and reprinted in *Early Lessons* (1801). The latter was a series of books which combined straightforward narratives involving children with practical lessons in a variety of subjects.

One particular contradiction between Rousseau's ideas and real life, again reflected in later literature, was that few children are brought up in isolation and hence the ideal of 'negative education', or shielding children from vice, is largely impractical (other than for the aristocracy, where children were often taught by private tutors in isolation from other children). This led to stories, many set in schools, which focussed on misbehaviour, punishment and either rebellion or reform, accepting that vice cannot be ignored but revealing the consequences of indulging in it.

Rousseau's picture of the ideal life of a child in *Émile* had other effects on children's literature, most notably, perhaps, being his love of nature and the way this was incorporated into subsequent children's fiction, numerous children's stories and novels containing lessons on natural history, botany, astronomy, science, geology and geography.

Rousseau's influence was also felt in the development of the school story, despite his objection to schools as places for children to learn and develop. Instead, Rousseau placed the onus of education on a tutor or a tutor-figure, who guides his or her pupil and steers them in the right direction, allowing them to learn from experience and from their mistakes, before they embark on more practical lessons. Such a figure is central to many of the children's books in the late eighteenth century, be it a governess, tutor, parent or guardian, or, in some cases, a schoolmaster or schoolmistress who sees his or her role extending beyond that of simply being an educator. One feature of many of these books was the inclusion of inset stories, lectures and digressions which either served the purpose of illustrating a moral or simply imparting information, in many cases echoing Rousseau's idea that a child should want to learn, rather than be obliged to learn. Hence the tutor-figure will often contrive a situation where the child's curiosity is aroused and he or she will begin demanding answers to questions.

Of course, some writers rejected Rousseau's ideas and used their school stories to condemn, mock or satirise them. Nevertheless, the fact that his philosophy was treated in this way is a clear indication of the extent of his influence.

9

The Genre Established: School Stories, 1749–85

Up until the mid eighteenth century, fictional representations of education, school and pupils either had a distinct pedagogic purpose – the texts and dialogues written by teachers and educationalists as teaching and translation exercises – or were written for an adult readership or audience. The school story as a genre for children was born in 1749 and it was an important step in the development of literature for children.

Studies of the history of children's literature are replete with examples of printed books from the fifteenth century onwards, although there is no clear consensus as to what is exactly meant by 'children's literature', and therefore no consensus as to when children's literature was born. F.J. Harvey Darton, in his ground-breaking *Children's Books in England*, defines his subject as 'printed works produced ostensibly to give children spontaneous pleasure, and not primarily to teach them, nor solely to make them good, nor to keep them *profitably* quiet'.[1]

Darton's study therefore excludes schoolbooks, alphabets, primers, spelling books, didactic and religious treatises and adult-minded descriptions of child life. Whilst acknowledging that books which meet his criteria were published in the seventeenth century, Darton takes as his starting point 1744, when John Newbery published his first children's book, *A Little Pretty Pocket Book*, and almost single-handedly founded

---

1. F.J. Harvey Darton, *Children's Books in England: Five Centuries of Social Life* (Cambridge: Cambridge University Press, 1932; rev. edns 1958 and 1982), p. 1.

the commercial children's book trade. On the other hand, after brief references to illuminated books and books which only existed in manuscript (for example, schoolbooks, including Aelfric's *Colloquy*), Jane Bingham and Grayce Scholt, in *Fifteen Centuries of Children's Literature*, suggest that the very first printed children's book, or at least the first printed book that had an appeal to children as well as to adults, was William Caxton's *Book of the subtyl historyes and Fables of Esope*, translated by Caxton from the French and published in 1484.[2]

Chapbooks – crude and cheap booklets usually illustrated with inferior woodcuts, sold by itinerant pedlars – began appearing in the early 1600s and brought rhymes, legends, myths and stories (many of which had their roots in the oral tradition) to homes all across the social spectrum. Many of these were appropriated and read by children, and by the early 1700s large numbers of chapbooks were aimed specifically at a juvenile readership.

One of the first full-length books published for children was James Janeway's *A Token for Children, Being an Exact Account of the Conversion, Holy and Exemplary Lives, and Joyful Deaths of Several Young Children*, first published in London in 1671, and quickly followed by a *Second Part* in 1672. Janeway, a nonconformist Puritan minister, was born into a middle-class Church of England family in 1636. As an adult in London, he experienced both the Great Plague in 1665 and the Great Fire in 1666, before dying of tuberculosis in 1674. His experiences, plus the deaths of five of his eight brothers all before the age of 40, only served to increase his religious zeal, and his *Token for Children*, a series of supposedly true accounts of the pious deaths of young children, became a popular and long-lasting evangelical tract.

Early Girls' School Stories

Most commentators agree that the first full-length work of fiction, written exclusively for children, was Sarah Fielding's *The Governess; or, Little Female Academy*, first published in 1749 and which remained in print until 1903.[3] As well as being the first continuous children's story, this was only the second true work of fiction to be set solely in a school.

---

2. Jane Bingham and Grayce Scholt, *Fifteen Centuries of Children's Literature: An Annotated Chronology of British and American Works in Historical Context* (Westport, CT: Greenwood Press, 1980).
3. An indispensable facsimile reissue of the first edition, which includes a lengthy introductory essay and a very useful bibliography by Jill E.

Sarah Fielding had already written two novels for adults (including *The Adventures of David Simple* – see chapter seven above) when she published *The Governess*. Her aim was clearly didactic as well as to entertain, as indicated by the full title of the first edition: *The Governess; or, Little Female Academy. Being the History of Mrs Teachum, and Her Nine Girls. With their Nine Days Amusement. Calculated for the Entertainment and Instruction of Young Ladies in their Education.*

The story follows the lives of nine girls and their governess, through nine days at their boarding school, somewhere in the north of England, and mixes narrative with fairy tales and other 'instructive' stories to get across its precepts of obedience and good behaviour. The names Fielding gives her characters are mostly allegorical – the governess is Mrs Teachum (a name echoed by later writers) and the nine pupils are Jenny Peace, Sukey Jennett, Dolly Friendly, Lucy Sly, Patty Lockit, Nanny Spruce, Betty Ford, Henny Fret and Polly Suckling. The eldest, Jenny Peace, is fourteen and the others are all under twelve.

Mrs Teachum is the 40-year-old widow of a clergyman, who had lost both of her young children to early deaths. She runs a small school for girls, in which she can educate the children herself without relying on other teachers.[4] She is even-tempered and kind, but always ready to reprimand when necessary. The girls are taught reading, writing, needlework, gardening, 'all proper Forms of Behaviour' and 'an exact neatness in their Persons and Dress, and a perfect Gentility in their whole Carriage' (in preparation for their roles as wives). There are prayers twice a day and two church services every Sunday.

The story opens with a fight between the girls over an apple, the largest in a basket given to them by Mrs Teachum after lessons have finished. One girl, Jenny Peace, tries to stop them, but they carry on, until the fight is broken up by Mrs Teachum, with each girl being left holding a lock of hair or a piece of torn clothing. The girls then begin to proffer their excuses, blaming each other, but Mrs Teachum is not taken in by this and declares them all equally guilty. The remaining apples are taken away, and Mrs Teachum, after punishing the girls (in an unspecified

---

Grey, was published by the Oxford University Press in 1968, as part of its Juvenile Library series.

4. Many eighteenth- and early nineteenth-century girls' school stories were set in very small schools, which were designed to replicate the family home, with the teacher or governess a metaphor for the mother. This replicated the real world, where many advertisements for small girls' boarding schools emphasised their family-like atmosphere.

way) makes them promise to become friends again, although they all have their reasons for resisting this.

The following morning Jenny Peace has a lengthy conversation with Sukey Jennett, who, despite her pride, eventually accepts that her attitude, especially her antipathy towards her schoolfellows, is wrong. Jenny also persuades the other girls to become reconciled with each other and, after delivering a little homily in the garden, produces a second basket of apples, which she has bought with her pocket money, and which the girls share in a friendly and co-operative manner.[5]

Jenny then proposes that the girls tell the stories of their lives to each other, and proceeds to narrate her own life story, ending with her mother's death from scarlet fever, which leaves all her schoolfellows in tears. As she finishes, the supper bell rings, and Mrs Teachum watches the girls leaving the garden hand in hand and evidently all in good humour (despite the sadness of Jenny's story). Mrs Teachum later readily agrees that the girls may spend time each day in the garden 'reading Stories and such Things as she should think a proper and innocent Amusement'. In addition, Mrs Teachum 'desired Miss Jenny, as a Reward for what she had already done, to preside over these Diversions, and to give her an Account in what manner they proceeded'. This could be seem as an early example of the prefect system, with an older and more responsible pupil supervising the others outside the classroom.

On the succeeding days, the girls narrate their own life stories, and they are followed by three fictional tales, all of which contain strong moral lessons. Immediately after Jenny has read the final story, Mrs Teachum brings her a letter, revealing that her aunt has returned home from abroad and is sending a coach to collect her. All the girls are upset at this news, such is their affection for Jenny, and Jenny herself is torn between her desire to see her aunt and her desire to stay at school. Nonetheless, familial ties take precedence, Jenny leaves, never to return, although her name and her character lives on.

The Governess was first issued on 2 January 1749, 'Printed for the AUTHOR, and Sold by A. Millar, in the Strand, London', priced at two shillings and sixpence. This was at a time when the average wage

---

5. The use of apples, as opposed to cakes, sweets or other fruit, as the focus for discord is clearly a symbol of temptation and avarice. It had featured in Aelfric's *Colloquy* (see chapter one) and it went on to appear in numerous later school stories, although largely in the context of apples (or other fruit) being stolen from orchards and gardens, and therefore being a much stronger metaphor for forbidden fruit.

was less than ten shillings a week. Millar subsequently issued a second edition, which included small corrections and minor textual changes, in smaller type and with fewer pages, on 29 August 1749, priced at one shilling and sixpence.

In her introductory essay to the 1968 facsimile reissue, Jill Grey suggests that, with *The Governess*, Sarah Fielding was the first author to establish a distinct social environment with a set of characters taken from ordinary life and using everyday speech, although for many readers their lives would have been completely different. The author's choice of a school setting provided an element of romance for readers, most of whom would not attend a school of any sort, let alone an exclusive girls' boarding school. Having said that, popular fiction since the mid eighteenth century has often relied on the conceit of readers being transported into a world far-removed from their own.

The Governess was certainly a pioneer, not only being the first full-length work of fiction for children but also, almost, the first school story, although most of the narrative is wholly unrelated to school life. The story also created a template used by numerous later authors, namely, the use of stories inserted into the text in order to inculcate precepts of good behaviour, such as obedience, self-control, honesty, moderation, kindness, politeness, and consideration for others, and showing how children should lead their lives.

It may have taken some inspiration from the courtesy book, or conduct book, a guide to etiquette, manners and behaviour which can be traced back to thirteenth-century Italy and Germany. Amongst the earliest in Britain were *The Babees Book* (c. 1475), *The Book of Curtesye* (c. 1478), *The Boke of Nurture* (1513), and *A lytil Booke of good manners for chyldren* (1532). Later, John Newbery published *Letters on the Most Common, as well as Important, Occasions in Life* (1758) and *The Polite Lady; or, A Course of Female Education, in a Series of Letters from a Mother to Her Daughter* (1760). The first title to suggest a scholastic background was *The Polite Academy; or, Complete Instructions for a Genteel Behaviour and Polite Address in Masters and Misses*, published by R. Baldwin in 1758. This was revised and reissued as *The Polite Academy; or, School of Behaviour for Young Gentlemen and Ladies*, published by R. Baldwin and B. Collins in 1762. This comprises essays on behaviour and rules of conduct for various environments and social occasions, including instructions on how to dance a minuet.

Similarly, books of general instruction and education were occasionally given titles suggesting a scholastic setting – such as *The School of Wisdom; or, Repository of the Most Valuable Curiosities of Art and Nature* (Gainsborough, 1776), and *The School of Wisdom; or, New Preceptor:*

A General System of the Works of Art and Nature, Calculated for Advancing the Instruction of Youth (W. Lane, 1777).

Yet another form which existed before 1749 but which may have been given some impetus by *The Governess* was the book of letters, in which a parent or governess or tutor gave advice or discussed similar topics to those raised in novels which simply used the school as a background. One of the first of these which appeared after 1749 was Charles Allen's *The Polite Lady; or, A Course of Female Education, in a Series of Letters, from a Mother to Her Daughter*, first published by J. Newbery in 1760. This comprises 40 letters between Portia and her daughter, Sophia, who is at boarding school under a Mrs Bromley. The subjects range from the lessons Sophia is having – reading, writing, French, geography and sewing, for example – to those such as obedience, friendship, cleanliness, modesty, temperance, pride, chastity and religion.

This was followed, in 1766, by Sarah Maese's *The School: Being a Series of Letters between a Young Lady and Her Mother*, published by W. Flexney. The author was the owner of a boarding school in Bath, and her book was as much a reflection of her own educational ideas and methods as it was concerned with giving advice. Slightly different in approach was the anonymous *Pleasure Improved, by Being Made a Guide to Useful Knowledge, Religion and Politeness; or, An Account of Mrs Wishwell's Scholars Performance at Their Leaving School for the Holidays*, printed for the author in London in 1777. The setting is an evening's entertainment, at a girls' school, for parents, guardians and friends. Most of the girls, as before, have symbolic names, such as Miss Noble, Miss Genteel, Miss Upright and Miss Thoughtful, and the book is simply a collection of 'orations as to the advantages and usefulness of Education and Virtue' and 'select passages from some of the most approved authors, both in prose and verse, narrated by the pupils'. Again, these cover a wide range of topics, the school simply acting as the background.

Unsurprisingly, *The Governess* spawned many imitators, which followed its idea of providing moral lessons through the medium of conversations between a governess or a teacher and her pupils. Some of these successors used a school setting, although in many cases any description of school life is notable by its absence. Others took the narrative away from school, for example, using a governess living with a family to educate one or more daughters, or a tutor employed to teach boys. Many of these disparate works of fiction are often classified as school stories, although in truth they are anything but.[6]

---

6. See, for example, the list by Jill Grey in the 1968 Oxford University Press reprint of *The Governess* and the list in Sue Sims and Hilary Clare,

The first direct successor to *The Governess* was *The Young Misses Magazine: Containing Dialogues between a Governess and Several Young Ladies of Quality, Her Scholars*, written by Mme Jeanne-Marie Leprince de Beaumont, a French educational writer who lived in London for many years. This was first published in instalments, in French, as *Le Magasin des enfants* in 1756, before being translated and published in England by J. Nourse in either 1756 or 1757 (the exact date is not known). The setting is a small girls' school run by a Mrs Affable. There are only six pupils – Lady Sensible, Lady Mary, Lady Charlotte, Miss Molly, Lady Witty and Lady Tempest. Like *The Governess*, this includes several tales told by Mrs Affable and the girls, including biblical, historical and fairy stories. Mme de Beaumont followed this with three further titles, including *Le Magasin des adolescents*, translated as *The Young Ladies Magazine; or, Dialogues between a Discreet Governess and Several Young Ladies of the First Rank under Her Education* (J. Nourse, 1760). This uses the same characters plus a number of newcomers, again with a mixture of symbolic and ordinary names – Miss Rural, Lady Violent, Miss Frivolous, Miss Sophia and Miss Fanny, for example. The dialogues cover subjects such as philosophy, the Bible, polite behaviour, vanity and happiness, and are interspersed with fables, historical tales and stories with a moral dimension, all of which are followed by discussions between the girls and Mrs Affable. This was subsequently reissued as *The Polite Tutoress, or Young Lady's Instructor, Being a Series of Dialogues between Mrs Affable, a Sensible Governess, and Several of her Pupils of the First Rank* (J. Coote, 1761).[7]

The Encyclopaedia of Girls' School Stories (Aldershot: Ashgate, 2000). (This latter publication was revised and reissued in three volumes by Girls Gone By Publishers [Radstock, Somerset] in 2020.) While neither of these lay any claim to completeness, they are the only previous efforts to identify pre-1850 girls' school stories, although both lists include titles which, on close examination, fall outside any reasonable definition of 'school story'. Having said that, two of the most notable direct imitators of *The Governess* were: *Mrs Leicester's School; or, The History of Several Young Ladies, Related by Themselves*, written by Mary and Charles Lamb and originally published, anonymously, by M.J. Godwin in 1809; and Mrs Mary Sherwood's *The Governess; or, The Little Female Academy*, a more-or-less complete rewrite of the original, first published by F. Houlston & Son in 1820.

7. A further reissue, credited to Charles Stanhope, was *The New Polite Tutoress, Containing a Complete Course of Dialogues between a Sensible Governess and Several of Her Pupils of the First Rank* (Alex Hogg, date of

In 1770 T. Carnan published *The Little Female Orators; or, Nine Evenings Entertainment*, written by Richard Johnson.[8] This is set in a girls' boarding school just outside London, where, every Saturday evening, a pupil addresses the others on 'some moral and entertaining subject'. The girls, with names such as Deborah Grace, Dolly Goodchild, Penelope Lovebook and Betty Thoughtful, are model pupils, with Deborah Grace opening her recital by stressing the importance of learning (although one would have thought that ordinary lessons would have been enough): 'The best Method I can propose for filling up those empty Spaces of Time, which are tedious and burdensome to idle People, and which we little Ones often employ in the Pursuit of Trifles, is to apply ourselves to the Acquisition of useful Knowledge.'

The subjects chosen by the pupils mainly cover books they have read, although other subjects include the importance of dress and the correct use of a fan. The fictional tales include an Oriental story, a satire on London society, and a story set in North America, all of which are adaptations of earlier stories by other writers. Each tale is followed, as before, by a discussion amongst the girls and the governess, the latter drawing out morals and precepts and correcting any misjudgements or contrary views expressed by her pupils.

Another direct descendant of *The Governess* was the anonymous *School Occurrences: Supposed to Have Arisen among a Set of Young Ladies, under the Tuition of Mrs Teachwell and to Be Recorded by One of Them*, published by John Marshall in 1782. The author was actually Ellenor Fenn (1743–1813), who was a prolific writer of children's books, in particular, for John Marshall, and wrote under pseudonyms such as 'Mrs Teachwell', 'Mrs Lovechild' and 'A Lady'. Again, this was set in a small and exclusive girls' school, staffed by the governess, Mrs Teachwell, her assistant, Miss Friendly, a housekeeper, Mrs Care, and with pupils such as Miss Sprightly, Miss Pert, Miss Cheat and Miss Pry. The narrative comprises a series of moral escapades involving the girls, covering themes such as deceit, theft and self-denial, and a larger series of dramas, acted by the girls but set outside school. The overriding moral

---

publication not known, but *c.* 1786). Later reissues of the original *Young Ladies Magazine* carried the title *The Young Ladies Magazine, or Polite Tutoress, Containing Dialogues between a Governess and Several Young Ladies of Quality, Her Scholars*.

8. In the same year Carnan published Richard Johnson's *Letters between Master Tommy and Miss Nancy Goodwill*, which was loosely based on episodes from *The Governess*.

lesson is the importance of learning and the value of the appropriate behaviour suited to one's station.

A distinct offshoot of *The Governess* was the 'governess novel', set in private homes rather than schools, which initially used stories and incidents to illustrate a moral point, but which later became concerned with the lives of governesses and their relationships with their employers and the girls they were educating.[9] One of the earliest examples was *Tea-Table Dialogues between a Governess and Miss Thoughtful, Miss Sterling, Miss Prattle, Master Thoughtful, Master Goodwill and Master Poplin, Wherein Is Delineated the Charms of Innocence and Virtue, and the Pleasure of Rural Amusements*, attributed to Richard Johnson and first published by T. Carnan in 1771.[10] The governess is Mrs Goodwill and much of the narrative comprises reworked extracts from *The Young Misses Magazine*, with the girls' names reflecting their characters and with their faults and good points being drawn out in the dialogues which follow the tales, largely biblical, told by themselves and the governess. Many similar novels followed, with the moral and practical education of girls eventually giving way to comment on the working conditions and social position of governesses, reflecting real-life changes that were taking place from the 1830s onwards.

The most important descendant of *The Governess* was, of course, the school story proper. In the immediate post-*Governess* period, most of those which appeared were set in boys' schools, with a handful set in girls' and mixed schools. One of the most famous post-*Governess* school stories was the anonymous *The History of Little Goody Two-Shoes*, published by John Newbery (see below) in 1765, although this was far from being a conventional school story. It tells the rags-to-riches story of an orphan girl, Margery Meanwell, who comes to love her alphabet and, through her enthusiasm, becomes a popular teacher, first to children in her neighbourhood and then as the headmistress of a local school.

It begins with the death of Margery's parents, leaving Margery and her brother, Tommy, orphaned and homeless, initially surviving

---

9. For a comprehensive study, see Cecilia Wadsö-Lecaros, *The Victorian Governess Novel* (Lund: Lund University Press, 2001).
10. This was subsequently rewritten and reissued as *Tea-Table Dialogues between a Governess and Miss Sensible, Miss Thoughtful, Miss Bloom, Miss Hopeful, Miss Sterling, Miss Lively and Miss Tempest*. A later reprint by Darton & Harvey in 1796 carried the title, *Tea-Table Dialogues between a Governess and Mary Sensible, Eliza Thoughtful, Jane Bloom, Ann Hopeful, Dinah Sterling, Lucy Lively and Emma Tempest*.

on berries from hedgerows and gifts from local people, until they are rescued by a rich clergyman. Tommy is sent to sea and Margery determines to learn to read, which she does by borrowing books from the local schoolchildren whom she meets on their way home. Quickly becoming efficient, she then takes it upon herself to teach those children who cannot read, becoming a 'trotting Tutoress'. The book at this point becomes particularly pedagogic, with examples of how Margery set about learning for herself and then passing on her knowledge, followed by a series of 'Lessons for the Conduct of Life'. Eventually she is invited to take over a Mrs Williams' school.[11] The narrative at this point becomes somewhat surreal, with Margery rescuing a raven and then a pigeon from gangs of boys, who are mistreating the birds, and then teaching the birds to read. The school also gains a pet skylark, a pet lamb and a dog, who later rescues the entire school by warning Margery and her pupils that the roof is about to fall in. Margery is able to continue teaching thanks to the generosity of a local farmer, who not only gives her a room in his house, but also orders the school to be rebuilt at his expense. She later finds a rich husband, and six happy years of marriage follows, until her husband dies and she inherits his wealth, which she is able to put to good use, enabling bread and books to be distributed to the poor.

Like many of Newbery's children's books, it was a plea for education, reflecting the publisher's belief that a child could improve his or her social and economic standing and future prospects through reading. It was also, at least to begin with, overtly political, with an introduction which narrates how Margery's father, a farmer, is forced into bankruptcy by the machinations of the unscrupulous Farmer Graspall.

The strong tone of the introduction has led many to propose that the author of *Goody Two-Shoes* was Oliver Goldsmith. (The title page of the first edition claims that the work had been translated from a manuscript in the Vatican and that the woodcuts were by Michaelangelo, but this was purely a joke on the part of Newbery.) Goldsmith has been put forward as the author on the basis that he frequently worked for Newbery and that the sentiments expressed in the introduction echo those in his poem *The Deserted Village*, which was first published in 1770. However, John Rowe Townsend, in *Trade and Plumb-Cake for Ever, Huzza!*, suggests that the evidence for this was tenuous, pointing out that Newbery came from a farming family and may have had direct

---

11. Mrs Williams had previously appeared in *The History of Mrs Williams and Her Plumb Cake*, published by Newbery in 1750 (see below).

experience of landowners and unscrupulous farmers, and was himself, possibly, the author.[12]

Goody Two-Shoes was reprinted on numerous occasions and by a variety of publishers. Several editions were abridged, for example, an 1804 edition by Tabart & Co., which excluded everything which could have been regarded as political, although this was as much for reasons of space, given the format that the publisher had adopted for many of its children's books, as it was for political expediency. This edition also included a new second part to the story which told of Tommy Meanwell's adventures overseas; this was expanded on by Mary Elliott in *The Adventures of Tommy Two-Shoes*, published by William Darton Jr in 1818. This was, given its context, a surprisingly exciting tale, with a plot and narrative that would not have been out of place in a penny dreadful some 50 years later. However, this had far less impact than the original story, which remains one of the most influential children's stories of its era, and the first to emphasise the value of education in such a way that readers would have been unaware that they were being fed pedagogical propaganda.

In 1773 W. Tringham, appropriating John Newbery's 1751 title (see below), issued *The Lilliputian Magazine; or, Children's Repository, Containing what is whimsical, witty, and moral, calculated to entertain and improve the minds of youth of both sexes*, ostensibly written by 'Timothy Teachum and Co.' This was issued in twelve monthly instalments, with each two instalments issued as a small volume in its own right. Volume three included *Entertaining Memoirs of Little Personages; or, Moral Amusements for Young Ladies*[13] and this contained two girls' school stories, the first being *The History of Polly Pert*, in which the eponymous heroine is always talking, interrupting others, asking questions and using bad language. In order to cure this she is sent to a boarding school, where she very quickly becomes unpopular, in particular, because she is always eavesdropping on other girls' conversations. The governess is on the verge of asking her parents to take her away when she hatches a scheme in which two of the older girls talk confidentially about a closet which is strictly out of bounds. Polly finds the closet and steps inside, only to be locked in and kept there overnight. Of course, as a

---

12. John Rowe Townsend, *Trade and Plumb-Cake for Ever, Huzza! The Life and Work of John Newbery, 1713–1767, Publisher and Bookseller* (Cambridge: Colt Books, 1994).
13. Volume one included *Entertaining Memoirs of Little Personages, or Moral Amusements for Young Gentlemen*. Both volumes were subsequently issued separately *c*. 1783–85.

consequence she reforms and becomes 'as much respected and beloved as she was hated and despised before'.

The History of Miss Fanny Hewet, from the same collection of stories, follows a similar pattern. The over-indulged Fanny is an outcast at her day school and, after two or three instances of bad behaviour, is given a dunce's cap to wear and made to stand in the middle of the school, where she is seen by all the girls and even some of their servants when they come to collect their charges. Again, her mortification at this leads to reform and a growing popularity.

* * *

Although in its infancy, the girls' school story was, by 1785, beginning to exhibit the characteristics which were to become its defining features in future years. Most pre-1785 girls' school stories were heavily didactic in nature, with an emphasis on advice, guidance and moral education, with themes such as deceit, unpopularity and dishonesty just beginning to emerge. These, and other themes such as greed, pride, vanity, snobbery, friendship and rivalry, disobedience, laziness and bad behaviour, and, for a while, religion, were subsequently woven into longer narratives, and these came to define what was to become recognised as a fully-fledged genre.

In the meantime, school stories for boys were also developing, demonstrably at a faster rate than school stories for girls, with the pioneering publisher John Newbery at the forefront of this movement.

Early Boys' School Stories – John Newbery and His Successors

In 1744 John Newbery published *A Pretty Little Pocket Book*, one of the first books designed for the pleasure, rather than the instruction, of children. Newbery was born on 17 June 1713 in Waltham St Lawrence, Berkshire, the son of a farmer. In 1730 he began a long association with the printing and publishing family of William Carnan in Reading, Berkshire, and on William's death he became joint owner, with William's son Thomas, of the family business. He later married William Carnan's widow, Mary, with whom he had three children.

Newbery moved to London and in 1744 joined a long-established community of printers in St Paul's Churchyard, under the sign of the Bible and Sun. In 1750 he published two more children's books, *Nurse Truelove's Chistmas Box; or, The Golden Plaything for Children* and *Nurse Truelove's New Year's Gift; or, The Book of Books for Children*, and in 1751–52 he published three issues of *The Lilliputian Magazine; or,*

The Young Gentleman and Lady's Golden Library, thereby establishing him as one of the pioneers of publishing for children. He published several more children's books (as well as numerous other books) before his death in 1767, the business being continued by his son, Francis, and his stepson, Thomas Carnan. Francis withdrew from the trade in 1779 and Carnan carried on alone until his death in 1788. In the meantime, John's nephew, Francis, had established himself as a publisher in his own right, from 'the Corner of St Paul's Church Yard', in 1767, with his wife, Elizabeth, taking over the business on his death in 1780 until she sold up in 1801.[14]

Nurse Truelove's New Year's Gift is notable for containing the very first story set in a mixed school. *The History of Mrs Williams and Her Plumb Cake* is a short tale in which the division of a cake amongst her pupils by a schoolmistress on Twelfth Night leads to discord and a lecture on the value of trade, as opposed to inherited wealth. It is the source of the phrase most closely associated with Newbery, 'Trade and plumb cake for ever'.[15]

Mrs Williams is much-loved by her pupils, who are very careful not to do anything which will incur her displeasure. Having made a large cake and divided it into equal parts, she serves the girl pupils first, before asking Master Hawes to have first choice of the remaining slices. Master Long, the son of the lord of the manor, objects to this, on the grounds of his superior social status, with Master Hawes being 'only a tradesman's son'. Mrs Williams points out to Master Long that she treats the children on merit, not status, and then asks:

> Is not the Tradesman and the Farmer as useful to the Publick
> as the Gentleman? I think they are. Without the Farmer

---

14. There was little love lost between Francis, John's son, and Francis, John's nephew. The partnership of Francis the son and Thomas Carnan felt obliged to emphasise the difference between the two firms, with a statement published on the reverse of the title-page of many of their books: 'The Public are desired to observe, that F. Newbery, at the Corner of St. Paul's Church Yard, has not the least concern in any of the late Mr John Newbery's Entertaining Books for Children; and to prevent having paltry compilations obtruded on them, instead of Mr John Newbery's useful Publications, they are desired to particularly careful to apply for them to T. Carnan and F. Newbery, jun. (Successors to the late Mr John Newbery) at No. 65, near the Bar in St. Paul's Church Yard.'
15. The story was reprinted in *The House that Jack Built, Also, The History of Mrs Williams and her Plumb Cake* (Williamsburg, Virginia: 1956).

you would have no Corn, and without the Tradesman that Corn could not be ground and made into Bread. Nay, you are indebted to Trade for the very Cloaths that you wear and but for the Tradesman you would not have a Shoe to your Foot. Even this Cake before me, which you so long for, is the Product of Husbandry and Trade. Farmer Wilson sowed the Corn, Giles Jenkins reap'd it, Neighbour Jones at the Mill ground it, the Milk came from farmer Curtis, the Eggs from John Thomas the Higgler; that Plumb came from Turkey, and this from Spain; the Sugar we had from Jamaica, the candied Sweatmeats from Barbadoes, and the Spices from the East-Indies. And will you offer to set Trade at nought, when you see even a Plumb-Cake cannot be made without it?[16]

Mrs Williams goes on to tell Master Long that his father is respected throughout the country not because he is rich but because he is a good man. Riches have no consequence unless they are used to promote happiness. When she had finished, 'Master Long blush'd, and all the rest bow'd respectfully, and cry'd out, Trade and Plum-Cake for ever. Huzza!'[17]

The publishing history of *Nurse Truelove's New Year's Gift* is uncertain. S. Roscoe, the author of *John Newbery and His Successors*, could not find any copy or reference to it prior to 1753, when it was advertised in *The Public Advertiser* on 18 December.[18] It was then advertised in *The Public Ledger* on 12 January 1756 as 'just published'. However, Jill Grey, in her article '*The Lilliputian Magazine*', has shown that it was printed for Newbery by William Strahan in or before 1750 via an entry in the printer's ledger (recording 6,000 copies at a cost of £5 14s.).[19] The story of Mrs Williams was subsequently reprinted in *The Twelfth Day Gift*, published by Newbery in 1767.[20]

Both sides of the Newbery family published school stories, either as complete volumes or as short stories, in the years that followed. The

---

16. Ibid., pp. 18–19.
17. A similar point on the value of trade was made by Aelfric in his *Colloquy* (see chapter one).
18. S. Roscoe, *John Newbery and His Successors, 1740–1814* (Wormley: Five Owls Press, 1973).
19. Jill Grey, '*The Lilliputian Magazine* – A Pioneering Periodical?', *Journal of Librarianship* 2, no. 2 (April 1970).
20. Mrs Williams makes a second appearance in *Goody Two-Shoes* (see earlier in this chapter).

best-known was *The History of Little Goody Two-Shoes*. Another came from John Newbery's nephew Francis, who had been publishing from 'the Corner of St Paul's Church Yard' since 1767; *The Sister's Gift, or The Naughty Boy Reformed* was a brief tale (of 32 pages), which first appeared in 1769[21] and told the story of Kitty and George Somers. Kitty, aged twelve, is graceful, gentle, just and clever, whereas George, aged eight, is ill-tempered, cruel and indifferent to the feelings of others. Although he is clever, he never helps any of his schoolfellows, 'in hopes of having the pleasure of seeing them whipped all round'. When the children are orphaned, they are sent to different boarding schools – Kitty becomes popular, but George does not, always playing tricks on his fellow-pupils. He becomes an outcast after playing a malicious trick on another boy, Dick Rooksby (involving a case of a borrowed jacket and mistaken identity), and Rooksby is unjustly whipped, with George exulting in his punishment and distress, being 'one of the first to assist in horsing him and to render his punishment as severe as possible'.

During the holiday, Kitty witnesses George's cruelty to insects and animals, which culminates in him dropping a cat from the top of a church tower. Kitty subsequently lectures him at length, enforcing her words by references to the principles of Christianity and virtue. George is shocked by the picture Kitty paints, and promises to be good.

The story introduced two themes that were to become key elements of many later school stories – cruelty, exhibited by a boy with no moral or social feelings, and unjust punishment. Misbehaviour and the eventual reform of a bad character also featured in *The Necessity of Correction for Idleness and Perverseness*, a short story in the anonymous *The Mother's Gift; or, A Present for All Little Boys Who Wish to Be Good*, first published by Carnan and Newbery in 1769. This focusses on the elder son of Mrs Newland, who, because of ill health, had entrusted him to a nurse, who over-indulged him. When he refuses to learn to read or write, he is sent to a small boarding school under Mr Teachum, who is told to punish the boy if at all necessary, Mrs Newland vowing not to visit her son until she has received a report of his good behaviour. Despite this, the boy misbehaves on his first day and, after ignoring Mr Teachum's entreaties to be good, is caned, the first time the teacher has used the cane for a year. Master Newland is subsequently sent to Coventry and, when the boys are free to play outside, he is refused entry to their games. He therefore determines to mend his ways, behaving well the following morning, and, when he is praised by Mr Teachum, he bursts into tears.

---

21. It was reprinted, as *The Sister's Gift; or, The Bad Boy Reformed*, by J. Kendrew of York in 1826.

His mother subsequently receives a favourable report, visits him, and immediately notices a difference in his build and demeanour.

Francis Newbery followed *The Sister's Gift* in 1775, with *The Rival Pupils; or, A New Holiday Gift for a Boarding School*, similar to Sarah Fielding's *The Governess* in that, whilst it is set in a school (a boys' school), it consists of a series of unlinked stories, none of which relate to the school in any way. These are followed, rather incongruously, by a translation of part of an Italian opera (*Joseph Made Known to His Brethren*).

The school is a small and exclusive boarding school just outside London (or what was then London) of only twelve pupils, 'born of parents in rather a superior station of life', the proprietor being a Mr Loveworth. (Surprisingly, perhaps, the pupils who are mentioned do not have such allegorical names.)

We learn virtually nothing about the school other than that it was originally built as a large family house. Its surroundings are pleasant – including a two-acre paddock and a fruit garden, and an artificial 'canal' in which Mr Loveworth insists his pupils learn to swim. The most notable revelation is that the boys have their own beds (if not bedrooms) – in stark contrast to many schools where the sharing of beds was not uncommon. (Indeed, it occurs in school fiction at least as late as 1841, in Harriet Martineau's *The Crofton Boys*.) The author indicates that there was a particular reason for this, but tantalisingly does not go into any detail.

The only reference to academic work is the book's *raison d'être*. Mr Loveworth has an annual custom of awarding a prize to each of his six most senior boys in return for a public recitation of a story, illustrating some moral or philosophical point. The judges are two neighbours, and the prizes they are to hand out are a rather eclectic collection – three improving books, an inkstand, a pocket book and a silver penknife. The parents of the six boys are invited, plus two or three of Mr Loveworth's friends to hear the recitations. The boys are supposed to follow the telling of their story with comments on its meaning and usefulness – most do so, although one boy finishes his brief and comic narration by saying that he hopes to be excused 'from making a tedious comment upon so plain a text'.

The recitations provide the bulk of the text. Historical, comic, poetic – on the whole they make for rather heavy reading, and were it not for references in the text to 'young' readers and 'little friends' they would suggest an intended adult rather than juvenile readership.[22]

---

22. The publication date of *The Rival Pupils* is something of a mystery. The earliest date ascribed to the book is 1766, in Charles Welsh, *A Bookseller of the Last Century: Being Some Account of the Life of John Newbery, and*

One of the first school stories to feature an element of fantasy (or perhaps 'the fantastic' would be a more appropriate term) was *The History of Little King Pippin*, first published by E. Newbery in 1775.[23] This is the story of a small boy, Peter Pippin, initially aged six, who prefers to buy books rather than spend his money on sweets and apples, and who is obliged to work scaring crows for a farmer. His father cannot afford to send him to school but, nevertheless, Peter is an angel, saying his prayers every night, always telling the truth, never swearing and never quarelling with other boys.

When Lady Bountiful finds him crying because he can't afford to buy a new book, she decides to pay for his schooling. Sent to a boarding school, he becomes so popular, giving good advice and settling quarrels and disagreements, that he is elected 'king', and his fellow pupils buy him a cap with 'Peter Pippin King of the Good Boys' embroidered on it.

Other pupils are Billy Meanwell, Sammy Sober, Bobby Bright, Tommy Telltruth, and the less savoury George Graceless and Ned Neverpray. One lunchtime, these latter two, with others including Harry Harmless, find themselves late for afternoon school and they decide instead to play truant and go attacking birds' nests. Despite protestations from Harry, they destroy several nests, until George falls off a tree trying to reach a turtle dove's nest, and plunges into the river, and drowns. The others are afraid to go back, and they wander about until they eventually fall asleep under some bushes. In the night they are woken by the roar of wild animals. Harry begs them to pray, but they cannot, not knowing how to – consequently, they are all eaten by lions, except Harry. Instead, the lions lie down next to him.

---

of the Books He Published, with a Notice of the Later Newberys (London: Griffith, Farren, Okeden & Welch, 1885). This describes the book as 'printed for J. Newbery, at the Corner of St. Paul's Churchyard'. However, J. Newbery did not operate from this address, and all known copies of *The Rival Pupils* (apart from an edition published in Dublin) carry the imprint of F. Newbery (John Newbery's nephew). The second recorded date, and probably the correct one, is 1775, when its forthcoming publication by F. Newbery was announced in the *London Chronicle* in January 1775. All the known copies are undated, although some carry dated inscriptions ranging from 1775 to 1786. So it is probably safe to assume it was published in 1775, with a reissue by Caleb Jenkins, of Dublin, in 1776.

23. The full title was *The History of Little King Pippin: with an Account of the Melancholy Death of Four Naughty Boys, Who Were Devoured by Wild Beasts: Likewise the Wonderful Delivery of Master Harry Harmless, by a Little White Horse.*

Harry is then rescued by a white horse and returns to school. George's parents, on learning of their son's fate, die of broken hearts within a month, and the lives of the other boys' parents are rendered miserable by the loss of their sons. As with *The Sister's Gift*, this reinforced one of the central tenets of the philosopher, John Locke, and the boys who exhibited cruelty to animals, in this case those who destroyed the birds' nests, were doomed to die, although Harry, who prayed, was saved.

Pippin is befriended by the father of one of his schoolfellows, who gives him a job and sends him to the West Indies to manage an estate – the voyage ends in tragedy, with Pippin the only survivor of a shipwreck. Inspired by Robinson Crusoe, he survives on a desert island, and is soon rescued. He then makes a success of managing the estate, and is eventually elected governor by the natives.

One of the commonest themes in the early school story was the robbing of orchards or the theft of fruit from gardens.[24] The first school story in which this appeared was *Juvenile Trials for Robbing Orchards, Telling Fibs and Other High Misdemeanours*, first published by T. Carnan in 1772.[25] Although published anonymously (its title continued *by Master Tommy Littleton, Secretary to the Court*), it is known that it was written by Richard Johnson (1734–93), a hack writer who wrote several books for the Newbery family as well as for other publishers. Many of these were plagiarised from other sources – for example, he wrote a chapbook version of Thomas Day's *Sandford and Merton*.

Set in a mixed boarding school, *Juvenile Trials* established the principle of children sitting in judgement on each other. The tutor and the governess admit their reluctance to use corporal punishment except in the most extreme cases, while at the same time recognising that children are individuals. They therefore decide to establish a court, with one of the boys sitting as judge, in order to deal with misdemeanours and 'all complaints against any one who should be accused of telling tales, taking from another that which did not belong to him, and other such offences', including quarrelling. The punishments to be meted out

---

24. This first appeared in one of Aelfric Bata's *Colloquies* – see chapter one.
25. It was subsequently reprinted several times, most notably by Darton & Harvey from 1796 onwards. Most of these new editions carried subtly different titles, for example *Juvenile Trials for Telling Fibs, Robbing Orchards and Other Heinous Offences*. A facsimile of an edition from 1786 was published in 1973 by Herbert Lang & Co. (Bern and Frankfurt) in conjunction with Toronto Public Library and with an introduction by Kathryn Dixon.

will range from depriving the guilty party of cakes and fruit for a time, to being sent to Coventry.

Twelve-year-old Master Meanwell is recommended by the tutor as the judge, and there is also to be a jury, although no indication is given as to whether this comprises all the pupils or just a few. Miss Sterling is chosen as a judge for when one of the accused is a girl. The initial reaction of the children is one of 'shame, that they should have been so naughty and unruly as to oblige their governor to erect such a tribunal among them'.

The first trial pits Master Tommy Telltruth against Billy Prattle. At the beginning, Master Meanwell makes a long speech to the school, the style of which suggests that he has a maturity far beyond his years. The basis of the trial is that Prattle has robbed an orchard, belonging to Telltruth's uncle, damaging a tree in the process. One of the witnesses is Jeremiah Trusty, an usher, who admits to accepting fruit from the accused and wondering where it came from but never asking. He is subsequently admonished by Meanwell for his attitude of indifference to obvious wrongdoing.

Prattle is found guilty but is pardoned on condition he begs forgiveness, which he does. The author goes on tell us that he is so ashamed by all of this he instantly reforms and becomes 'the best boy in the world'.

The second trial sees one of the girls, Miss Delia, charged with raising strife and disturbing the peace, precipitated by an argument over a sweet. This was, in fact, taken almost intact from Sarah Fielding's *The Governess*.[26] The third trial is Tommy Halifax versus Harry Lenox, with Lenox accused of substituting pebbles for the plums in a tart given to Halifax as a reward by the tutor. While Lenox's guilt appears to be obvious, all the evidence against him is circumstantial. When the jury cannot reach a verdict, the case is taken over by the tutor, who immediately finds Lenox guilty, not only of the crime of which he is accused but also of lying in his defence. Thus caught out, Lenox admits his guilt and is forgiven.

The fourth trial sees Master Flirt – rich, proud and snobbish – accused of bullying and mistreating another boy. Faced with the evidence of several witnesses (although not his victim), Flirt immediately recognises his faults, reforms and (establishing a tradition which countless school stories followed) becomes a close friend of the boy he has tormented. In many respects this is the most intriguing trial, and the one with the

---

26. Richard Johnson also imitated *The Governess* in *The Little Female Orator; or, Nine Evenings Entertainment*, first published by T. Carnan in 1770 – see above.

strongest moral message – that bullying is an insidious and hurtful crime which harms both the bully and the bullied.

The last trial (of the original edition) sees a farmer accusing a boy of trespassing on his land and damaging his property (hedges, trees and corn). However, the evidence provided turns the tables on the farmer, who ends up facing a charge of assault on the boy he had accused.

At the end of the first edition, we are told that the tutor and governess 'now dissolved this court of justice, plainly perceiving there was no further need of it, as peace, harmony, and tranquility, were perfectly established among their scholars'. However, a sixth trial appeared in 1793, in volume three of *Evenings at Home; or, The Juvenile Budget Opened*, by Dr John Aikin and his sister, Mrs Barbauld, and published by J. Johnson. This, like *The Governess* and other earlier books, was a series of tales told over a period of time, in this case over a number of evenings. *The Trial*, of Evening XIII, was 'meant as a sequel of that very pleasing and ingenious little work, Juvenile Trials'. In it, Henry Luckless is brought before the court accused of breaking the windows of Widow Careful, although the evidence is circumstantial. Unable to reach a decision, the court decides to compensate Widow Careful out of the school's own funds and the truth, that another boy was responsible, only emerges after a separate 'court of enquiry'. This extra trial was subsequently incorporated into reprints of *Juvenile Trials* by Darton & Harvey.

Juvenile Trials gets its message across by using children to right wrongs, to assess evidence and sit in judgement on their peers. Only rarely do adults intervene – indeed, in the first trial an adult, one of the teachers, is severely ticked off by the twelve-year-old judge. Such a form of justice was to appear in several later school stories, where boys took it upon themselves to act as judge and jury, although in many cases this was with more sinister motives and almost always without official sanction. *Juvenile Trials* was an honest attempt at illustrating how children, even those of a comparatively young age, could recognise not only right and wrong but also see the effects of their actions and appreciate that sometimes the solution to their problems was in their hands, and not those charged with looking after them.

Unfortunately, the story did not meet the approval of the editor of *The Guardian of Education*, Mrs Trimmer,[27] who remarked:

> It is certainly very proper to make British youth fully acquainted with the great privilege of trials by jury; but to

---

27. That is Sarah Trimmer (1741–1810), a writer and critic of children's literature.

suffer children thus to ape judges and jurymen, and sit in judgement on each other's conduct, is the very way to lessen, in their estimation, the solemnity of real trials, to bring courts of judicature into contempt; to destroy the authority of school-masters, and to fill boys' minds with vanity and conceit.[28]

The children portrayed in *Juvenile Trials* could be said to have shown a remarkable sagacity, far removed from the type of child which featured in many other stories and which was used as a vehicle for strong and sometimes tearjerking moral lessons. Many such stories used the lives of two children of contrasting characters to illustrate the folly of misbehaviour, idleness and ignorance, their nature usually delineated by their names. One of the earliest examples of this type of story was the anonymous *Virtue and Vice; or, The History of Charles Careful and Harry Heedless*, first published by E. Newbery in 1780.[29] Charles and Harry are close friends – good-natured, clever and God-fearing, although in all other respects they are opposites. Charles is careful with his money, spending it only on books or other useful items, or giving it to the poor, whereas Harry is a spendthrift. Charles is careful in what he reads, consulting his parents before buying his books, whereas Harry will read anything, showing no discernment in his tastes. Finally, Charles is steady and sensible, whereas Harry is reckless and headstrong, often finding himself in dangerous situations of his own making. Unlike most other 'bad' boys in school stories, Harry is not particularly wicked, but rather lacks common sense and is easily led astray. Charles goes on to university and inherits a fortune on his employer's death, while Harry gets into bad company and ends up homeless. A fortuitous meeting between Charles and Harry leads to Harry being set up as an assistant to a merchant and going on to lead a useful life.

Harry Heedless was the victim of his own shortcomings and could only blame himself for his faults. However, there was another type of child frequently portrayed in fiction at this time with similar

---

28. *The Guardian of Education*, no. 14, June 1803, published by J. Hatchard and F.C. and J. Rivington.
29. Its full subtitle was *Shewing the Good Effects of Caution and Prudence and the Many Inconveniences that Harry Heedless Experienced from His Rashness and Disobedience, While Master Careful Became a Great Man only by His Merit*. It is not known if it was ever reprinted by Newbery, but two editions, in 1804 and 1815, were published by J. Harris.

characteristics. This was the child of over-indulgent parents – such children, boys in particular, were shown as being ill-tempered, tyranical, demanding, passionate, lazy, duplicitous, cruel to animals, rude to servants, ungrateful and cowardly, yet whose every wish is granted and who is forgiven every time he misbehaves. In short, he is a boy who can do no wrong, at least as far as his mother, who is usually the parent at fault, is concerned.

An early exemplar of this trope was *The History of Tommy Playlove and Jacky Lovebook, wherein is shewn the superiority of virtue over vice, however dignified by birth or fortune*, first published by E. Newbery in 1783.[30] Tommy Playlove has been brought up by Lady Playlove, a rich widow, to expect anything he asks for and never to be punished. When he had reached the age of eight, Lady Playlove employed a private tutor, who soon resigned because of Tommy's refusal to co-operate. A boarding school was out of the question, as Lady Playlove would not be parted from her son. Accordingly, she tries to get him admitted to Westminster School nearby, but only with the provisos that he will not be beaten and that he starts school at ten o'clock in the morning.

Not surprisingly, admission is refused and Tommy ends up going to a small private school under a Dr Syntax, who is as indulgent to his pupils as their parents are, and is generally unconcerned as to whether they do any work or not. There, Tommy befriends Bill Wilful, an obstinate and uncontrollable boy, Tom Hardy, who is bold and daring, Bobby Scapegrace, an accomplished thief, Dick Funny, described as an arch, sly rogue, and Ned Slippery, an idle blockhead. He also, for ulterior motives, makes a friend of Jacky Lovebook, who is adept at Latin and French and helps Tommy with his exercises. Jacky, of course, is the antithesis of Tommy – God-fearing, hardworking, honest and obedient and, when Lady Playlove learns of his character, she is anxious that he should visit Tommy at home as much as possible. Jacky is initially reluctant, but agrees and spends an eventful and eventually pleasant afternoon with Tommy while Lady Playlove is away. However, after the two boys have parted, Tommy falls in with his other friends and they indulge in a spree of mischief, until they are caught by two servants and severely horsewhipped. Later that night, Tommy has a vision, being visited by Wisdom, the son of Experience, who lectures him and urges him to make a true friend of Lovebook. Thus begins Tommy's repentance and reformation.

---

30. It was reprinted in 1788, 1789, 1793 and 1800, with a fifth reprint, by J. Lumsden of Glasgow, appearing in 1819.

Early Boys' School Stories – Common Themes

The first, full-length, eighteenth-century school story to be set in a real school was the anonymous *The Fortunate Blue-Coat Boy; or, Memoirs of the Life and Happy Adventures of Mr Benjamin Templeman, Formerly a Scholar in Christ's Hospital*, by 'An Orphanotrophian', published in 1770 in two volumes by J. Cooke.[31] This was set in the 1720s and, while the author is unknown, he clearly wrote from experience, as many of the novel's characters have been shown to be based on real people.

The story follows the school career of Ben Templeman, sent to Christ's Hospital in London at the age of nine following the death of his father and being placed in the Writing School. Having learnt a little writing, Latin and arithmetic from his father, he progresses quickly, but is high-spirited and anxious to get into the King's Ward, which prepares boys for a career in the navy. He is described as a dab hand at 'marbles, chuck, huzzle-cap, jumping' and other games, but is an inveterate rule-breaker, often caught misbehaving in church and leaving the school without permission. He is, therefore, well-known to the steward, Mr Henchman, who is responsible for punishments. As a senior, and after having achieved his ambition of entering the King's Ward (the school authorities having decided that he is only fit for a life at sea), he is spotted by a rich, young, city widow on a visit to the school, who is attracted by his singing voice. She rapidly falls in love with him, offers her hand in marriage and transforms him into a young gentleman.

While the story is highly improbable – it was described as 'arrant make-believe' by Reginald Watters in its 1987 reissue – it does paint a vivid and authentic picture of school and London life in the early eighteenth century. The perils of school life are far from glossed over – Ben is shown to be an unscrupulous moneylender, extracting extortionate rates of interest, and being severely thrashed by the steward for it. As the author claims:

> in all great schools, you will find the same fraud and deceit, treachery and tricking carried on among the boys, in all their little bargains, as you will among the trading part of mankind; and in their gaming, as much gambling, as you may behold, either at White's or Newmarket, with this difference only, that

---

31. A second edition appeared from publishers, A. Millar, W. Law & R. Cater and Wilson & Spence of York, in 1789. It was later reissued, with a lengthy introduction and notes by Reginald Watters, by Christ's Hospital in 1987.

the one is for marbles, or at the most for a few pence, but the other too often for whole estates; and that both become ruined in the end by sharpers.[32]

Both lending and borrowing is condemned – the even-handed steward, having thrashed Ben for his greed and charging such a high rate of interest that a loan of one penny has become a debt of half a crown, insists that Ben's victim should pay the full debt, observing that 'if he made such foolish bargains he ought in justice to make them good'. Ben does, however, have his good points. He is a good scholar and much liked by his master – and, of course, in spite of his faults, he ends up on top.

The novel was reprinted only once prior to 1987 and, presumably, had only a limited readership. The author recognised this in an opening statement, addressed to 'The Gentlemen who have been, are, or may be, educated in Christ's Hospital'. His readership would also have been restricted as a result of its critical reception – one review suggested that its dialogues, between working-class characters, such as the steward and a porter, would not appeal 'to readers of a higher class'.[33]

* * *

Several school stories appeared in *Entertaining Memoirs of Little Personages, or Moral Amusements for Young Gentlemen*, published by W. Tringham and comprising short tales from his *Lilliputian Magazine; or, Children's Repository*, first issued in 1773. (As noted above, there was also a companion volume for girls.) The stories all tell the story of a boy from the age of around seven or eight to around fifteen, each having a name signalling their character, with each story encompassing a moral lesson.

Billy, in *The History of Billy Trifler*, is indulged by his parents, who are always buying him toys but never insist on him learning to read. However, he decides on his own account to learn to read after catching a butterfly and asking questions about it of his father, who satisfies his curiosity but tells him that, if he learnt to read, he could learn a lot more. After some thought, Billy says that he will give away all his toys if he can go to school and, after having his wish granted, turns out to be a quick learner and soon becomes the school's best scholar. Nevertheless, education is not just about classroom lessons – he learns a particular

---

32. Watters (Christ's Hospital), p. 9.
33. *The Critical Review: or Annals of Literature*, Vol. 29 (1770).

lesson when he becomes trapped in a hollow tree whilst attacking nesting birds. He also earns the mockery of his schoolfellows after falling into a pond whilst chasing a butterfly. As his father told him after he fell into the pond, 'all that glitters is not gold'.

Another quick learner is Simon in *Simple Simon's History*, the only child of a member of an old and distinguished family. Sent to school, he is soon a favourite of the master, being obedient, trusting and respectful. When he is encouraged to rob an orchard and to bring apples back to his schoolfellows, he refuses his own share, saying that there are plenty of apples in his father's garden and leaves the boys to divide the spoils amongst themselves. Unfortunately, he was spotted in the orchard and the farmer arrives at the school, catches the boys in the act of dividing the apples, and horsewhips them. When the master finds out, Simon, after he explains what had happened, is let off and the boys punished again. He is later coerced by the farmer's son into riding a bull. When the bull bolts, the son tells his father that Simon has stolen it. Simon then realises that he should not accept things at face value and he grows up to be more serious. The moral of the story is that, while simplicity is a virtue, it should not stand in the way of keeping a good name.

The risks involved in playing truant and lying are explored in *The Truant*, although the story begins with a brief sermon on idleness and the importance of education. The author, however, goes on to recognise that children are not all alike, that 'some are more capable at ten years, than others are at fourteen' and goes on to refer to Alexander Pope and Jonathan Swift, one an excellent writer whilst at school and the other a dunce.

The story itself revolves around Master Playful, the son of a rich businessman in the country. Sent to a day school in a nearby market town, he is initially a good scholar but he soon begins to play truant, arriving at school later and later, all the time inventing ingenious excuses which the master takes at face value. Thus, he commits two faults – playing truant and lying. He is at last caught out when his father visits the school unexpectedly and is surprised not to find his son there. When Master Playful eventually turns up, he makes his usual untruthful excuse, only for his father to reveal himself and his lie is exposed. He is subsequently severely flogged and as a result reforms his behaviour. He becomes one of the best scholars in the school and in later life a successful merchant.

The archetypal schoolboy dilemma of telling or not telling the truth is explored in *The History of Master Trueworth, Commonly Called Tommy Telltruth*. Tommy is born to the second wife of a retired and rich businessman and his first ever words are 'Tell truth!' When the bootboy is late and trying to think of an excuse, Tommy says 'Tell truth!' and the bootboy confesses. This has an immediate effect on all the other servants. When Tommy is sent to school, he keeps to the precept of truth-telling and urges his schoolfellows to do the same. Some, who habitually tell lies, pretend to respect him, but this 'was more out of fear than love.'

One of his enemies, Timothy Tearbook, who is incorrigibly bad and idle and who is frequently punished, determines to bring Tommy into disgrace. He takes his opportunity when Tommy, who is allowed to stay in the school at playtime to learn his lessons, decides to go out for some exercise, and Timothy sneaks into the classroom and tears all the boys' books, blots their writing and rubs out the sums on their slates. When the boys return, they find that the only pupil whose possessions have not been damaged is Tommy. The master is only half inclined to believe the boy's protestations of innocence, at which point Tommy bursts into tears and urges every boy to tell the truth. The master questions each boy individually. Timothy becomes flustered, thereby giving away his guilt, and tries to run away, only to find that the master has locked the door. After confessing, he is spared physical punishment but expelled, 'his master being determined to have no such wicked boys in the school, for fear they might corrupt others'.

Tommy grows up to be a successful businessman, knighted and made lord mayor, the moral of the story being that telling the truth can lead to great things.

A fifth school story in *Entertaining Memoirs* is an implicit condemnation of servants who tell children ghosts stories. The hero of *Francis Fearful* is the only son of a retired businessman and his wife, who have been content to leave their son in the care of a nurse, who is also his tutor. She is very fond of telling Francis stories, especially those concerning ghosts, witches and hobgoblins. Unfortunately, Francis takes all these at face value and becomes very timorous, refusing to go anywhere after dark without someone with him. When he is sent to school, he learns quickly and his schoolfellows are unaware of his disposition, until a bat flies out of the chimney and Frank has hysterics, claiming he has seen a spirit. He immediately becomes a laughing stock. Several days later he comes across a bird scarer in a tree, which he takes to be a ghost. His master has to prove to him that it is no such thing and, concerned as to Francis' timidity, tells his father. When the source of this – the nurse – is discovered, she is dismissed. The story ends with the father acknowledging to himself that he should have been more involved in his son's upbringing, and that care is needed when parents entrust their children to someone else, as what they take in as infants they can often carry to the grave.

* * *

A key theme in school stories is friendship, with one of the first school stories to focus on this being the anonymous *The Friends; or, The History of Billy Freeman and Tommy Truelove*, first published by J. & J. Robertson (Glasgow) in 1777.[34] Billy Freeman is the son of a retired merchant, who, at the age of four, is unable to read, his father having been unable to persuade him to learn. Billy meets a gentleman who, on learning that he cannot read, offers him books as a reward for learning. So Billy gets his father to teach him and he later starts attending the academy kept by Mr Allworthy. There he becomes friendly with Tommy Truelove, the school's best scholar. Both become popular with their schoolfellows, 'spending their vacant time in reading some instructive story' to them. (This prompted the journalist and essayist William Caldwell Roscoe to remark, 'What shocking prigs the whole set would have appeared in the eyes of a modern schoolboy.'[35]) After a few of these stories are told, the two boys go to sea, are captured and sold as slaves, resist the urge to commit suicide, are rescued by Indians, and eventually return home to their grateful families. The story ends with a long essay on friendship.

* * *

Punishment was, not surprisingly, a key feature of many school stories, with one particularly novel form, mentioned in at least two late eighteenth-century school stories, that of a boy having a log tied to his leg in order to immobilise him. One occurrence was in Rev. George Burder's *The Entertaining History of Master Billy and Miss Betsey Goodchild*, a short story in his *Early Piety; or, Memoirs of Children Eminently Religious*, published by H. Trapp in 1777. This is also one of the very first overtly religious school stories. Bill and Betsey are sent to a preparatory boarding school under Mrs Lovegood, who is very pious and who encourages the children to be diligent in reading their Bible, in learning their catechism and giving a good account of the sermons they hear on a Sunday in church. Over the Christmas holidays, on Twelfth Day, various friends

---

34. Its full title was *The Friends; or, The History of Billy Freeman and Tommy Truelove, Proper to Be Imitated by all Those Who Desire to Be Good and Great*.
35. 'Fictions for Children' in *The Prospective Review*, February 1855.

come and see Billy and Betsey before they go back to school and, instead of playing games, they are encouraged to tell stories. One story is about Jack Perverse, who is sent to a good school but is a dunce – he is always in trouble, cruel, plays truant to avoid punishment and, when he is caught, he is flogged and 'a heavy log was also fastened to his leg, and a great fool's cap put upon his head; so that he became the sport and derision of all that beheld him'. The master continually reminds Jack that the purpose of going to school is to gain useful knowledge. His behaviour is equally as bad at home – eventually, in a forerunner of the fate of bad characters in later stories, he and a friend drown in a river.

Several more punishments are vividly described in Dorothy Kilner's *The Village School; or, A Collection of Entertaining Histories for the Instruction and Amusement of All Good Children*, first published in two volumes by J. Marshall in 1783.[36] This is set in a small school of some 20 children kept by a Mrs Bell and is little more than a litany of bad behaviour and harsh discipline, interspersed with short moral tales read by the children. In volume one, two girls are punished for playing with toys after being told not to, a boy deliberately kicks a two year-old in the face and, after being severely caned by Mrs Bell, has his hands and feet tied together and is locked in a closet for the night. Two boys are punished by their fathers after being sent home for fighting and other similar punishments follow, including one boy who is 'horsewhipped all the way home through the village' by his father.

At the beginning of volume two a boy is punished after being caught persuading another boy to sell his watch and tell a lie that he lost it. The boy's father regales his son with a story of a series of vicious punishments handed out to a boy he once knew – flogged with a rod fashioned out of twigs from a hedge, whipped by Mrs Bell and denied entry to his home before bedtime for a month (surely an incitement to further misbehaviour). Nonetheless, the boy's conduct goes from bad to worse – he is forever telling lies and getting found out, until ultimately his parents refuse to believe anything he tells them. When he is run over by a horse and cart, his insistence that he is seriously hurt is not taken seriously until it is too late and he dies. Another boy is about to be sent away by his father to work in a Cornish tin mine but, before he leaves the school, he is locked in a closet with no food. Finally, in a rather abrupt ending, Mrs Bell perishes when her cottage goes up in flames.

---

36. The exact publication date is uncertain. It was originally published under the pseudonym 'M.P.', i.e. Mary Pelham. There were at least two subsequent editions in one volume published by J. Harris in 1828 and 1831.

It is difficult to see that children reading *The Village School* would have garnered much in the way of enjoyment or amusement from it, other than, perhaps, a degree of schadenfreude as a result of all the punishments portrayed. The story is full of moral lessons, in particular, the consequences that can arise from telling lies, refusing to learn and ignoring adult guidance. The point is also made that the behaviour of children is not linked to class or their station in life. The school's pupils come from a wide range of backgrounds, and the better-off children are just as likely to behave badly as those that are poor.

* * *

What may have been the first appearance of Eton in children's fiction was contained in a very short character sketch in volume two of Thomas Percival's *A Father's Instructions: Consisting of Moral Tales, Fables and Reflections*, first published by Robert Dodsley in 1777. Under the heading, *Habits of Sensuality May Be Formed in Early Youth*, a sorry picture is painted of Florio and Alonzo, inseparable companions who are 'profusely supplied with money by their too indulgent parents', which they spend on food rather than books. Florio, with a poor digestion, will only eat food 'such as afforded the most savoury and exquisite relish' and soon becomes pale and emaciated. On the other hand, Alonzo becomes 'lusty and corpulent' and dies of apoplexy at the age of 30. Why the author, who was a physician and health reformer, chose Eton as Florio's and Alonzo's school is a mystery, unless it was a subtle dig at the aristocracy.

Food was also at the centre of *The Three Cakes*, a short story which first appeared in the fourth volume of Anna Laetitia Barbauld's *Lessons for Children*, published by J. Johnson in 1779. Barbauld (1743–1825) (born Ann Laetitia Aikin) was a prolific children's author, poet, essayist, educationalist and literary critic. *Lessons for Children* was a series of four books aimed at very young children (two to four years old) and depicts a mother teaching her son. It was written for her and her husband's adopted child (and her nephew), Charles. *The Three Cakes* was subsequently rewritten and expanded (it is not known by whom) and published by Whitrow & Co. in 1792.

The story is set in a boys' boarding school and tells of three boys and what happens when they each receive a cake from home. Henry, who receives a cake after winning a prize, eats it very quickly, and consequently becomes seriously ill. Francis receives a cake after writing a perfect letter to his mother – he keeps the cake to himself, eating small pieces at a time, but after a week the remains of the cake become dry and then mouldy and he has to throw it away. The third cake is sent to

Gratian, for no other reason than that his mother loves him. Gratian chooses to share it with his friends, but decides to save his piece until the following day. While the boys are playing shortly afterwards, a blind beggar enters the schoolyard and entertains the boys with tunes on his fiddle. When Gratian sees that he is weeping, he asks him what is making him weep, and the old man replies that he is hungry. Gratian weeps also and then rushes and gets his piece of cake, which he gives to the beggar.

The story ends there. There is no moralising, no concluding statement, the author being quite content to let the three contrasting stories speak for themselves.

* * *

Most early school stories were educational in some way, imparting moral and occasionally practical lessons, some more overtly than others. One of the most explicit examples of a boys' school story aimed at instruction was *School Dialogues for Boys, Being an Attempt to Convey Instruction to Their Tender Minds, and Instill the Love of Virtue*, written by 'A Lady' (i.e. Ellenor Fenn) and published, in two volumes, by John Marshall in 1783. *School Dialogues* was written, as explained in an 'Address to the Reader', 'for one particular boy, who is on the point of emerging ... into that LITTLE WORLD, a SCHOOL ... with a view to fortify him against the contagion of bad example'. Yet, while most of the dialogues that follow are clearly aimed at boys, some are aimed at parents, containing anecdotes about faulty mothers and nursery maids, and boys who are indulged too much.

The *Critical Review* summed up its contents succinctly:

> Some of the principal topics, which form these Dialogues, are cautions to new scholars, ready obedience, encouragement to a diligent application, docility, piety, progress in learning, neatness, pleasure of obliging, importance of seeming trifles, forgiveness, brotherly affection, transgressing bounds, pride, false modesty, danger of too easy compliance, incitement to industry, oeconomy, riots, behaviour at church, punishments, rewards, &c.[37]

All the characters are given allegorical names: the masters are Mr Aweful, Mr Wiseman, Mr Sage and Mr Straight, and the boys include Sensible (Head Boy), Worthy (Second Boy), Goodwill, Careful, Haughty,

---

37. *The Critical Review*, June 1784, pp. 480–81.

Sneer, Flippant, Spiteful, Gentle, Sly and Meek. The dialogues themselves are either rather bland, or excessively flowery, giving the impression it is how the author would like boys to speak rather than how they actually speak. As the *Monthly Review* (July 1784) put it: '[These dialogues] contain a great deal of good advice; but it is delivered with somewhat too much sententious formality to suit the characters of the piece.' Nevertheless, the *Monthly Review* felt that the book 'is not without merit. The incidents, if not interesting, are natural, the language is easy, tolerably correct, and the moral is always good.' The *Critical Review* was of the opinion, arguably misguided, that: 'Boys will listen to the conversation of boys, and receive their decisions without prejudice or suspicion.'[38]

Dorothy Kilner's sister-in-law, Mary Ann Kilner (1753–1831) was less concerrned with imparting moral lessons than showing how children could improve their general behaviour whilst also being entertaining. She was most famous for *The Adventures of a Pin Cushion* (first published in 1782), closely followed by *Memoirs of a Peg-Top*, first published (anonymously) by John Marshall in around 1785. These were amongst the first books for children in which the hero, and narrator, was an inanimate object. The aim, of both books, as explained in the author's preface to *Memoirs of a Peg-Top*, was 'to promote the cause of virtue, and to blend the hints of instruction with incidents of an amusing nature'.

The peg-top is bought by ten-year-old Henry, who is sent off to boarding school with a series of admonitions from his mother – ignore boys who laugh at his devotion to God, always tell the truth, do not give in to temptation and do not fight. When he arrives at school, he is ridiculed for not understanding the concept of boys being called by their surnames, rather than 'master' or 'sir'. The top then passes to fourteen-year-old Frank, who is 'sprightly and active, and esteemed by his companions one of the cleverest boys in the school'. He is certainly clever and the envy of his schoolfellows, but he is also loved and respected by them because of his good nature and honesty. Admired, too, by the

---

38. In a completely different vein was *Letters from a Tutor to His Pupils*, written by William Jones and published by G. Robinson in 1780. This was part of the tradition of improving literature, designed to instruct, rather than entertain, through the format of letters and lectures, also found in books for girls. It was, according to the author, based on the conversations he had had with his own pupils and published for the benefit of other boys, although how much of the author's turgid prose readers will have appreciated is a moot point.

master, he is in charge of distributing the weekly pocket money to some of the boys. One of the boys, Jack, subsequently unknowingly drops a sixpence and accuses Frank of cheating him. When he finds the coin, rather than admit his mistake he slips it into Frank's pocket, where it is discovered, and, although Frank protests his innocence, he is told he is guilty of deceit, lying and fraud, and confined to a punishment room. His toys, including his top, are confiscated, and they join several other confiscated toys. Frank is subsequently vindicated after the master overhears Jack boasting of his deceit to a friend, and Jack is flogged and deprived of his pocket money.

The top is later exchanged for a bat and ball, the new owner being Ben. He thinks little of his studies and is behind boys who are three years younger than him, but he is a leader when it comes to games. When Ben breaks a glass belonging to a gardener, the top is taken from him and thrown into the fire by the Master (luckily it survives) – meanwhile, Ben is given a long lecture on the consequences of not learning. The top is then returned to him, but later falls through a hole in his pocket, and is picked up by the baker's boy. The rest of the story concerns the top's adventures elsewhere.

* * *

By 1785, the school story had become established as a distinct literary genre, although for the most part early school stories were very different from those by which the genre is recognised today. Many pre-1785 school stories were strongly didactic, imparting moral lessons and revealing little about school life. This soon began to change, with schools quickly becoming a fertile environment for exploring themes such as friendship and rivalry, honesty and dishonesty, tale-telling, disobedience, indolence, cheating, cruelty and bullying. Boarding schools, in particular, became a popular setting, although it took until the second half of the nineteenth century for the boarding school story to become dominant, with its emphasis on sport and sporting rivalry, hierarchy, customs, and its focus on the life of the school and its organisation playing a vital role. This was buttressed by its exploration of the schoolboy code – manliness, honesty, sportsmanship, chivalry and loyalty – exemplified by Thomas Hughes' *Tom Brown's Schooldays*, first published in 1857. Indeed, for a long time it was assumed that *Tom Brown's Schooldays* was the very first boys' school story but, as has been shown, this was far from the case.

The years between 1785 and 1857 saw a rapid growth in the number of school stories, both for boys and girls, and an expansion of their ambition, in terms of narrative and the issues they explored. Some writers were trenchant critics of schools – some writers for girls condemned the 'genteel' education offered by some private girls' schools, with their emphasis on deportment, manners, dancing and dress, seen as nothing more than preparation for marriage; and some writers of boys' school stories exposed the iniquities of the fagging system, bullying, the exercising of prefectorial power, harsh punishments and the curriculum. (One notable critic was Charles Dickens, who has been almost wholly neglected in previous studies of the school story but who, while never writing a full-length school novel, created some of fiction's most memorable schools – Dotheboys Hall, Salem House – and schoolmasters – Wackford Squeers, Mr Creakle, Thomas Gradgrind and Mr M'Choakumchild.)

However, these later stories must remain the subject of a future study. This book has the sole purpose of showing how the school story was born, out of early teaching aids, translation exercises, stage plays, and explorations of education outside school, ending wth the gradual establishment of the school story as its own distinctive category of children's literature.

Further Reading

Adams, Gillian, 'Ancient and Medieval Children's Texts', in Peter Hunt (ed.), *International Companion Encyclopedia of Children's Literature* (London: Routledge, 2004)
Adams, Gillian, 'The First Children's Literature? The Case for Sumer', *Children's Literature* 14 (1986), 1–30
Avery, Gillian, *Childhood's Pattern: A Study of the Heroes and Heroines of Children's Fiction, 1770–1950* (London: Hodder & Stoughton, 1975)
Avery, Gillian, *Nineteenth Century Children: Heroes and Heroines in English Children's Stories, 1780–1900* (London: Hodder & Stoughton, 1965)
Barney, Richard A., *Plots of Enlightenment: Education and the Novel in Eighteenth-Century England* (Stanford, CA: Stanford University Press, 1999)
Barry, Florence V., *A Century of Children's Books* (London: Methuen & Co., 1922)
Bingham, Jane, and Grayce Scholt, *Fifteen Centuries of Children's Literature: An Annotated Chronology of British and American Works in Historical Context* (Westport, CT: Greenwood Press, 1980)
Clark, Beverly Lyon, *Regendering the School Story: Sassy Sissies and Tattling Tomboys* (New York, NY, and London: Routledge, 1996)
Colgrave, Bertram, 'Dobson's Drie Bobs', *Durham University Journal* 43, no. 3 (New Series 12, no. 3) (June 1951)
Cooper, Helen, *Oxford Guides to Chaucer: The Canterbury Tales* (Oxford: Oxford University Press, 1989)
Cribiore, Raffaella, *Gymnastics of the Mind: Greek Education in Hellenistic and Roman Egypt* (Princeton, NJ: Princeton University Press, 2001)
Darton, F.J. Harvey, *Children's Books in England: Five Centuries of Social Life* (Cambridge: Cambridge University Press, 1932; 3rd edn, rev. Brian Alderson, 1982)
Erasmus, *The Colloquies of Erasmus*, trans. N. Bailey (London: Reeves & Turner, 1878)
Erasmus, Desiderius, *Colloquies*, trans. Craig R. Thompson, Collected Words of Erasmus, Vols 39–40 (Toronto: University of Toronto Press, 1997)

Erman, Adolf (ed.), *The Ancient Egyptians: A Sourcebook of Their Writings* (New York, NY: Harper & Row, 1966) (Originally published in Germany, 1923)

Erman, Adolf, (ed.), *Life in Ancient Egypt*, trans. H.M. Tirard (London: Macmillan, 1894)

Field, E.M., *The Child and His Book: Some Account of the History and Progress of Children's Literature in England* (London: Wells Gardner, Darton & Co., 1891)

Friedman, Albert, 'The Prioress's Tale and Chaucer's Anti-Semitism', *Chaucer Review* 9 (1974), 118–29

Gardiner, Alan H., *Egyptian Hieratic Papyri: Series I: Literary Texts of the New Kingdom: Part I* (Leipzig: J.C. Hinrichs'sche Buchhandlung, 1911)

Garmonsway, G.N. (ed.), *Aelfric's Colloquy*, Exeter Medieval Texts and Studies Series, rev. edn (Liverpool: Liverpool University Press, 1991)

Gem, S. Harvey, *An Anglo-Saxon Abbot: Aelfric of Eynsham* (Edinburgh: T. & T. Clark, 1912)

Goldstone, Bette P., *Lessons to be Learned: A Study of Eighteenth Century English Didactic Children's Literature* (New York, NY: Peter Lang, 1984)

Grantley, Darryll, *Wit's Pilgrimage: Drama and the Social Impact of Education in Early Modern England* (Aldershot: Ashgate, 2000)

Grisbrooke-Campbell, Gulliver, 'Aelfric Bata's *Colloquia*: Reassessing an Eleventh-Century Latin Textbook' (unpublished MA thesis, University of Wales, Trinity Saint David, 2021)

Gwara, Scott, (ed.) and David W. Porter (trans.), *Anglo-Saxon Conversations: The Colloquies of Aelfric Bata* (Woodbridge: Boydell Press, 1997)

Herodas, *The Mimes and Fragments*, with notes by Walter Headlam, ed. A.D. Knox (Cambridge: Cambridge University Press, 1922)

Herren, Michael, *The Hisperica Famina: 1. The A-Text* (Toronto: Pontifical Institute of Medieval Studies, 1974)

Hilton, Mary, Morag Styles and Victor Watson (eds), *Opening the Nursery Door: Reading, Writing and Childhood, 1600–1900* (London: Routledge, 1997)

Hollyband, Claudius, and Peter Erondell, *The Elizabethan Home: Discovered in Two Dialogues*, ed. M. St Clare Byrne (London: Frederick Etchells & Hugh Macdonald, 1925; rev. edn, London: Methuen & Co., 1949)

Hope, Ascott R., *A Book about Schools, Schoolboys, Schoolmasters and Schoolbooks* (London: A. & C. Black, 1925)

Hoppit, Julian, *A Land of Liberty? England 1689–1727* (Oxford: Oxford University Press, 2000)

Hürlimann, Bettina, *Three Centuries of Children's Books in Europe* (Oxford: Oxford University Press, 1967)

Irving, Washington, *The Life of Oliver Goldsmith* (New York, NY: Harper & Brothers, 1840)

Jackson, Mary V., *Engines of Instruction, Mischief, and Magic: Children's Literature in England from Its Beginnings to 1839* (Lincoln, NE: University of Nebraska Press, 1989)

Kirkpatrick, Robert J., *Bullies, Beaks and Flannelled Fools: An Annotated Bibliography of Boys' School Fiction, 1742–2000* (1st edn published by the author, 1990; 2nd rev. edn, expanded and updated, 2001)

Kirkpatrick, Robert J., *The Encyclopaedia of Boys' School Stories* (Aldershot: Ashgate, 2000)

Kramer, Samuel Noah, *History Begins at Sumer: Thirty-Nine Firsts in Recorded History* (London: Thames & Hudson, 1958)

Kramer, Samuel Noah, *The Sumerians: Their History, Culture, and Character* (Chicago, IL: University of Chicago Press, 1963)

Lapidge, Michael, 'Aelfric's Schooldays', in S. Rosser and E. Treharne (eds), *Early Medieval English Texts: Studies Presented to Donald G. Scragg*, Medieval and Renaissance Texts and Studies Series, Volume 252 (Tempe: Arizona Centre for Medieval and Renaissance Studies, 2003)

MacDonald, Ruth K., *Literature for Children in England and America from 1646 to 1774* (Troy, NY: Whitston Pub. Co., 1982)

Mack, Edward C., *Public Schools and British Opinion, 1780–1860* (London: Methuen & Co., 1938)

Manly, John Matthews, *Some New Light on Chaucer: Lectures Delivered at the Lowell Institute* (Gloucester, MA: Henry Holt & Co., 1926)

Marks, Sylvia Kasey, *Writing for the Rising Generation: British Fiction for Young People 1672–1839*, English Literary Studies Monograph (Victoria, BC: University of Victoria, 2018)

Marrou, Henri, *A History of Education in Antiquity*, trans. George Lamb (London: Sheed & Ward, 1956)

Meigs, Cornelia, Anne Eaton, Elizabeth Nesbitt, Ruth Hill Viguers and Vera Bock, *A Critical History of Children's Literature: A Survey of Children's Books in English from Earliest Times to the Present, Prepared in Four Parts under the Editorship of Cornelia Meigs* (New York, NY: Macmillan, 1953)

Motter, T.H. Vail, *The School Drama in England* (London: Longmans, Green & Co., 1929)

Muir, Percy, *English Children's Books 1600–1900* (London: B.T. Batsford, 1954)

Nelson, William (ed.), *A Fifteenth Century School Book: From a Manuscript in the British Museum (Ms. Arundel 249)* (Oxford: Clarendon Press, 1956)

O'Brien, Avril S., 'Dobsons Drie Bobbes: A Significant Contribution to the Development of Prose Fiction', *Studies in English Literature, 1500–1900* 12, no. 1 (Winter 1972), 55–70

Orme, Nicholas, *Education and Society in Medieval and Renaissance England* (London: Hambledon Press, 1989)

Orme, Nicholas, *English School Exercises, 1420–1530* (Toronto, ON: Pontifical Institute of Medieval Studies, 2013)

Orme, Nicholas, *English Schools in the Middle Ages* (London: Methuen, 1973)

Orme, Nicholas, *Medieval Schools: From Roman Britain to Renaissance England* (New Haven, CT: Yale University Press, 2006)

Patterson, Sylvia W., *Rousseau's Émile and Early Children's Literature* (Metuchen, NJ: The Scarecrow Press, 1971)

Pickering, Samuel F., *John Locke and Children's Books in Eighteenth-Century England* (Knoxville: University of Tennessee Press, 1981)
Pickering, Samuel F., *Moral Instruction and Fiction for Children, 1749–1820* (Athens: University of Georgia Press, 1995)
Potter, Ursula, 'Pedagogy and Parenting in English Drama, 1560–1610' (PhD thesis, University of Sydney, 2001)
Protherough, Robert, 'The Figure of the Teacher in English Literature 1740–1918' (unpublished doctoral thesis, University of Hull, 1980)
Roscoe, S., *John Newbery and His Successors, 1740–1814* (Wormley: Five Owls Press, 1973)
Sill, Geoffrey, (ed.), *Satire, Fantasy and Writings on the Supernatural by Daniel Defoe* (London: Pickering & Chatto, 2003), Volume 3
Sullivan, Paul Vincent, '*Ludi Magister*: The Play of Tudor School and Stage' (PhD dissertation, University of Texas, 2005)
Swanton, Michael (ed. and trans.), *Anglo-Saxon Prose* (London: J.M. Dent & Sons, 1975)
Thwaite, Mary, *From Primer to Pleasure in Reading: An Introduction to the History of Children's Books in England from the Invention of Printing to 1914, With an Outline of Some Developments in Other Countries*, 2nd edn (London: Library Association Publishing, 1972)
Townsend, John Rowe, *Trade and Plumb-Cake for Ever, Huzza! The Life and Work of John Newbery, 1713–1767, Publisher and Bookseller* (Cambridge: Colt Books, 1994)
Tracy, James D., *Erasmus of the Low Countries* (Berkeley: University of California Press, 1966)
Walker, Jonathan, and Paul D. Streufert (eds), *Early Modern Academic Drama* (Farnham: Ashgate, 2008)
Watson, Foster, *Tudor School-Boy Life: The Dialogues of Juan Luis Vives* (London: J.M. Dent & Co., 1908)
Weedon, M.J.P., 'Richard Johnson and the Successors to John Newbery', *Transactions of the Bibliographical Society*, 5th series, vol. 4 (1949), 37 and 59
Whalley, Joyce Irene, *Cobwebs to Catch Flies: Illustrated Books for the Nursery and Schoolroom, 1700–1900* (London: Elek Books, 1974)
White, Beatrice (ed.), *The Vulgaria of John Stanbridge and the Vulgaria of Robert Whittinton* (London: Kegan Paul, Trench, Trubner & Co., 1932)
Zitter, Emmy Stark, 'Anti-Semitism in Chaucer's *Prioress's Tale*', *Chaucer Review* 25, no. 4 (1991), 277–84

Index

Adams, Gillian, 5(n1), 6(n3), 9, 10
Adventures of a Pin Cushion, The, 220
Adventures of David Simple, The, 154-155
Adventures of Peregrine Pickle, The, 159-163
Adventures of Roderick Random, The, 156-159
Adventures of Tommy Two-Shoes, The, 200
Aelfric, 21-24
Aelfric Bata, 24-30
Aelfric's Colloquy, 21-24
Aitken, Dr John, 209
Allen, Charles, 195
Anastasi Papyrus, 11(n13), 11(n15)
Anglo-Saxon Conversations: The Colloquies of Aelfric Bata, 26-30
Animals, cruelty to, 182, 204, 207, 211
Ankwyll, John, 39, 42
Apollo Shroving, 107-109
Austen Jane, 119

Babees Book, The, 194
Bacchides (The Two Bacchises), 16
Barbauld, Mrs Anna Laetitia, 209, 218
Bede, 19
Beer (and wine etc.), 23, 25, 28, 113, 126, 163, 173
Bellot, Jacques, 60
Best, Thomas W., 86(n23)
Bingham, Jane, 191

Boarding School, or The Sham Captain, 114
Boke of Nurture, The, 194
Book of Curtesye, The, 194
Bookseller of the Last Century, Being Some Account of the Life of John Newbery, A, 205(n22)
Brimley, John, 130
Brinsley, John, 66, 73, 96-97
Brooke, Henry, 177
Brothels, 16, 85-86, 91, 173
Burder, Rev. George, 216
Busby, Richard, 55(n45)
Byrne, Muriel St Clair, 61

Chaucer, 31-37
Camp di Fior, 61
Campbell, John (Duke of Argyll), 135
Canterbury Tales, The, 31
Carnan, Thomas, 202
Chapman, George, 106
Charles Spencer (Earl of Sunderland), 136
Chaste Maid in Cheapside, A, 107
Children of St Paul's, 78(n9)
Children of the Chapel, 78(n9)
Children of the Revels, 87
Children's Books in England: Five Centuries of Social Life, 190
Children's Talk, English and Latin, 68(n73)
Churchill, John (Duke of Marlborough), 134-135
Cibber, Colley, 109

Clarke, John, 73
Clothes, 28, 47, 62, 127
Coffey, Charles, 114
Colgrave, Bertram, 123
Colloquirum Scholasticorum, 73
Comedy of Errors, A, 100-101
Cooke, Joshua, 99
Corderius, Mathurin, 73
Coventry, Francis, 172
Cribiore, Raffaella, 18(n24)

d'Urfey, Thomas, 114
Darton, F.J. Harvey, 190
Dawson, Giles, 94
Day, Thomas, 181-182
de Beaumont, Mme Jeanne-Marie Leprince, 196
De Raris Fabulis, 20-21
Death, 37, 191
  murder, 35
  execution, 86, 91, 94, 152
  accident, 206, 217
  ill-health/disease, 44, 47, 113, 218
Defoe, Daniel, 132
Deserted Village, The, 199
Dickens, Charles, 42(n13), 118(n91), 169, 222
Discipline, see Punishment
Disgraced Page, The, 144-145
Dishonesty, 29, 208
Disobedient Child, The, 87
Dobsons Drie Bobbes, 122-131
Drury, John, 39
Durham Cathedral School, 122, 129-130

Early Piety, or Memoirs of Children Eminently Religious, 216
Edgeworth, Maria, 188
Edgeworth, Richard Lovell, 176
Education and Society in Medieval and Renaissance England, 38-39
Education, attitudes to and criticism of, 77, 190, 107, 115-116, 117-118, 149-150, 167, 170, 185-186
Egypt, schools in Ancient 10-11
Egyptian Hieratic Papyri, 11(n14)
Elizabethan Home: Discovered in Two Dialogues, The, 61
Elliott, Mary, 200

Émile, ou de l'education, 174-176
English Schoolmaster, The, 61
English School Exercises, 1420-1530, 40, 45(n22)
English Schools in the Middle Ages, 79(10)
Entertaining History of Master Billy and Miss Betsey Goodchild, The, 216
Entertaining Memoirs of Little Personages, or Moral Amusements for Young Gentlemen, 213
Entertaining Memoirs of Little Personages, or Moral Amusements for Young Ladies, 200
Erasmus of the Low Countries, 51(n38)
Erasmus, Desiderius, 51
Erman, Adolf, 11(n13), (n15)
Eton College, 50, 149, 168, 218
Evenings at Home, or, The Juvenile Budget Opened, 209
Exeter Grammar School, 41

Father's Instructions: Consisting of Moral Tales, Fables and Reflections, A, 218
Fenn, Ellenor, 197, 219
Fielding, Henry, 148
Fielding, Sarah, 154, 191
Fifteen Centuries of Children's Literature, 191
Fifteenth Century School Book, A, 42
Food, 19, 23, 40, 43, 23, 54, 59, 65, 125, 128, 170-171, 184, 187, 218
Fool of Quality, or, The History of Henry Earl of Moreland, The, 177-181
Foote, Samuel, 169
Forsett, Edward, 97
Fortunate Blue-Coat Boy, or, Memoirs of the Life and Happy Adventures of Mr Benjamin Templeman, The, 212
Francis Fearful, 216
French Littleton, The, 61
French Schoolmaster, The, 61
Friends, or The History of Billy Freeman and Tommy Truelove, The, 216
Friendship, 12, 27, 44, 89, 117, 144, 154-155, 161, 193, 195, 201, 210, 211, 216, 221
Fruit, theft of, 29, 47, 48, 80, 151, 157, 193(n5), 207-208, 214
Fulwell, Ulpian, 86

Index

Gallus, Evaldus, 68
Gambling, 13, 54, 84, 91, 109, 144, 145, 212
Games, see Leisure
Gardiner, Alan H., 11(n14)
Garmonsway, G.N., 22(n34)
Gascoigne, George, 92
George I, 132, 137
Glass of Government, The, 87, 92-93
Goldsmith, Oliver, 165-166, 199
Governess, or Little Female Academy, The, 191, 208
Governess, or The Boarding School Dissected, The, 115-119, 185(n19)
Governess, or The Little Female Academy, The (Sherwood), 196(n6)
Grantley, Darryll, 80(n13)
Greece, schools in Ancient, 12-14
Greed, see Food
Grey, Jill E., 191(n3), 194, 203
Guardian of Education, The, 210
Gulliver's Travels, 145-148
Gwara, Scott, 21(n31), 24()n40), 25
Gymnastics of the Mind: Greek Education in Hellenistic and Roman Egypt, 18(n24)

Harvey Gem, S., 22(n34)
Hawkins, William, 106
Henry St. John (Viscount Bolingbroke), 136
Hermeneumata Pseudodositheana, 17
Herodas, 13
Hill, Rowland, 37(n7)
Hisperica Famina, 19-20
History Begins at Sumer, 6(n2)
History of Billy Trifler, The, 213
History of Education in Antiquity, A, 12(n17)
History of Fanny Hewet, The, 201
History of Little Goody Two-Shoes, The, 198
History of Little King Pippin, The, 206
History of Master Trueworth, Commonly Called Tommy Telltruth, The, 214-215
History of Mrs Williams and Her Plumb Cake, The, 202
History of Polly Pert, The, 200
History of Pompey the Little, or The Life and Adventures of a Lap-Dog, The, 172-173
History of Sandford and Merton, The, 182-188
History of the Adventures of Joseph Andrews ...., The, 148-150
History of the Curate of Craman, The, 170
History of the Life of the Late Mr Jonathan Wild, the Great, The, 150-152
History of Tom Jones, A Foundling, The, 152-154
History of Tommy Playlove and Jacky Lovebook, The, 211
Hollyband, Claudius, 60
Hoole, Charles, 68, 72, 73
Hoppit, Julian, 133(n1)
Horman, William, 49
Hornbook, 100, 102, 119-120, 123-124
Hornbye, William, 119
Hornbyes Hornbook, 119-120
Horsman, E.A. 123
How a Man May Choose a Good Wife from a Bad, 99
Hugh of Lincoln, 36
Hygeine, 20-21, 28, 47, 70

Idleness, 9, 11, 13, 84, 111, 204, 214, 215
Indulgent parent(s), 83, 85-87, 89, 90, 112, 114, 116, 117, 173, 183, 211, 218
Ingelend, Thomas, 87
Instructions for Children, or A Token of Love for the Rising Generation, 37(n7)
Insults, 9-10, 28

Janeway, James, 37, 191
Jenner, Charles, 170
John Newbery and His Successors, 203
Johnson, Richard, 160, 184(n18), 197, 198, 207
Jones, William, 220(n38)
Jonson, Ben, 77
Jowett, B. 13(n18)
July and Julian, 94-95
Juvenal and Persius, 15(n20)
Juvenal, 15

Juvenile Trials for Robbing Orchards, Telling Fibs and Other High Misdemeanours, 160, 207

Kilner, Dorothy, 217
Kilner, Mary Ann, 220
Kramer, Samuel Noah, 6(n2), 7-10

l'Hermite, Francois, 144
Lady of May, The, 95-97
Lamb, Charles and Mary, 196(n6)
Lapidge, Michel, 21(n33)
Leisure, 26-27, 40, 50, 53-54, 71, 74, 162, 212
Lessons for Children, 218
Lessons, 7, 8, 11, 14, 15, 17-18, 22, 27, 59, 60, 63, 93, 99, 103, 105, 192, 197, 199
Letters Between Master Tommy and Miss Nancy Goodchild, 197(n8)
Letters from a Tutor to His Pupils, 220(n38)
Letters on the Most Common, as well as Important, Occasions in Life, 194
Life and Adventures of Nicholas Nickleby, The, 42(n13), 118(n91), 159(n22), 169
Life and Adventures of Peter Wilkins, The, 164-165
Like Will to Like, 86
Lilliputian Magazine, or The Young Gentleman and Lady's Golden Library, The, 201-202
Lilliputian Magazine, or, Children's Repository, The, 200, 213
Little Female Orators, or Nine Evenings Entertainment, The, 197
Locke, John, 148
Londe, Robert, 40
Longer Thou Livest, The More Fool Thou Art, The, 87
Love for Money, or The Boarding School, 114
Love's Labour's Lost, 100
Ludi Magister: The Play of Tudor School and Stage, 78
Ludus Literarius, 66, 96
Lusty Juventus, 87
Lyar, A Comedy in Three Acts, The, 169-170
Lysis, 12

Lytil Booke of good manners for children, A, 194

Macropedius, 82
Maese, Sarah, 195
Magdalen Grammar School, 41, 42, 48-49
Malim, William, 76
Marriage of Wit and Science, The, 81
Marriage, 81, 88, 94, 114
Marrou, Henri, 12(n17)
Marston, John, 104
Martial, 16
Memoirs of a Peg-Top, 220
Merry Wives of Windsor, The, 100, 103, 105
Middleton, Thomas, 107
Monsieur D'Olive, 106-107
Mother's Gift, or A Present for All Little Boys Who Wish to be Good, The, 204
Motter, T.H. Vail, 76
Mrs Leicester's School, or The History of Several Young Ladies, 196(n6)
Mulcaster, Richard, 76

Nash, Thomas, 106
Necessity of Correction for Idleness and Perverseness, The, 204
Nelson, William, 42
New Polite Tutoress, The, 196(n7)
Newbery, Elizabeth, 202
Newbery, Francis, 202, 204
Newbery, John, 190, 194, 198, 201-203
Newgate School, Bristol, 40
Nice Wanton, 87
Northbrooke, John, 77
Nurse Truelove's Christmas Box, 201
Nurse Truelove's New Year's Gift, 201, 202

O'Brien, Avril, 123(n3), 131
Orchards, robbing of, see Fruit, theft of
Original Stories, from Real Life, 176, 188
Orme, Nicholas, 33, 38, 40, 45, 79(n10)

Paltock, Robert, 164
Parson's Tale, The, 34(n4)
Pedagogy and Parenting in English Drama, 1560-1610, 79
Pedantius, 97-99

Index   231

Percival, Thomas, 218
Petriscus, 82, 85-86
Placid Man, or Memoirs of Sir Charles Beville, The, 170
Plato, 12
Plautus, 16
Play of Wit and Science, The, 81
Pleasure Improved, by Being Made a Guide to Useful Knowledge, Religion and Politeness, 195
Polite Academy, or Complete Instructions for a Genteel Behaviour..., 194
Polite Academy, or, School of Behaviour for Young Gentlemen and Ladies, The, 194
Polite Lady, or a Course of Female Education, The, 194, 195
Polite Tutoress, or Young Lady's Instructor, The, 196
Porter, David W., 24(n40), 25
Potter, Ursula, 79
Poverty, 40, 56, 70, 74
Practical Education, 176
Pretty Interlude Called Nice Wanton, A, 89-92
Pretty Little Pocket Book, A, 201
Prioress's Tale, The, 32-37
Pueriles confabulatiunculae, 66
Punishment, 7, 8, 11, 12, 16, 34(n4), 44, 49, 55, 64, 67, 81, 95, 154, 160, 162, 192, 201, 217
   unjust, 104-105, 124, 130-131, 157, 168, 204, 221
   excessive, 13-14, 29, 83, 84, 88, 90, 111, 120, 152-153, 179-180, 213, 214
Purple Jar, The, 188

Quarrel of the School-Boys at Athens, The, 132-142

Rebellion by schoolboys, 120, 158
Rebels, The, 82-85
Redford, John, 81
Religion, 19, 23, 25, 29, 32-37, 56-57, 121, 175, 191, 195, 201, 216
Remorse and reformation, 30, 131, 201, 204, 208, 211
Rival Pupils, or A New Holiday Gift for a Boarding School, The, 205

Rome, schools in Ancient, 14-18
Roscoe, S., 203
Roscoe, William Caldwell, 216
Rousseau, Jean-Jacques, 174

Scholt, Grayce, 191
School Dialogues (Vives), 57
School Dialogues for Boys, 219
School Drama in England, The, 76
School Occuurences, Supposed to Have Arisen among a Set of Young Ladies, 197
School of Wisdom, or Repository of the Most Valuable Curiosities of Art and Nature, The, 194
School of Wisdom, or, New Preceptor, The, 194
School-Boy, or The Comical Rival, The, 109-110
School-Boy's Mask, The, 110-114
School, Being a Series of Letters between a Young Lady and Her Mother, The, 195
Schoolmaster, pompous, 96, 97-100, 101-103
Schools, criticism of, see Education, attitudes to and criticism of
Schoolwork, see Lessons
Schort, Thomas, 40
Shakespeare, William, 100
Shapiro, Michael, 87
Sherwood, Mary, 196(n6)
Sidney, Philip, 95
Simple Simon's History, 214
Sister's Gift, or The Naughty Boy Reformed, The, 204
Smollett, Tobias, 156
Some Thoughts Concerning Education, 148
Spateman, Thomas, 110
St. Paul's School, 51
Stanbridge, John, 48
Stanhope, James (Earl Stanhope), 135
Staple of News, The, 77
Sullivan, Paul, 78
Sumeria, schools in, 6-10
Sumerians: Their History, Culture and Character, The, 6(n2)
Summer's Last Will and Testament, 106
Sutton, Dana F., 97(n47)

Swift, Jonathan, 145-146

Tale-Telling, 29, 64, 69
Tea-Table Dialogues between a Governess and Miss Thoughtful, Miss Sterling etc., 198
Teachers, status of, 15, 46, 70, 79-80, 102
Theft, 8, 29, 85,90, 95, 100, 206, 214, 217 (see also Fruit, theft of)
Three Cakes, The, 218
Token for Children, A, 37, 191
Tom Brown's Schooldays, 221
Townsend, John Rowe, 199
Townshend, Charles, 134
Tracy, James D., 51
Trade and Plumb Cake Forever, Huzza!, 199
Trade, attitudes to, 23, 178, 202-203
Trimmer, Sarah, 210
Tringham, W., 200
Truancy, 13, 41, 85, 90, 100, 206, 214, 214
Truant, The, 214
Tutors, private, 144, 152-153, 172-173, 178-181
Twelfth Day Gift, The, 203
Two Noble Kinsmen, The, 100, 103-104

Vicar of Wakefield, The, 166-167
Vicesimus Knox, 171
Victorian Governess Novel, The, 198(n9)
Village School, or A Collection of Entertaining Histories for the Instruction and Amusement of all Good Children, The, 217

Vindication of the Rights of Women, A, 176
Virtue and Vice, or The History of Charles Careful and Harry Heedless, 210
Vives, Juan Luis, 57
Vulgaria of John Stanbridge and the Vulgaria of Robert Whittinton, The, 48(n32)

Wadsö-Lecaros, Cecilia, 198(n9)
Wager, William, 87
Walpole, Robert, 133, 150
Watson, Foster, 58(n51)
Watters, Reginald, 212
Webbe, Joseph, 68, 72
Welsh, Charles, 205(n22)
Westminster School, 77, 55(n45), 110, 173
Wever, Robert (or Richard), 86
What You Will, 104-105
White, Beatrice, 48
Whittinton, Robert, 49
Winchester School, 107, 162
Winter Evenings, 171
Wit's Pilgrimage: Drama and the Social Impact of Education in Early Modern England, 80(n 14)
Woolstonecraft, Mary, 176
World and the Child, The, 80

Young Ladies Magazine, The, 196
Young Misses Magazine, The, 196

You may also be interested in:

From the Dairyman's Daughter to Worrals of the WAAF

The RTS, Lutterworth Press and Children's Literature

Edited by Dennis Butts and Pat Garrett

by Julian Lovelock

A collection of essays based on the Children's Books History Society study conference marking the bicentenary of the Religious Tract Society and the Lutterworth Press. The book analyses the children's literature it produced, charting the development of the genre from the evangelical tract through to the popular school story, spanning the period from the late eighteenth to the mid-twentieth centuries. It shows how publishing worked within the context of a missionary society with a global reach.

The book details the nature and development of the tract genre both in Britain and America, before looking at the range of RTS and Lutterworth output of children's titles, including its movement into magazine publishing. The work studies the two great magazines for which the RTS and Lutterworth were known to generations of children, the *Boy's Own Paper* and the *Girl's Own Paper*, as well as other magazines, such as *The Child's Companion*. There are also chapters on popular tracts, such as *The Dairyman's Daughter*, and successful authors, from Hesba Stretton and Mrs Walton to W.E. Johns and Laura Ingalls Wilder.

These essays explore how, in order to reflect an increasingly secular age, the subject matter widened, providing more non-fiction in its periodicals as well as an increasingly broad range of fiction, mostly secular in nature. It was also necessary for the Society to alter its didactically religious tone in order to present its Christian values with more subtlety.

This collection is a major contribution to publishing history in the nineteenth and twentieth centuries.

Dennis Butts, a former Chairman of The Children's Books History Society, teaches the MA Course in Children's Literature at Reading University. He has written on many aspects of nineteenth-century literature and children's books.

Pat Garrett is a former librarian and teacher. She has been Secretary of the Children's Books History Society, and is its current Chairman.

Published 2018
Paperback ISBN: 978 0 7188 9540 2
ePub ISBN: 978 0 7188 4773 9
PDF ISBN: 978 0 7188 4772 2

You may also be interested in:

A Complete Identity

The Youthful Hero in the Work of G.A. Henty and George MacDonald

by R.E. Johnson

A Complete Identity is an examination of the hero figure in the works of G.A. Henty (1832-1902) and George MacDonald (1824-1905) and a reassessment of oppositional critiques of their writing. It demonstrates the complementary characteristics of the hero figure, which construct a complete identity commensurate with the Victorian ideal hero.

The relationship between the expansion of the British Empire and youthful heroism is established through investigation of the Victorian political, social and religious milieu, the construct of the child, and the construct of the hero. A connection between the exotic geographical space of empire and the unknown psychological space is drawn through examination of representation of the "other" in the work of Henty and MacDonald.

This book demonstrates that Henty's work is more complex than the stereotypically linear, masculine, imperialistic critique of his stories that historical realism allows, and that MacDonald's work displays more evidence of historical embedding and ideological interpellation than the critical focus on his work as fantasy and fairy tale considers.

> 'This remarkable piece of scholarship offers a bold, unexpected and exciting juxtaposition of G.A. Henty and George MacDonald, exploring their work as part of the same tradition and the product of the same culture and ideology.'
> – **Maria Nikolajeva**, Professor of Education, Professorial Fellow of Homerton College, Cambridge

R.E. Johnson is an Associate Researcher attached to The International Forum for Research in Children's Literature at the University of Worcester.

Published 2014
Paperback ISBN: 978 0 718 9359 0
PDF ISBN: 978 0 7188 4271 0

You may also be interested in:

How Did Long John Silver Lose his Leg?

and Twenty-Six Other Mysteries of Children's Literature

by Dennis Butts and Peter Hunt.

How Did Long John Silver Lose his Leg? is a diverting tour through some of the best-loved classics of children's literature, addressing may of the unanswered questions that inspire intense speculation when the books are laid down.

Could Bobbie's train really have stopped in time (*The Railway Children*)? Did Beatrix Potter have the 'flu in 1909, and did this lead to a certain darkness in her work (*The Tale of Mr Tod*)? Would the 'rugby football played by Tom Brown be recognised by sportsmen today (*Tom Brown's Schooldays*)? The authors speculate entertainingly and informatively on the anomalies and unexplained phenomena found in chidren's literature and, having established the cultural importance of children's books in the modern age, also consider the more serious issues raised by the genre. Why are we so defensive of the idyllic worlds presented in children's books? Why have some of our best-loved authors been outed as neglectful parents to their own children? Should we ever separate the book from its creator and appreciate the works of writers convicted of crimes against children?

Dennis Butts has taught Children's Literature at reading University and is former Chairman of The Childrne's Books History Society. he is co-editor of *From the Dairyman's Daughter to Worrla of the WAAF (The Lutterworth Press*, 2006).

Peter Hunt is Professor Emeritus at the School of English, Cardiff University, Visiting Professor at Newcastle University, and Visiting Professor at the Università Ca' Foscari, Venice. In 2003 he was awarded the Brothers Grimm Award for services to children's literature.

Published 2013
Paperback ISBN: 978 0 7188 9310 1
ePub ISBN 978 0 7188 4194 2
PDF ISBN 978 0 7188 4193 5

You may also be interested in:

Childrens Literature and Social Change

Some Case Studies from Barbara Hofland to Philip Pullman

by Dennis Butts

While there are many books about children's literature, few discuss it within its social context or investigate the ways writers reflect or react to change in society. Dennis Butts explores how shifting attitudes and historical upheavals from the 1840s onwards affected and continue to affect books written for younger audiences. Spanning the period of the industrial revolution to the sexual revolution, this book reveals the impact that these external events have had on writers as diverse as moral storyteller Barbara Hofland and the controversial Melvin Burgess.

G.A. Henty, Robert Louis Stevenson and Philip Pullman are included in the discussion, as Butts identifies commonalities between books of the past and present, arguing that trends shown in most of the early children's literature are being displayed again now, albeit in a more subtle manner.

This book will appeal to undergraduate students attending complementary courses in children's literature during their degree in English Literature or Cultural Studies. It will also be of use to postgraduate research students working in the field of Children's Literature.

'Butts range of reference is truly astounding'
– **David Rudd,** in *Children's Literature Association Quarterly,* Vol. 38, No 4

Dennis Butts a former Chairman of The Children's Books History Society, taught children's literature at Reading University. He has a lifelong interest in the relationship between politics, society and literature, and has written on many aspects of children's books and nineteenth-century literature.

Published 2010
Paperback ISBN: 978 0 7188 9208 1

You may also be interested in:

From Morality to Mayhem

The Fall and Rise of the English School Story

by Julian Lovelock

The stories we read as children are the ones that stay with us the longest, and from the nineteenth century until the 1950s stories about schools held a particular fascination. Many will remember the goings-on at such earnest establishments as Tom Brown's Rugby, St Dominic's, Greyfriars, the Chalet School, Malory Towers and Linbury Court. In the second part of the twentieth century, with more liberal social attitudes and the advent of secondary education for all, these moral tales lost their appeal and the school story very nearly died out. More recently, however, a new generation of compromised schoolboy and schoolgirl heroes – Pennington, Tyke Tiler, Harry Potter and Millie Roads – have given it a new and challenging relevance.

Focusing mainly on novels written for young people, *From Morality to Mayhem* charts the fall and rise of the school story, from the grim accounts of Victorian times to the magic and mayhem of our own age. In doing so it considers how fictional schools not only reflect but sometimes influence real life. This captivating study will appeal to those interested in children's literature and education, both students and the general reader, taking us on a not altogether comfortable trip down memory lane.

'tackles this neglectec canon with... evident enjoyment'
– **Dr John Drew,** Professor of English Literature,
University of Buckingham

Julian Lovelock has spent almost all his life in education - as schoolboy, student, teacher and, for twenty-five years, headmaster. More recently, he lectured in English Literature at theUniversity of Buckingham, where he became Dean of Arts and Languages and Pro Vice-Chancellor.

Published 2006
Paperback ISBN: 978 0 7188 3055 7

BV - #0038 - 230724 - C0 - 234/156/14 - PB - 9780718897369 - Matt Lamination